The Media and Modernity

The Media and Modernity

A SOCIAL THEORY OF THE MEDIA

JOHN B. THOMPSON

Stanford University Press
Stanford, California
1995

Stanford University Press
Stanford, California
© 1995 John B. Thompson
Originating publisher Polity Press, Cambridge
   in association with Blackwell Publishers Ltd
First published in the U.S.A. by
   Stanford University Press, 1995
Printed in Great Britain
Cloth ISBN 0-8047-2678-7
Paper ISBN 0-8047-2679-5
LC 95-74796
This book is printed on acid-free paper.

Contents

Preface

This book is an elaboration and refinement of some of the ideas initially sketched in my *Ideology and Modern Culture*. There I put forward the view that, if we wish to understand the cultural transformations associated with the rise of modern societies, then we must give a central role to the development of communication media and their impact. In this book I seek to redeem this claim. I examine in some detail the nature of communication media and their changing forms; I discuss the emergence of the media industries and analyse some recent trends; but above all I try to show that the development of the media was interwoven in fundamental ways with the major institutional transformations which have shaped the modern world. My primary concern is to explore these interconnections, to trace their contours and consider their implications, and hopefully to shed some light on our contemporary, media-saturated world while avoiding a myopic preoccupation with the present.

I owe a substantial debt to numerous friends and colleagues with whom I have discussed these issues over the years, and who took the time to read and comment on earlier drafts of the text. Lizbeth Goodman deserves special mention: she gave me many helpful suggestions and has been a constant source of encouragement and support. Conversations with Anthony Giddens and David Held helped to shape the concerns of this book; they also read an earlier draft and provided much valuable feedback. Peter Burke, James Lull, William Outhwaite and Annabelle Sreberny-

Mohammadi were generous with their time and their comments; I am grateful to them for their probing criticisms and their numerous references to relevant works in their areas of expertise. Michelle Stanworth, Henrietta Moore, Helga Geyer-Ryan and Peter and Karin Groombridge have been wonderful friends and have always advised me well. I should also like to thank Avril Symonds for her patient word-processing; Ann Bone for her careful copy-editing; and the many people at Polity Press and Blackwell Publishers – especially Gill Motley, Julia Harsant, Nicola Ross, Pam Thomas, Lin Lucas and Ginny Stroud-Lewis – who have helped, at one stage or another, to prepare this book for publication.

J.B.T., Cambridge, December 1994

Introduction

'I have said that, in my opinion, all was chaos, that is, earth, air, water, and fire were mixed together; and out of that bulk a mass formed – just as cheese is made out of milk – and worms appeared in it, and these were the angels. The most holy majesty decreed that these should be God and the angels, and among that number of angels, there was also God, he too having been created out of that mass at the same time, and he was made Lord . . .'[1] These words, spoken by a sixteenth-century miller from Montereale, a small village of the Friuli in what is now northern Italy, strike us today like the remnants of another age. It is not easy for us to take seriously the vision of the world they convey, or to understand why the person who uttered them – one Domenico Scandella, also known as Menocchio – should have to pay so dearly for his eccentric beliefs. (Menocchio was interrogated, imprisoned and eventually put to death.) But despite the distance that separates our world today from the world of this sixteenth-century miller, there is a social trait of fundamental importance that ties him to us. For, unlike many of his fellow villagers, Menocchio could read.

Among other things, Menocchio had read *Il cavallier Zuanne de Mandavilla*, a translation of the popular book of travels attributed to Sir John Mandeville. Originally written in the mid-fourteenth century, the book was reprinted many times in the sixteenth century and diffused widely throughout Europe. Here Menocchio had read of distant lands where people practised different cus-

toms, obeyed different laws and held different beliefs; he had read
of places where some people worshipped the sun, some worshipped fire and some worshipped images and idols; he had read
of islands apparently inhabited by cannibals, pigmies and men
with the heads of dogs. These descriptions deeply troubled
Menocchio and led him to question the foundations of his own
beliefs. They provided him with a window on to another world, a
world into which he could step temporarily and from which he
could view – with the kind of discomfort that often accompanies
the discovery of alternatives – the world of his daily life in
Montereale.

There can be no doubt that Menocchio was a man of uncommon imagination. His strange cosmogony was his own creation,
and his ideas were probably viewed by his fellow villagers with a
mixture of caution, bewilderment and awe. In the course of his
interrogation, Menocchio repeatedly insisted that his ideas were
his own invention ('Sir, I have never met anyone who holds these
opinions; my opinions come out of my own head'), but this was
only partly true. For Menocchio had read many books and culled
many ideas from them. His vivid imagination had reworked these
ideas, infused them with meaning, mixed them together with one
another and with ideas drawn from the oral traditions of rural life.
Menocchio's views were undoubtedly the product of a unique and
restless mind, but they were made possible by a social transformation whose origins lay elsewhere and whose impact extended far
beyond the villages of the Friuli.

By the time that Menocchio's trial began in 1584, printing
presses had been in operation throughout Europe for more than a
hundred years. They were producing a growing avalanche of
printed materials which would gradually transform the life conditions of most individuals. Initially the impact of print was felt most
strongly in the large urban centres, among educated elites who
held the reigns of power. But printed materials spread quickly,
and it was not long before ordinary individuals like Menocchio –
this self-taught miller of humble origins – were able to gain access
to the worlds opened up by print. However strange Menocchio's
opinions may seem to us today, he was the harbinger of a new era
in which symbolic forms would spill far beyond the shared locales
of daily life, and in which the circulation of ideas would no longer
be restricted by the exchange of words in contexts of face-to-face
interaction.

My aim in this book is to trace the contours of this and subsequent transformations in what I shall describe as the social organization of symbolic power, and to explore some of their consequences for the kind of world in which we live today. I shall try to show that the development of communication media – from early forms of print to recent types of electronic communication – was an integral part of the rise of modern societies. The development of communication media was interwoven in complex ways with a number of other developmental processes which, taken together, were constitutive of what we have come to call 'modernity'. Hence, if we wish to understand the nature of modernity – that is, of the institutional characteristics of modern societies and the life conditions created by them – then we must give a central role to the development of communication media and their impact.

It is perhaps surprising that, among the works of social theorists who have concerned themselves with the rise of modern societies, there are so few which have treated communication media with the seriousness they deserve. There is a substantial body of work by social and cultural historians on the impact of printing in early modern Europe and elsewhere, and there is a large literature dealing with more recent developments in the media industries; but in the writings of social theorists, a concern with communication media is most noticeable for its absence. Why this neglect? Partly it is due, no doubt, to a certain attitude of suspiciousness towards the media. For theorists interested in long-term processes of social change, the media may seem like a sphere of the superficial and the ephemeral, a sphere about which, it may seem, very little of any substance can be said. But there are other reasons, more deeply rooted historically and intellectually, which help to explain this neglect.

When social theorists today reflect on the broad developmental contours of modernity, they generally do so in ways that are profoundly shaped by the legacy of classical social thought. They take their terms of reference from the work of authors who, writing in the nineteenth and early twentieth centuries, were struggling to make sense of the industrial societies taking shape around them. For the most part, the classical social thinkers did not attribute a significant role to the development of communication media. For them, the key cultural dynamic associated with the rise of modern societies lay elsewhere: it consisted above all in processes of rationalization and secularization, through which modern societies would, it was thought, gradually discard the traditional encumbrances of the past. This was a lofty vision, a grand narrative in the tradition of epic story-telling, which pitched the progressive forces of reason and enlightenment against the darkened ramparts of myth and superstition. And it is a vision which has continued to grip the theoretical imagination, dividing contemporary theorists into opposing camps of those who wish to defend and refine the narrative and those who are inclined to reject it as another myth.

The account I shall offer here shares little in common with the high drama of the grand narrative. In contrast to this somewhat ethereal battle between the forces of reason and myth, I shall be concerned with a series of developments which can be reasonably well documented and which have clear institutional bases, from the small printing presses of the late fifteenth century to the huge communication conglomerates of today. I shall be concerned with the gradual expansion of networks of communication and information flow, networks which, since the mid-nineteenth century, have become increasingly global in scope. I shall be concerned with the ways in which these networks are interwoven with other forms of power – economic, political and military – and how they have been used by actors, both individual and collective, to pursue their aims. But I shall also be concerned to show that, notwithstanding the worldly character of these developments, their consequences are far-reaching.

A central argument of this book is that we can understand the social impact of the development of new networks of communication and information flow only if we put aside the intuitively plausible idea that communication media serve to transmit information and symbolic content to individuals whose relations to others remain fundamentally unchanged. We must see, instead, that the use of communication media involves the creation of new forms of action and interaction in the social world, new kinds of social relationship and new ways of relating to others and to oneself. When individuals use communication media, they enter into forms of interaction which differ in certain respects from the type of face-to-face interaction which characterizes most encounters of daily life. They are able to act for others who are physically absent, or act in response to others who are situated in distant locales. In a fundamental way, the use of communication media transforms the spatial and temporal organization of social life, creating new forms of action and interaction, and new modes of exercising power, which are no longer linked to the sharing of a common locale.

It is easier to call attention to this transformation in a general way than it is to analyse it rigorously and to follow through its implications for social and political life. Many of the chapters that follow are an attempt – certainly partial, and no doubt faltering in places – to analyse this transformation and to explore its wider implications. The first two chapters prepare the way, both theoretically and historically. In chapter 1 I analyse the nature of communication media within the framework of a more comprehensive social theory; this chapter lays the foundations for a social theory of the media by analysing the structured social contexts within which all communication – including mediated communication – takes place and with reference to which it must be understood. Chapter 2 shifts the analysis on to a historical plane. Drawing on the theoretical framework elaborated in the first chapter, I offer a broad reinterpretation of the main transformations associated with the rise of modern societies, placing particular emphasis on the development of media institutions and on the growth of new networks of communication and information flow.

In chapter 3 I develop the argument that the use of communication media has created new forms of action and interaction in the modern world, and I try to analyse these forms as rigorously and precisely as possible. The argument is pursued in chapter 4, where I explore the impact of communication media on the relation between the public and the private and on the changing nexus of visibility and power. I try to show that phenomena which have become pervasive and troubling features of the political arena today – such as the frequent occurrence of scandals of various kinds – are rooted in a series of fundamental transformations concerning the mediated visibility of power.

The development of communication media has not only rendered power visible in new ways, it has also rendered it visible on an unprecedented scale: today mediated visibility is effectively global in scope. This circumstance is the outcome of a complex process of globalization whose origins can be traced back at least as far as the mid-nineteenth century, and whose characteristics and consequences are the concern of chapter 5. Here I seek to show how the globalization of communication was interwoven with other developmental processes constitutive of modern societies; and I argue that, if we wish to understand the consequences of these developments, we must take account of the specific contexts within which globalized media products are received and understood.

Chapters 6 and 7 are concerned to explore some of the ways in which the development of communication media has affected the daily lives of individuals. In chapter 6 I focus on the nature of tradition and its changing role: has the growing diffusion of media products helped to undermine traditional ways of life, as many commentators have assumed? Or is there a sense in which the media have breathed new life into traditions, uprooting them from their contexts of origin, embedding them in cultural diaspora and providing individuals with sources of identity which are no longer linked to particular locales? Chapter 7 is focused on the nature of the self and on the ways in which the process of self-formation is affected by the profusion of mediated materials. What is it like to live in a world where the capacity to experience events is no longer determined by the possibility of encountering them on the time-space paths of daily life?

The final chapter addresses questions of a more normative kind concerning the role that media institutions can play, and ought to play, in the cultivation of an autonomous and responsible way of life. I argue that many of our traditional ways of thinking about social and political matters are shaped by a certain model of public life which stems from the ancient world, from the *agora* of classical Greece, and which envisions the possibility of individuals coming together in a shared space to discuss issues of common concern. But this traditional model of publicness as co-presence bears little resemblance to the practical realities of the late twentieth-century world. Today we must reinvent the idea of publicness in a way that reflects the complex interdependencies of the modern world, and in a way that recognizes the growing importance of forms of communication and interaction which are not face-to-face in character.

Throughout the book I have drawn on a rich and varied litera-ture in cultural history and the history of communications, in communications theory and research, and in contemporary media and cultural studies. But this book was written primarily as a work of social theory, not as a contribution to a specialist literature in the field of communications. I have tried to redress the neglect of communication media within the literature of social theory and to show that, if we take the media seriously, we find that they have serious consequences for some of the core concerns of social and political thought. At the same time, while wishing to redress the neglect of the media, I have tried to avoid an equally one-sided preoccupation with the media, as if one could plausibly study the development of communication media independently of broader social and historical processes. Social theory has as much to offer communications research as it has to gain from it; and a social theory of the media may help to situate the study of the media where, in my view, it belongs: among a set of disciplines concerned with the emergence, development and structural characteristics of modern societies and their futures.

In developing the arguments in this book I also draw liberally on the literature of contemporary social and cultural theory. But there are three traditions of thought which are particularly relevant to my concerns, and which have helped to shape the general orientation of my account. One is the tradition of critical social theory stemming from the work of the Frankfurt School.[2] I doubt whether much can be salvaged today from the writings of the early Frankfurt School theorists, such as Horkheimer, Adorno and Marcuse; their critique of what they called 'the culture industry' was too negative and was rooted in a questionable conception of modern societies and their developmental trends.[3] But Habermas's early account of the emergence and transformation of the public sphere is a work that still merits careful consideration.[4] The great strength of Habermas's early work is that it treats the development of the media as an integral part of the formation of modern societies. He argued that the circulation of printed materials in early modern Europe played a crucial role in the transition from absolutist to liberal-democratic regimes, and that the articulation of critical public opinion through the media was a vital feature of modern democratic life. There are many respects in which Habermas's argument is unconvincing, as we shall see; and I think it is clear that his argument could no longer be sustained in anything like its original form. But the vision which lies behind Habermas's account is one that continues, with some justification, to command our respect.

A second tradition of thought on which I draw loosely here is a tradition stemming from the work of the so-called media theorists. The most well known of these theorists was, of course, Marshall McLuhan; but the most original and insightful was probably McLuhan's compatriot and mentor, Harold Innis. Writing in the 1940s and early 1950s, Innis was one of the first to explore systematically the relations between media of communication, on the one hand, and the spatial and temporal organization of power, on the other.[5] His theory of the 'bias' of communication – simply put, that different media favoured different ways of organizing political power, whether centralized or decentralized, extended in time or space, and so on – was no doubt too crude to account for the complexities of the historical relations between communication and power. But Innis rightly emphasized the fact that communication media as such are important for the organization of power, irrespective of the content of the messages they convey. This approach has been taken up and developed by others – by McLuhan, certainly, but also by more recent theorists like Joshua Meyrowitz, who insightfully combines an analysis of electronic media inspired by McLuhan with an account of social interaction derived from Goffman.[6] This tradition is less helpful, however, when it comes to thinking about the social organization of the media industries, about the ways in which the media are interwoven with the unequal distribution of power and resources, and about how individuals make sense of media products and incorporate them into their lives.

The third tradition which informs my account is that of hermeneutics, a tradition concerned, broadly speaking, with the contextualized interpretation of symbolic forms. Among the recent contributions to this tradition I include the work of Gadamer and Ricoeur, but also the more ethnographically oriented writings of Clifford Geertz.[7] Hermeneutics highlights the fact that the reception of symbolic forms – including media products – always involves a contextualized and creative process of interpretation in which individuals draw on the resources available to them in order to make sense of the messages they receive. It also calls our attention to the fact that the activity of 'appropriation' is part of an extended process of self-formation through which individuals develop a sense of themselves and others, of their history, their place in the world and the social groups to which they belong. By emphasizing the creative, constructive and socially embedded character of interpretation, hermeneutics converges with some of the recent ethnographic work on the reception of media products, while at the same time enriching this work by bringing to bear on it the resources of a tradition concerned with the link between interpretation and self-formation.

Some readers may find it surprising that in a book concerned with social theory and the media I draw so little on the literature generally referred to (no doubt rather crudely) with the labels 'post-structuralism' and 'postmodernism'. This is not the place to spell out the reasons for my dissatisfaction with much of this literature; some of these reasons will emerge in the pages that follow. Here it will suffice to say that, for all the talk of postmodernism and postmodernity, there are precious few signs that the inhabitants of the late twentieth-century world have recently entered a new age, and that the doors opened up by the advent of modern societies have now closed behind them. If the debates sparked off by postmodernism have taught us anything, it is not that the developmental processes characteristic of modern societies have propelled us beyond modernity to some new and as yet undefined age, but rather that our traditional theoretical frameworks for understanding these processes are, in many respects, woefully inadequate. What we need today is not a theory of a new age, but rather a new theory of an age whose broad contours were laid down some while ago, and whose consequences we have yet fully to ascertain. If we put aside the fashionable rhetoric and focus our attention on the deeply rooted social transformations that shape our lives, we may find that we share more in common with our predecessors – perhaps even with the ill-fated miller from Montereale – than some contemporary theorists would like us to believe.

1

Communication and Social Context

In all societies human beings engage in the production and exchange of information and symbolic content. From the earliest forms of gesture and language use to the most recent develop-ments in computer technology, the production, storage and circu-lation of information and symbolic content have been central aspects of social life. But with the development of a range of media institutions from the late fifteenth century to the present day, the processes of production, storage and circulation have been trans-formed in certain ways. These processes have been caught up in a series of institutional developments which are characteristic of the modern era. By virtue of these developments, symbolic forms have been produced and reproduced on an ever-expanding scale; they have been turned into commodities which can be bought and sold on a market; they have become accessible to individuals who are widely dispersed in space and time. In a profound and irreversible way, the development of the media has transformed the nature of symbolic production and exchange in the modern world.

In this chapter I shall begin to explore the contours of this trans-formation by analysing some of the characteristics of mediated communication. I shall develop an approach to the media which is fundamentally 'cultural', by which I mean an approach which is concerned *both* with the meaningful character of symbolic forms *and* with their social contextualization.[1] On the one hand, it is important to stress that communication media have an irreducible symbolic dimension: they are concerned with the production, storage and circulation of materials which are *meaningful for* the individuals who produce and receive them. It is easy to lose sight of this symbolic dimension and to become preoccupied with the technical features of communication media. These technical features are certainly important, as we shall see; but they should not be allowed to obscure the fact that the development of communication media is, in a fundamental sense, a reworking of the symbolic character of social life, a reorganization of the ways in which information and symbolic content are produced and exchanged in the social world and a restructuring of the ways in which individuals relate to one another and to themselves. If 'man is an animal suspended in webs of significance he himself has spun,' as Geertz once remarked,[2] then communication media are spinning wheels in the modern world and, in using these media, human beings are fabricating webs of significance for themselves.

On the other hand, it is also important to emphasize that mediated communication is always a contextualized social phenomenon: it is always embedded in social contexts which are structured in various ways and which, in turn, have a structuring impact on the communication that occurs. Once again, it is easy to lose sight of this aspect. Since mediated communication is generally 'fixed' in a material substratum of some kind – words inscribed on paper, for example, or images captured on film – it is easy to focus on the symbolic content of media messages and to ignore the complex array of social conditions which underlie the production and circulation of these messages. This is a tendency which I shall seek resolutely to avoid. Without neglecting the symbolic content of media messages, I shall develop an approach which emphasizes that mediated communication is an integral part of – and cannot be understood apart from – the broader contexts of social life.

In the first section of this chapter I shall outline some of the features of the social contexts within which communication in general, and mediated communication in particular, should be understood. Against this backcloth, I shall then analyse some of the characteristics of technical media of communication (section 2) and some of the peculiarities of what is commonly described as 'mass communication' (section 3). The fourth section will be concerned with the ways in which communication media reorder relations of space and time and alter our experience of them. In the final section of the chapter I shall explore, in a preliminary way, the relation between mediated communication and the practical social contexts within which such communication is received and understood.

Action, Power and Communication

It has become commonplace to say that communication is a form of action. Ever since Austin observed that to utter an expression is to perform an action and not merely to report or describe some state of affairs,[3] we have become sensitive to the fact that speaking a language is a social activity through which individuals establish and renew relations with one another. But if communication is a form of action, then the analysis of communication must be based, at least in part, on an analysis of action and on an account of its socially contextualized character. Austin, and most subsequent speech act theorists, did not pursue the argument in this direction; hence their accounts of speech acts tend to be rather formal and abstract, divorced from the actual circumstances in which individuals use language in the course of their day-to-day lives. Today we can take up Austin's observation only by abandoning his approach and by developing a substantive social theory of action and of the kinds of power, resources and institutions on which it is based.

The account I shall develop here is based on the assumption that social phenomena can be viewed as purposive actions carried out in structured social contexts.[4] Social life is made up of individuals who pursue aims and objectives of various kinds. In so doing they always act within sets of circumstances which are given in advance, and which provide different individuals with different inclinations and opportunities. These sets of circumstances can be conceptualized as 'fields of interaction', to use a term fruitfully developed by Pierre Bourdieu.[5] Individuals are situated at different positions within these fields, depending on the different kinds and quantities of resources available to them. In some cases these positions acquire a certain stability by being institutionalized – that is, by becoming part of a relatively stable cluster of rules, resources and social relations. Institutions can be viewed as determinate sets of rules, resources and relations which have some degree of durability in time and some extension in space, and which are bound together for the purposes of pursuing some overall objectives. Institutions give a definite shape to pre-existing fields of interaction and, at the same time, they create new positions within these fields, as well as new sets of life trajectories for the individuals who occupy them.

The position that an individual occupies within a field or institution is closely related to the *power* that he or she possesses. In the most general sense, power is the ability to act in pursuit of one's aims and interests, the ability to intervene in the course of events and to affect their outcome. In exercising power, individuals employ the resources available to them; resources are the means which enable them to pursue their aims and interests effectively. Hence by accumulating resources of various kinds, individuals can augment their power – in the way, for instance, that an individual may build up personal savings in order to purchase a property. While resources can be built up personally, they are also commonly accumulated within the framework of institutions, which are important bases for the exercise of power. Individuals who occupy dominant positions within large institutions may have vast resources at their disposal, enabling them to make decisions and pursue objectives which have far-reaching consequences.

Understood in this general way, power is a pervasive social phenomenon that is characteristic of different kinds of action and encounter, from the recognizably political actions of state officials to the mundane encounter between individuals in the street. If today we commonly associate power with political power, that is, with the actions of individuals acting on behalf of the state, this is because states have become particularly important centres of concentrated power in the modern world. But the importance of state institutions should not blind us to the fact that overt political power is only one rather specialized form of power, and that individuals commonly exercise power in many contexts which have little or nothing to do with the state. In so doing, they both express and help to establish relatively stable relations or networks of power and domination between individuals, and between groups of individuals, who occupy different positions in fields of interaction.

It is helpful to distinguish broadly between several different forms of power. Following Michael Mann and others, I shall distinguish four main types – what I shall call 'economic', 'political', 'coercive' and 'symbolic' power.[6] These distinctions are primarily analytical in character. They reflect the different kinds of activity in which human beings typically engage, and the different kinds of resources on which they typically draw in exercising power. But in reality these different forms of power commonly overlap in complex and shifting ways. A particular institution or type of institution may provide the framework for the intensive accumulation of a certain kind of resource, and hence a privileged basis for the exercise of a certain form of power – in the way, for instance, that present-day commercial enterprises provide a framework for the intensive accumulation of material resources and a privileged basis for the exercise of economic power. I shall describe institutions which provide privileged bases for the exercise of certain forms of power as 'paradigmatic institutions'. But even paradigmatic institutions typically involve a complex mixture of different kinds of activity, resources and power, even if they are geared primarily towards the accumulation of a certain kind of resource and the exercise of a certain type of power.

Economic power stems from human productive activity, that is, activity concerned with the provision of the means of subsistence through the extraction of raw materials and their transformation into goods which can be consumed or exchanged in a market. Productive activity involves the use and the creation of various kinds of material and financial resources, which include raw materials, instruments of production (tools, machinery, land, buildings, etc.), consumable products and financial capital (money, stocks and shares, forms of credit, etc.). These resources can be accumulated by individuals and organizations for the purposes of expanding their productive activity; and, in so doing, they are able to increase their economic power. In earlier epochs, productive activity was predominantly agrarian, and the paradigmatic institutions of economic power were typically small-scale organizations oriented towards subsistence farming or towards the production of small surpluses for trade. With the development of modern societies, the paradigmatic institutions of economic power have become much larger in the scale and scope of their activities and more varied in character, with manufacturing and, subsequently, industrial production assuming a fundamental importance.

Economic power can be distinguished from *political power*, which stems from the activity of coordinating individuals and regulating the patterns of their interaction. All organizations involve some degree of coordination and regulation, and hence some degree of political power in this sense. But we can identify a range of institutions which are concerned *primarily* with coordination and regulation, and which pursue these activities in a manner that is relatively centralized within a territory that is more or less circumscribed. These institutions comprise what is generally referred to as the state – the paradigmatic institution of political power. Historically there have been many different forms of the state, from traditional imperial states and classical city-states to the modern form of nation-state. All states, or state-like institutions, are essentially systems of authority. They involve a complex system of rules and procedures which authorize certain individuals to act in certain ways. In some cases these rules and procedures are explicitly encoded in the form of laws which are enacted by sovereign bodies and administered by a judicial system.

However, as Max Weber among others has noted, the capacity of a state to command authority is generally dependent on its capacity to exercise two related but distinct forms of power, which I shall describe as coercive power and symbolic power. Ultimately the state can make recourse to various forms of coercion – that is, to the actual or threatened use of physical force – in order to back up the exercise of political power, both with regard to external conquest or threat and with regard to internal unrest or disobedience. The authority of the state can also be backed up by the diffusion of symbolic forms which seek to cultivate and sustain a belief in the legitimacy of political power. But to what extent do particular symbolic forms actually succeed in creating and sustaining a belief in legitimacy? To what extent are such beliefs actually shared by the various groups and members of a subject population, and to what extent is the sharing of such beliefs necessary for the stable and effective exercise of political power? There are no simple and clear-cut answers to these questions, and it is this uncertainty (among other things) which renders the political use of symbolic power a risk-laden and open-ended affair.

Although there is a close historical and empirical connection between political power and coercive power, it is sensible to distinguish analytically between them. *Coercive power* involves the use, or threatened use, of physical force to subdue or conquer an opponent. Physical force can be applied in differing ways, with differing degrees of intensity and with differing results. But there is a close and fundamental connection between coercion and bodily injury or death: the use of physical force carries with it the risk of maiming or destroying the opponent. Physical force does not consist simply in brute human strength. It can be augmented by the use of weapons and equipment, by training and tactics, by intelligence and planning, etc. Historically the most important

institutions for the accumulation of resources of this kind are
military institutions, and the most important form of coercive
power is *military power*. It is clear that military power has played an
enormously important role in shaping social and historical processes, both past and present. Throughout history states have
oriented a significant part of their activities towards the build-up
of military power, and towards the extraction – through conquest
and plunder, or through various kinds of taxation – of the material
resources necessary to sustain the institutions of armed force.
Traditionally military power has been used both for the purposes
of external defence and conquest, and for the purposes of internal
pacification and control. In modern societies, however, there is a
somewhat sharper differentiation between military institutions,
which are concerned primarily with maintaining (or expanding)
the territorial boundaries of nation-states, and the various paramilitary organizations (such as the police) and related institutions
(such as carceral institutions) which are concerned primarily with
internal pacification and control. But this institutional differentiation is by no means clear-cut, and there are many examples in
recent history when military power has been used to quell internal
unrest.

   The fourth type of power is cultural or *symbolic power*, which
stems from the activity of producing, transmitting and receiving
meaningful symbolic forms. Symbolic activity is a fundamental
feature of social life, on a par with productive activity, the coordination of individuals, and coercion. Individuals are constantly
engaged in the activity of expressing themselves in symbolic forms
and in interpreting the expressions of others; they are constantly
involved in communicating with one another and exchanging
information and symbolic content. In doing so, individuals draw
on various kinds of resources which I shall describe loosely as the
'means of information and communication'. These resources include the technical means of fixation and transmission; the skills,
competences and forms of knowledge employed in the production, transmission and reception of information and symbolic
content (what Bourdieu refers to as 'cultural capital'[7]); and the
accumulated prestige, recognition and respect accorded to certain
producers or institutions ('symbolic capital'). In producing symbolic forms, individuals draw on these and other resources to
perform actions which may intervene in the course of events and
have consequences of various kinds. Symbolic actions may give
rise to reactions, may lead others to act or respond in certain ways,
to pursue one course of action rather than another, to believe or

disbelieve, to affirm their support for a state of affairs or to rise up in collective revolt. I shall use the term 'symbolic power' to refer to this capacity to intervene in the course of events, to influence the actions of others and indeed to create events, by means of the production and transmission of symbolic forms.[8]

While symbolic activity is a pervasive feature of social life, nevertheless there are a range of institutions which have assumed a particularly important role historically in the accumulation of the means of information and communication. These include religious institutions, which are concerned primarily with the production and diffusion of symbolic forms pertaining to salvation, spiritual values and other-worldly beliefs; educational institutions, which are concerned with the transmission of acquired symbolic content (or knowledge) and the inculcation of skills and competences; and media institutions, which are oriented towards the large-scale production and generalized diffusion of symbolic forms in space and time. These and other cultural institutions have provided important bases for the accumulation of the means of information and communication, as well as material and financial resources, and have shaped the ways in which information and symbolic content are produced and circulated in the social world.

Table 1.1 Forms of power

Forms of power	Resources	Paradigmatic institutions
Economic power	Material and financial resources	Economic institutions (e.g. commercial enterprises)
Political power	Authority	Political institutions (e.g. states)
Coercive power (especially military power)	Physical and armed force	Coercive institutions (especially the military, but also the police, carceral institutions, etc.)
Symbolic power	Means of information and communication	Cultural institutions (e.g. the Church, schools and universities, the media industries, etc.)

Table 1.1 summarizes the four forms of power in relation to the resources on which they typically depend and the paradigmatic institutions in which they are typically concentrated. This typology does not purport to be a comprehensive classification of forms of power and types of institution. Moreover, as I indicated earlier, many actions will in practice draw on resources of various kinds, and many actual institutions will provide bases for differing forms of power: in the murky reality of social life, distinctions are rarely clear-cut. Nevertheless, this typology provides a helpful framework for analysing social organization and social change. And, as I shall undertake to show in the following chapter, this framework can be used effectively to analyse the institutional transformations associated with the rise of modern societies.

The Uses of Communication Media

I have characterized communication as a distinctive kind of social activity which involves the production, transmission and reception of symbolic forms, and which involves the implementation of resources of various kinds. I now want to examine some of these resources in more detail. I want to begin by considering the nature of communication media and some of the uses to which they can be put. I shall then consider some of the skills, competences and forms of knowledge which are presupposed by the use of communication media.

In producing symbolic forms and transmitting them to others, individuals generally employ a *technical medium*. The technical medium is the material substratum of symbolic forms – that is, the material elements with which, and by means of which, information or symbolic content is fixed and transmitted from producer to receiver. All processes of symbolic exchange involve a technical medium of some kind. Even the exchange of utterances in face-to-face interaction presupposes some material elements – the larynx and vocal cords, air waves, ears and hearing drums, etc. – by virtue of which meaningful sounds are produced and received. But the nature of the technical medium varies greatly from one type of symbolic production and exchange to another, and the properties of different technical media both facilitate and circumscribe the kinds of symbolic production and exchange which are possible.

We can examine these issues further by distinguishing several general aspects or attributes of technical media. One attribute is that the technical medium generally allows for a certain degree of *fixation* of the symbolic form, that is, it allows the symbolic form to be fixed or preserved in a medium which has varying degrees of durability. In the case of conversation – whether face-to-face conversation or that transmitted by technical media such as loudspeakers or telephones – the degree of fixation may be very low or effectively non-existent; any fixation that does occur may be dependent on the faculty of memory rather than on the distinctive properties of the technical medium as such. But in other cases, such as writing on parchment or paper, carving in wood or stone, engraving, painting, printing, filming, recording, etc., there may be a relatively high degree of fixation. The degree of fixation depends on the specific medium employed – a message carved in stone, for example, will be more durable than one written on parchment or paper. And just as different media allow for different degrees of fixation, so too they vary in the extent to which they enable a fixed message to be altered or revised. A message written in pencil is more susceptible to alteration than one written or printed in ink, and an utterance recorded on tape is more difficult to renounce than words exchanged in the flux of day-to-day interaction.

By virtue of the capacity for fixation, technical media are able to store information or symbolic content. Hence technical media may be regarded as differing kinds of 'information storage mechanisms' which are able, to differing degrees, to preserve information or symbolic content and make it available for subsequent use. Technical media, and the information or symbolic content stored in them, can thus be used as a resource for the exercise of different forms of power. It seems likely that the earliest forms of writing – those developed by the Sumerians and ancient Egyptians around 3000 BC – were used primarily for the purposes of recording information relevant to the ownership of property and the conduct of trade.[9] The development of economic activity in later historical periods, such as late medieval and early modern Europe, depended crucially on the availability of various means of recording and protecting information concerning the production and exchange of goods. Moreover, the exercise of power by political and religious authorities has always been closely linked to the collation and control of information and communication, as exemplified by the role of scribes in earlier centuries and the role of diverse agencies – from organizations compiling official statistics to public relations officers – in our societies today.

A second attribute of technical media is that they allow for a certain degree of *reproduction*. By 'reproduction' I mean the capacity of a technical medium to allow for the production of multiple copies of a symbolic form. With some kinds of technical media, such as stone carvings, the degree of reproducibility may be very low: it would require a great deal of effort to produce, in the medium of stone itself, multiple copies of a symbolic form carved in stone. The development of systems of writing and technical media like parchment and paper increased significantly the reproducibility of symbolic forms. Throughout the Middle Ages scribes were employed in considerable numbers to reproduce texts of a religious, literary and philosophical kind. But the decisive development in this regard was the invention of the printing press, which allowed written messages to be reproduced on a scale and with a speed that had not been possible previously. Similarly, the development of lithography, photography, the gramophone and the tape recorder were significant not only because they allowed visual and acoustic phenomena to be fixed in a durable medium, but also because they fixed those phenomena in a medium that enabled them in principle to be reproduced.

The reproducibility of symbolic forms is one of the key characteristics that underlies the commercial exploitation of technical media of communication. Symbolic forms can be 'commodified', that is, turned into commodities which are bought and sold in a market; and a principal means of commodifying symbolic forms is to develop ways of augmenting and controlling the capacity for reproduction. Many of the major innovations in the media industries – such as the introduction of Koenig's steam press in 1814 and the rotary printing press in 1848 – were directly concerned with increasing reproductive capacity for commercial purposes. But the commercial viability of media organizations also depends on the fact that they are able to exercise some degree of control over the reproducibility of a work. Hence the protection of 'copyright', or the right to reproduce, license and distribute a work, is of crucial significance for the media industries. In terms of its origins and its principal beneficiaries, the development of copyright law had less to do with safeguarding the rights of authors than with protecting the interests of printers and booksellers, who had a great deal to lose from the unauthorized reproduction of books and other printed material.[10]

While the reproductive capacity of technical media lends itself to commercial exploitation, it also has far-reaching implications for the notion of an 'original' or 'authentic' work.[11] The fact that an original or authentic work is *not* a reproduction becomes an increasingly important feature of the work; and as the reproduction of symbolic forms becomes more pervasive, the non-reproductive character of the original work becomes an increasingly important factor in determining the value of the work in the market for symbolic goods. Of course, with the development of techniques of printing and photography, it becomes possible to produce multiple copies or replicas of original works. But these replicas are not the same as the original, precisely because they are replicas; and they therefore command a much lower value in the market for symbolic goods.

However, many reproduced symbolic forms are not reproductions of an original work at all. Rather, the work *consists of* the copies or reproductions that are produced. As controlled reproduction becomes increasingly central to the process of production itself, the notions of originality and authenticity are gradually prised apart from the idea of uniqueness. So, for example, in the case of books, what typically become collectors' items are not unique texts but rather first editions, which comprise all the copies produced in the first printing of a work. Similarly, films and musical recordings are always produced in multiple copies, and all copies have roughly comparable status (provided that they are all of good quality or 'high fidelity'). Thus, whereas the economic valorization of works of art is generally based on the uniqueness of the work (and on the defence of this uniqueness from the claims of forgers and pretenders), the commercial exploitation of books, musical recordings, etc., is based on the capacity to produce the work in multiple copies and to control this reproductive process in a profitable way.

A third aspect of technical media is that they allow for some degree of *space-time distanciation*. Any process of symbolic exchange generally involves the detachment of a symbolic form from its context of production: it is distanced from this context, both spatially and temporally, and re-embedded in new contexts which may be located at different times and places. I shall use the expression 'space-time distanciation' to refer to this process of distancing.[12] All forms of communication involve some degree of space-time distanciation, some degree of movement through space and time. But the extent of distanciation varies greatly, depending on the circumstances of communication and on the type of technical medium employed.

In the case of face-to-face conversation, there is relatively little space-time distanciation. The conversation takes place in a context of co-presence: the participants in the conversation are physically present to one another and they share a similar set (or very similar sets) of spatial-temporal referents. The utterances exchanged in the conversation are generally available only to the interlocutors, or to individuals located in the immediate proximity, and the utterances will not endure beyond the transient moment of their exchange or the fading memory of their content.

The supplementation of speech by technical media of various kinds can endow it with extended availability in space or time or both. By amplifying speech, a loudspeaker can make utterances available to individuals who are beyond the reach of ordinary conversation: the utterances acquire extended availability in space, although their temporal durability remains limited to the moment of their exchange. By using other technical media, like tape recorders or various forms of inscription, utterances can be given extended availability in time. A message that is recorded or inscribed can be preserved for subsequent occasions; it can be played back or read by individuals located in other contexts which may be remote in time and space from the original context of production.

By altering the spatial and temporal conditions of communication, the use of technical media also alters the spatial and temporal conditions under which individuals exercise power.[13] Individuals are able to communicate across spatial and temporal distances, and hence are able to act and interact at a distance. They may be able to intervene in and influence the course of events which take place in locales that are spatially and temporally remote. The use of technical media provides individuals with new ways of organizing and controlling space and time, and new ways of using space and time for their own ends. The development of new technical media may also have a profound impact on the ways in which individuals experience the spatial and temporal dimensions of social life. We shall pursue these implications in more detail later.

Finally, let us consider briefly the kinds of *skills, competences and forms of knowledge* which are involved in using technical media. The use of a technical medium generally presupposes a process of codification; that is, it involves the use of a set of rules and procedures for encoding and decoding information or symbolic content. Individuals who employ the medium must have a mastery, at least to some extent, of the relevant rules and procedures. To have a mastery of these rules and procedures is not necessarily to be able to formulate them in a clear and explicit fashion; rather, it is to be able to use them in practice, to know how to go on, as Wittgenstein would say. We are rarely called on to formulate these rules and procedures explicitly, but we are required to use them practically every time we employ a technical medium of communication.

In considering the kinds of skills and competences involved in using a technical medium, it is important to distinguish between those required in order to encode information or symbolic content, and those required in order to decode the message. In practice these skills and competences may go together or overlap to a considerable extent (for instance, someone who knows how to write a particular language will also generally be able to read it). But these skills do not coincide and they may, on occasion, diverge significantly. Most individuals who watch a television programme, for example, are able to make some sense of the programme even though they may know relatively little about how the programme is produced.

When individuals encode and decode messages, they employ not only the skills and competences required by the technical medium, but also various forms of knowledge and background assumptions which comprise part of the cultural resources they bring to bear on the process of symbolic exchange. These forms of knowledge and background assumptions shape the ways they understand the messages, how they relate to them and how they integrate them into their lives. The process of understanding is always an interplay between encoded messages and situated interpreters, and the latter always bring an array of cultural resources to bear on this process. Again, we shall return to this issue below.

Some Characteristics of 'Mass Communication'

So far we have been considering some of the attributes of technical media of communication and some of the uses to which they can be put. I have been using the phrase 'technical medium of communication' in a general way, to refer to the material elements by means of which information or symbolic content is fixed and transmitted. But when we use the term 'communication media' we often think of a more specific set of institutions and products: we think of books, newspapers, television and radio programmes, films, tapes, compact discs and so on. That is, we think of a set of institutions and products which are commonly subsumed under the label 'mass communication'. But what is 'mass communication'? Is this a term to which we can give a clear and coherent sense?

It has often been noted that 'mass communication' is an infelicitous phrase. The term 'mass' is especially misleading. It conjures up the image of a vast audience comprising many thousands, even millions of individuals. This may be an accurate image in the case of some media products, such as the most popular modern-day newspapers, films and television programmes; but it is hardly an accurate representation of the circumstance of most media products, past or present. During the early development of the periodical press, and in some sectors of the media industries today (for instance, some book and magazine publishers), the audiences were and remain relatively small and specialized. So if the term 'mass' is to be used, it should not be construed in narrowly quantitative terms. The important point about mass communication is not that a given number of individuals (or a specifiable proportion of the population) receives the products, but rather that the products are available in principle to a plurality of recipients.

There is another respect in which the expression 'mass' may be misleading. It suggests that the recipients of media products constitute a vast sea of passive, undifferentiated individuals. This is an image associated with some earlier critiques of 'mass culture' and 'mass society', critiques which generally assumed that the development of mass communication has had a largely negative impact on modern social life, creating a kind of bland and homogeneous culture which entertains individuals without challenging them, which absorbs their attention without engaging their critical faculties, which provides instant gratification without questioning the grounds on which that gratification is based. This traditional line of cultural criticism is not without interest; it has raised some important issues which still deserve to be addressed today, albeit in a rather different fashion. But this critical perspective is also imbued with a set of assumptions which are untenable, and which can only hinder an understanding of the media and their impact in the modern world. We must abandon the assumption that the recipients of media products are passive onlookers whose senses have been permanently dulled by the continuous reception of similar messages. We must also abandon the assumption that the process of reception itself is an unproblematic, uncritical process through which products are absorbed by individuals, like a sponge absorbing water. Assumptions of this kind have little to do with the actual character of reception activities and with the complex ways in which media products are taken up by individuals, interpreted by them and incorporated into their lives.

If the term 'mass' may be misleading in certain respects, the term 'communication' may be as well, since the kinds of communication generally involved in mass communication are quite different from those involved in ordinary conversation. In the communicative exchanges which take place in face-to-face interaction, the flow of communication is generally two-way: one person speaks, another replies, and so on. In other words, the communicative exchanges of face-to-face interaction are fundamentally dialogical. With most forms of mass communication, by contrast, the flow of communication is overwhelmingly one-way. Messages are produced by one set of individuals and transmitted to others who are typically situated in settings that are spatially and temporally remote from the original context of production. Hence the recipients of media messages are not so much partners in a reciprocal process of communicative exchange but rather participants in a structured process of symbolic transmission. Hence I shall generally speak of the 'transmission' or 'diffusion' of media messages rather than of 'communication' as such. Yet even in the structured circumstances of mass communication, recipients do have some capacity to intervene in and contribute to the course and content of the communicative process. They can, for instance, write letters to the editor, phone television companies and express their views, or simply refuse to purchase or receive the products concerned. Hence, while the communicative process is fundamentally asymmetrical, it is not entirely monological or one-way.

There is a further reason why the term 'mass communication' may seem somewhat inappropriate today. We generally associate this term with certain kinds of media transmission – for example, with the diffusion of mass-circulation newspapers, with radio and television broadcasting, and so on. Yet today we seem to be witnessing changes of a fundamental kind in the nature of mediated communication. The shift from analog to digital systems of information codification, combined with the development of new systems of transmission (including high-powered satellites and high-capacity cables), are creating a new technical scenario in which information and communication can be handled in more flexible ways. We shall consider some of these developments in more detail at a later stage. Here I shall simply note that, if the term 'mass communication' is misleading as a description of the more traditional forms of media transmission, then it seems particularly ill-suited to the new kinds of information and communication network which are becoming increasingly common today.

In view of these considerations, the term 'mass communication' should be used with a good deal of circumspection. I shall generally use other terms – such as 'mediated communication' or, more simply, 'the media' – which are less laden with misleading assumptions. Nevertheless, we should not let these conceptual difficulties obscure the fact that, through a series of historical developments which can be documented quite precisely, a new range of communicative phenomena emerged. In so far as I use the term 'mass communication', I shall use it to refer to this interrelated set of historical developments and communicative phenomena. What we now describe rather loosely as 'mass communication' is a range of phenomena that emerged historically through the development of institutions seeking to exploit new opportunities for gathering and recording information, for producing and reproducing symbolic forms, and for transmitting information and symbolic content to a plurality of recipients in return for some kind of financial remuneration.

Let me be more precise: I shall use the term 'mass communication' to refer to *the institutionalized production and generalized diffusion of symbolic goods via the fixation and transmission of information or symbolic content*. I shall unpack this account by elaborating on five characteristics: the technical and institutional means of production and diffusion; the commodification of symbolic forms; the structured break between production and reception; the extended availability of media products in time and space; and the public circulation of mediated symbolic forms. Not all of these characteristics are unique to what we would call 'mass communication'. But together they highlight a set of features which are typical and important aspects of the kind of communicative phenomena to which we have come to refer with this term.

The first characteristic of mass communication is that it involves certain technical and institutional means of production and diffusion. It is this characteristic that has received most attention in the specialist literature on the media. For it is clear that the development of the media, from early forms of printing to the most recent developments in the field of telecommunications, has been based on a series of technical innovations which were capable of being exploited commercially. It is also clear that the exploitation of these innovations is a process that has taken place within a range of institutions and institutional frameworks, and that these institutions continue to shape the ways in which the media operate today. In other words, the development of mass communication is inseparable from the development of the *media industries* – that is, the array of organizations which, from the late Middle Ages to the present day, have been concerned with the commercial exploitation of technical innovations that enabled symbolic forms to be produced and diffused in a generalized fashion. In the next chapter I shall examine some of the technical and institutional aspects of the media, beginning with the commercial exploitation of the printing press in the second half of the fifteenth century. But unlike much of the specialist literature on media technologies, I shall try to relate the development of technical media to the broader institutional aspects of the development of modern societies.

The fact that mass communication typically involves the commercial exploitation of technical innovations is made explicit by the second characteristic – what I have called the commodification of symbolic forms. I discussed this characteristic briefly in the previous section, in relation to the reproductive capacity of technical media; here I shall elaborate in a more general way. I regard commodification as a particular type of 'valorization', that is, as one of the ways in which objects can be ascribed a certain value. Symbolic forms can be subjected to two principal types of valorization.[14] 'Symbolic valorization' is the process through which symbolic forms are ascribed 'symbolic value'. This is the value that objects have by virtue of the ways in which, and the extent to which, they are esteemed by individuals – that is, praised or denounced, cherished or despised by them. 'Economic valorization' is the process through which symbolic forms are ascribed 'economic value', a value for which they can be exchanged in a market. By virtue of economic valorization, symbolic forms are constituted as *commodities*: they become objects which can be bought and sold in a market for a price. I shall refer to commodified symbolic forms as 'symbolic goods'.

Mass communication typically involves the commodification of symbolic forms in the sense that the objects produced by media institutions are symbolic forms subjected, in one way or another, to the process of economic valorization. The modes of valorizing symbolic forms vary greatly, depending on the technical media and the institutional frameworks within which they are deployed. The commodification of some printed materials, such as books and pamphlets, relies largely on the capacity to produce and sell multiple copies of the work. Other printed materials (newspapers, for instance) combine this mode of valorization with other modes, such as the capacity to sell advertising space. In the case of radio and television broadcasting, the sale of air-time to advertisers has played an important role in some national contexts as a means of economic valorization. In other national contexts the recipients of radio and television programmes have been charged directly (through a licence fee) or indirectly (through taxation) for the right to receive broadcast material. Recent technological developments associated with cable and satellite transmission have created new opportunities for economic valorization, such as the payment of subscription fees or the use of credit cards which enable viewers to decode scrambled messages.

Of course, the commodification of symbolic forms is not unique to mass communication. There are other kinds of symbolic forms, such as paintings and other works of art, which are routinely subjected to the process of economic valorization. The development of a market for works of art – the art galleries, auction houses, etc. – can be seen as the development of a set of institutions which govern the economic valorization of works of art, and within which these works can be bought and sold as commodities. The more symbolic value has been ascribed to these works and their producers, that is, the more they are regarded as 'great works' and 'great artists', the greater the price, generally speaking, for which the works change hands in the art market. So the media industries are not the only institutions concerned with the economic valorization of symbolic forms. But in the modern world they are certainly among the most important of these institutions, and those most likely to impinge on the day-to-day lives of most individuals.

The third characteristic of mass communication is that it institutes a structured break between the production of symbolic forms and their reception. In all types of mass communication, the context of production is generally separate from the context or contexts of reception. Symbolic goods are produced in one context or set of contexts (namely, the institutions which form the media industries) and transmitted to recipients located in contexts which are distant and diverse (such as the varied settings of domestic households). Moreover, unlike many other cases of communication involving a separation of contexts, in the case of mass communication the flow of messages is, as I noted earlier, predominantly one-way. The context of production is not also (or not to the same extent) a context of reception, nor are the contexts of reception also (or to the same extent) contexts of production. Hence the flow of messages is a *structured* flow in which the capacity of recipients to intervene in or contribute to the process of production is strictly circumscribed.

This characteristic of mass communication has important implications for processes of production and reception. On the side of production, it means that the personnel involved in producing and transmitting media messages are generally deprived of the direct and continuous forms of feedback characteristic of face-to-face interaction. Hence the processes of production and transmission are characterized by a distinctive kind of *indeterminacy*, since these processes take place in the absence of cues provided by recipients. (Compare the difference between a speech delivered to an assembled audience, which can express approval or disapproval by laughing, clapping or remaining silent, and a speech delivered to a television camera.) Of course, media personnel have developed a variety of techniques to cope with this indeterminacy, from the use of well-tried formulae which have a predictable audience appeal (such as television series and film sequels) to market research and the regular monitoring of audience size and response.[15]

On the side of reception, the structured break implies that the recipients of mediated messages are, so to speak, left to their own devices. Recipients can make of a message more or less what they will, and the producer is not there to elaborate or to correct possible misunderstanding. It also implies that recipients are in a fundamentally unequal position with regard to the communicative process. They are, by the very nature of mass communication, unequal partners in the process of symbolic exchange. Compared with the individuals involved in the processes of production and transmission, the recipients of mediated messages have relatively little power to determine the topic and content of communication. But this does not imply that they are powerless, nor does it imply that they are simply the passive spectators of a show over which they have little or no control.

A fourth characteristic of mass communication is that it extends the availability of symbolic forms in space and time. This characteristic is closely connected to the previous one: since the media institute a separation between contexts of production and contexts of reception, it follows that mediated messages are available in contexts that are remote from the contexts in which they were originally produced. They can be, and generally are, received by individuals who are far removed in space, and perhaps also in time, from the individuals who produced them. The extended availability of mediated messages is a feature which has far-reaching consequences, and hence I shall discuss this feature in more detail below. Once again, the extended availability of symbolic forms is not unique to mass communication. All symbolic forms, simply by virtue of being exchanged between individuals who do not occupy identical positions in space and time, involve some degree of space-time distanciation. But with the development of institutions oriented towards the large-scale production and generalized diffusion of symbolic goods, the extended availability of symbolic forms becomes a much more significant and pervasive social phenomenon. Information and symbolic content are made available to more individuals across larger expanses of space and at greater speeds. The extended availability of symbolic forms becomes both more pronounced and more routine, in the sense that it becomes increasingly taken for granted as a routine feature of social life.

This brings us to a fifth characteristic of mass communication: it involves the public circulation of symbolic forms. The products of the media industries are available in principle to a plurality of recipients. They are produced in multiple copies or transmitted to a multiplicity of receivers in such a way that they are available in principle to anyone who has the technical means, abilities and resources to acquire them. In this respect, mass communication differs from forms of communication – such as telephone conversations, teleconferencing, or private video recordings of various kinds – which employ the same technical media of fixation and transmission but which are oriented towards a single or highly restricted range of recipients. The line to be drawn here is not clear-cut, and the distinction may be increasingly blurred in the coming decades by the deployment of new communication technologies which allow for more personalized services. Nevertheless, it is characteristic of mass communication as it has developed hitherto that its products are available in principle to a plurality of recipients – even if in fact, for a variety of reasons, these products may circulate among a relatively small and restricted sector of the population.

The availability of the products of mass communication has important implications for the ways in which we think about the distinction between the public and private domains. The fact that media products are available in principle to a plurality of recipients means that they have an intrinsically *public* character, in the sense that they are 'open' or 'available to the public'. The content of media messages is thereby rendered public, that is, made visible and observable to a multiplicity of individuals who may be, and typically are, scattered across diverse and dispersed contexts. The impact of communication media on the nature of the 'public sphere', and on the relation between public and private domains, is a theme that will be explored in detail in later chapters.

The Reordering of Space and Time

We noted earlier how the use of technical media of communication can alter the spatial and temporal dimensions of social life. By enabling individuals to communicate across extended stretches of space and time, the use of technical media enables individuals to transcend the spatial and temporal boundaries characteristic of face-to-face interaction. At the same time, it enables individuals to reorder the spatial and temporal features of social organization, and to use these reordered features as a means of pursuing their objectives.

All technical media have a bearing on the spatial and temporal aspects of social life, but the development of telecommunication technology in the second half of the nineteenth century was particularly significant in this regard. Prior to the advent of telecommunication, the extension of availability of symbolic forms in space generally required their physical transportation: with a few notable exceptions (for instance, semaphore), significant spatial distanciation could be achieved only by transporting symbolic forms from one place to another. But with the development of early forms of telecommunication, such as the telegraph and telephone, significant spatial distanciation could be achieved without physically transporting symbolic forms, and hence without incurring the temporal delays involved in transportation. The advent of telecommunication thus resulted in *the uncoupling of space and time*, in the sense that spatial distanciation no longer required temporal distanciation. Information and symbolic content could be transmitted over vast distances with relatively little delay; once the transmission wires had been installed, messages could be relayed in little more than the time required to encode and decode the information. Spatial distanciation was greatly enhanced, while temporal delays were virtually eliminated.

The uncoupling of space and time prepared the way for another transformation, closely linked to the development of tele-communication: *the discovery of despatialized simultaneity*.[16] In earlier historical periods the experience of simultaneity – that is, of events occurring 'at the same time' – presupposed a specific locale in which the simultaneous events could be experienced by the individual. Simultaneity presupposed locality; 'the same time' presupposed 'the same place'. But with the uncoupling of space and time brought about by telecommunication, the experience of simultaneity was detached from the spatial condition of common locality. It became possible to experience events as simultaneous despite the fact that they occurred in locales that were spatially remote. In contrast to the concreteness of the here and now, there emerged a sense of 'now' which was no longer bound to a particular locale. Simultaneity was extended in space and became ultimately global in scope.

The transformations of space and time brought about in part by the development of new communication technologies, and in part by the development of quicker means of transport, gave rise to increasingly acute problems of space-time coordination, problems that were eventually resolved through a series of conventions on the standardization of world time.[17] Until the mid-nineteenth century, each city, town or village had its own standard of time; there was a plurality of local times which were not coordinated with one another. But with the development of mail-coach services in the late eighteenth century and the construction of the railways in the early nineteenth, there was growing pressure for the standardization of time reckoning on a supralocal level. The introduction of the standardized railway timetable, based on Greenwich Mean Time, gradually led to the adoption of GMT as the uniform standard of time throughout Britain. The task of standardizing time reckoning on a larger territorial scale gave rise to new problems which were resolved through the introduction of standard time zones. Time zones were initially established on the North American continent in the 1870s and early 1880s, and in 1884 an International Meridian Conference was convened in Washington, D.C., for the purpose of establishing a global system for the standardization of time. The world was divided into 24 one-hour time zones and an international date line was established. The date line was agreed to be the 180th meridian at the same distance east and west of Greenwich; travellers crossing it eastwards gain a day, while those crossing it westwards lose a day. Thenceforth, the standardized system of world time provided a framework for the coordination of local times and for the organization of networks of communication and transport.

The development of new media of communication and new means of transport also affected the ways in which individuals *experienced* the spatial and temporal characteristics of social life. The standardization of world time was accompanied by a growing interest in the personal experience of time and space, of speed and simultaneity, and of the uncoupling of space and time. This interest found expression in the art and literature of the late nineteenth and early twentieth centuries, from Proust and Baudelaire to James Joyce, from cubism and futurism to surrealism. The literary and artistic impact of these developments has been explored perceptively by Stephen Kern, Marshall Berman and others.[18] Here I wish to consider in a more general fashion some of the ways in which the development of communication media has affected the sense of space and time of ordinary individuals.

Prior to the development of the media industries, most people's sense of the past and of distant places was shaped primarily through the symbolic content exchanged in face-to-face interaction. The telling of stories played a central role in forming people's sense of the past and of the world beyond their immediate locales. For most people the sense of the past and the sense of distant places, as well as the sense of the spatially delimited and historically continuous communities to which they belonged, were constituted primarily by oral traditions that were produced and handed down in the social contexts of everyday life. But the increasing availability of mediated symbolic forms has gradually altered the ways in which most people acquire a sense of the past and of the world beyond their immediate milieu. The role of oral traditions was not eliminated, but these traditions were supplemented, and to some extent reconstituted, by the diffusion of media products.

The development of communication media has thus created what we may describe as a 'mediated historicity': our sense of the past, and our sense of the ways in which the past impinges on us today, become increasingly dependent on an ever expanding reservoir of mediated symbolic forms. Most individuals in Western societies today have derived their sense of the major events of the past, and even the major events of the twentieth century (the two world wars, the Russian Revolution, the Holocaust, etc.), primarily from books, newspapers, films and television programmes. As events recede further and further into the past, it becomes less and less likely that individuals will derive their understanding of these events from personal experience, or from the personal experience of others whose accounts are handed down to them through face-to-face interaction. Oral tradition and face-to-face interaction continue to play important roles in shaping our sense of the past, but they operate increasingly in conjunction with a process of understanding which draws its symbolic content from the products of the media industries.

If the media have altered our sense of the past, they have also created what we could call a 'mediated worldliness': our sense of the world which lies beyond the sphere of our personal experience, and our sense of our place within this world, are increasingly shaped by mediated symbolic forms. The diffusion of media products enables us in a certain sense to experience events, observe others and, in general, learn about a world that extends beyond the sphere of our day-to-day encounters. The spatial horizons of our understanding are thereby greatly expanded, for they are no longer restricted by the need to be physically present at the places where the observed events, etc., occur. So profound is the extent to which our sense of the world is shaped by media products today that, when we travel to distant parts of the world as a visitor or tourist, our lived experience[19] is often preceded by a set of images and expectations acquired through extended exposure to media products. Even in those cases where our experience of distant places does not concur with our expectations, the feeling of novelty or surprise often attests to the fact that our lived experience is preceded by a set of preconceptions derived, at least to some extent, from the words and images conveyed by the media.

By altering their sense of place and of the past, the development of communication media also has some bearing on individuals' sense of belonging – that is, on their sense of the groups and communities to which they feel they belong. The sense of belonging derives, to some extent, from a feeling of sharing a common history and a common locale, a common trajectory in time and space. But as our sense of the past becomes increasingly dependent on mediated symbolic forms, and as our sense of the world and our place within it becomes increasingly nourished by media products, so too our sense of the groups and communities with which we share a common path through time and space, a common origin and a common fate, is altered: we feel ourselves to belong to groups and communities which are constituted in part through the media. We shall return to this phenomenon of 'mediated sociality' in later chapters, where we shall consider some examples in detail.

So far we have been considering some of the ways in which the development of communication media has altered individuals' sense of the past and of the world beyond their immediate locales. But let us now consider a somewhat different issue. Our sense of space and time is closely linked to our sense of *distance*, of what is near and what is far away; and our sense of distance is shaped profoundly by the means at our disposal to move through space and time. The means of transport are clearly crucial in this regard. For rural peasants in earlier centuries, London was much more distant than it is for country dwellers in Britain today. In the seventeenth century, when roads were poor and the average speed of horse-drawn carriages in provincial regions was probably around 30 miles a day, a journey to London from a county like Norfolk would have taken several days;[20] today it can be done in a couple of hours. The means of communication also play a crucial role in shaping our sense of distance. When communication was dependent on the physical transportation of messages, then the sense of distance was dependent on the time taken to travel between the origin and destination. As the speed of transportation-communication increased, the distance seemed to diminish. But with the uncoupling of space and time brought about by telecommunication, the sense of distance was gradually prised apart from its exclusive dependence on travel time. From then on, the sense of distance was dependent on two variables – travel time and speed of communication – which did not necessarily coincide. The world was shrinking in both dimensions, but more quickly in one than the other.

It is this transformation in the sense of distance that underlies what has been aptly described as 'space-time compression'.[21] With the development of new means of transportation and communication, coupled with the ever more intensive and extensive expansion of a capitalist economy oriented towards the rapid turnover of capital and goods, the significance of spatial barriers has declined and the pace of social life has speeded up. Previously remote parts of the world are drawn into global networks of interdependency. Travel time is steadily reduced and, with the development of telecommunication, the speed of communication becomes virtually instantaneous. The world seems like a smaller place: no longer a vast expanse of unchartered territories but a globe thoroughly explored, carefully mapped out and vulnerable to the meddlings of human beings.

We have yet to gain a clear understanding of the impact of these transformations on the ways in which individuals experience the flow of history and their place within it. In earlier forms of society, when most individuals lived on the land and derived their subsistence from it, the experience of the flow of time was closely connected to the natural rhythms of the seasons and to the cycles of birth and death. As individuals were increasingly drawn into an urban, factory-based system of employment, the experience of the flow of time became increasingly linked to the time-keeping mechanisms required for the synchronization of labour and the organization of the working week.[22] As time was disciplined for the purposes of increasing commodity production, there was a certain trade-off: sacrifices made in the present were exchanged for the promise of a better future. The notion of progress, elaborated in Enlightenment philosophies of history and in evolutionary social theories, was experienced in day-to-day life as the gap between past and present experience, on the one hand, and the continuously shifting horizon of expectation associated with the future, on the other.[23]

This way of experiencing the flow of time may be changing today. As the pace of life speeds up, the future no longer stretches out ahead of us like a promised land. The continuously shifting horizon of expectation begins to collapse, as it runs up against a future that repeatedly falls short of past and present expectations.

It becomes more and more difficult to hold on to a linear conception of history as progress. The idea of progress is a way of colonizing the future, a way of subsuming the future to our present plans and expectations. But as the shortcomings of this strategy become clearer day by day, as the future repeatedly confounds our plans and expectations, the idea of progress begins to lose its hold on us.

It is too early to say whether this shift will continue and, if so, what its consequences will be. There can be no doubt that, thanks in part to the development of new forms of communication and transportation, our ways of experiencing space and time have changed in a quite profound manner. This will be a central theme in the chapters that follow. But how far the developments discussed here have begun to reshape our experience of the flow of history and our place within it, our sense of the future and our orientation towards it: these are questions that I shall, for the most part, leave open.

Communication, Appropriation and Everyday Life

At several points in this chapter I have emphasized the importance of thinking about communication media in relation to the practical social contexts in which individuals produce and receive mediated symbolic forms. The neglect of these social contexts is a tendency that can be found throughout the history of theoretical reflection on, and practical analyses of, the media. For instance, under the influence of structuralism, semiotics and related orientations, a good deal of cultural criticism in recent years has been concerned with the constitutive features of 'texts' – not only texts in the narrow sense of literary works, but texts in the broader sense of meaningful cultural forms, from films and TV programmes to billboard ads and subway graffiti.[24] There is much to be gained from a rigorous analysis of the constitutive features of these 'texts'. But any such analysis is, at best, a very partial way of examining cultural phenomena (including literary texts). It is partial because the phenomena concerned are generally analysed without considering in a systematic and detailed way the conditions under which they were produced and received. The texts are generally analysed in and for themselves, without reference to the aims and resources of those who produce them, on the one hand, or the ways in which they are used and understood by those who receive them, on the other. The producers and recipients slip out of sight, while the analyst or critic focuses on a cultural form which is, somewhat artificially, abstracted from the social conditions of its production, circulation and reception.

Within the more empirical traditions of media research, the nature and role of recipients – or audiences – have been examined in considerable detail. Various research methods have been employed to study factors such as the size and composition of audiences, the degrees of attention and comprehension displayed by recipients, the short-term and long-term 'effects' of exposure to media messages, the social and psychological 'needs' fulfilled by consuming media products, and so on.[25] This research has produced a good deal of interesting and important material. But there are certain shortcomings in much of this earlier research. One shortcoming is this: by seeking above all to measure and quantify audiences and their responses, much of the earlier research has tended to neglect what we could describe as *the mundane character of receptive activity*. By this I mean the fact that the reception of media products is a routine, practical activity which individuals carry out as an integral part of their everyday lives. If we wish to understand the nature of reception, then we must develop an approach which is sensitive to the routine and practical aspects of receptive activity.

In recent years this type of approach has gained ground among media researchers. Some of the most insightful studies of reception processes have used a variety of methods, including participant observation, questionnaires and extended interviews, to probe in detail the conditions under which individuals receive media products, what they do with them and what sense they make of them.[26] These studies have firmly put to rest the idea that the recipients of media products are passive consumers; they have shown time and time again that the reception of media products is a much more active and creative process than the myth of the passive recipient suggests. They have also shown that the ways in which individuals make sense of media products vary according to their social background and circumstances, so that the same message may be understood in differing ways in different contexts.

I shall draw on some of these studies in later chapters, but here I wish to dwell on the general theoretical implications of viewing the reception of media products as a routine, practical activity. This orientation implies, in the first instance, that reception should be seen as an *activity*: not as something passive, but as a kind of practice in which individuals take hold of and work over the symbolic materials they receive. In the process of reception, individuals make use of symbolic materials for their own purposes, in ways that may be extremely varied but also relatively hidden, since these practices are not confined to a particular locale. Whereas production 'fixes' symbolic content in a material substratum, reception 'unfixes' it and frees it up to the ravages of time.[27] Moreover, the uses that recipients make of symbolic materials may diverge considerably from the uses (if any) that the producers of these materials had in mind. Even if individuals may have relatively little control over the content of the symbolic materials made available to them, they can use these materials, rework and elaborate them in ways that are quite alien to the aims and intentions of the producers.

This orientation also implies that reception is a *situated* activity: media products are received by individuals who are always located in specific social-historical contexts. These contexts are typically characterized by relatively stable relations of power and by differential access to accumulated resources of various kinds. The activity of reception takes place within these structured contexts and depends on the power and resources available to the potential recipients. One cannot generally receive television programmes, for instance, unless one has the means to acquire the necessary receiving equipment; and patterns of TV watching are commonly regulated in certain ways, reflecting broader relations of power between members of the domestic unit.[28] And yet, while reception is always a situated activity, it is also an activity which enables individuals to take some distance from the practical contexts of their daily life. By receiving materials which involve a substantial degree of spatial (and perhaps also temporal) distanciation, individuals can lift themselves out of their life contexts and, for a moment, lose themselves in another world.[29]

The reception of media products should be seen, furthermore, as a *routine* activity, in the sense that it is an integral part of the regularized activities that constitute everyday life. The reception of media products overlaps and interlocks with other activities in complex ways, and part of the significance that particular kinds of reception have for individuals derives from the ways in which they relate to other aspects of their lives. So, for instance, individuals may read newspapers to pass the time while travelling to work; put on the TV to ease the monotony of making dinner or to pacify children; read a book to relax and escape temporarily from the demands of daily life. The reception of media products can also serve to order the daily schedules of their recipients. Individuals may adapt their routines to fit in with the transmission timetables of broadcasting organizations – for instance, regularly watch the nine o'clock news, or reserve a weekly time-slot to see the unfolding episodes of a series. It is this aspect of reception – its capacity to impose order on daily routines – which is significantly attenuated by the use of video cassette recorders. By enabling recipients to record broadcast material and play it back at a time which suits them (or 'time-shift', as this practice is commonly known), VCRs allow recipients to free themselves to some extent from the temporal order imposed by broadcasting organizations and to integrate the process of reception into routines which are determined by other demands and constraints.

In addition to being a situated and routine activity, the reception of media products is a *skilled accomplishment*. It depends on a range of acquired skills and competences which individuals deploy in the process of reception. These skills and competences are extremely diverse. We have noted already that different technical media generally require differing kinds of skills and competences on the part of those who use them. But it is also important to see that, as socially acquired attributes, these skills and competences may vary in certain respects from one group or class to another, and from one historical period to another. They are attributes which are acquired through processes of learning or inculcation, and these processes may be socially differentiated in certain respects, or differentially accessible to individuals from differing backgrounds.[30] Once acquired, these skills and competences become part of the social make-up of individuals and may be deployed so automatically that they are no longer recognized as complex, and often very sophisticated, social acquisitions.

Finally, the reception of media products is fundamentally a *hermeneutic process*. By this I mean that the individuals who receive media products are generally involved in a process of interpretation through which they make sense of these products. Of course, the *acquisition* of media products does not necessarily involve a process of interpretation in this sense: a book can be purchased and never read, just as a television set can be left on while no one is watching it. To acquire is simply to take into one's possession, in the way that one acquires other objects of consumption like clothes and cars. But the reception of a media product involves more than this: it requires some degree of attention and interpretative activity on the part of the recipient. The individual who receives a media product must, to some extent, pay attention to it (read, watch, look, listen, etc.); and, in so doing, the individual is commonly engaged in making sense of the symbolic content conveyed by the product. Different media typically allow for, and require, differing degrees of attention, concentration and effort. Reading a book generally requires a good deal of concerted effort on the part of the reader, whereas a newspaper can be leafed through in a casual way, glancing at head-lines and occasionally reading pertinent articles. Television can be watched with varying degrees of attentiveness, from total absorption to intermittent observations which enable one to follow loosely the drift.

If we regard the reception of media products as a hermeneutic process, then we can draw on some of the insights of the hermeneutic tradition to characterize this phenomenon. Interpretation, as Gadamer would say, is not a presuppositionless activity: it is an active, creative process in which the interpreter brings a set of assumptions and expectations to bear on the message which he or she seeks to understand.[31] Some of these assumptions and expectations may be personal, that is, unique to a particular individual from whose life history they stem. But many of the assumptions and expectations that an individual brings to the process of interpretation are of a broader social and historical character. They are the common assumptions and expectations that are shared by a group of individuals who have broadly similar social origins and trajectories. They constitute a kind of implicit background knowledge which individuals acquire through a gradual process of inculcation, and which provides them with a framework for the interpretation and assimilation of what is new.

Since the interpretation of symbolic forms requires an active contribution from the interpreter, who brings a certain framework to bear on the message, it follows that the ways in which a media product is understood may vary from one individual (or group of individuals) to another, and from one social-historical context to another. As with all symbolic forms, the 'meaning' of a message conveyed by the media is not a static phenomenon, permanently fixed and transparent for all to see. Rather, the meaning or sense of a message should be regarded as a complex, shifting phenomenon which is continuously renewed, and to some extent transformed, by the very process of reception, interpretation and re-interpretation. The meaning that a message has for an individual will depend to some extent on the framework that he or she brings to bear on it. Of course, there are some limits to this process; a message cannot mean anything, and an individual must have some knowledge of the rules and conventions in accordance with which a message is produced in order to make some sense of it (for instance, he or she must have a rudimentary knowledge of the language). But these limits are quite wide and they leave ample room for the possibility that, from one individual or group of individuals to another, and from one social-historical context to another, the message conveyed by a media product may be understood differently.

The tradition of hermeneutics calls our attention to another aspect of interpretation which is relevant here: in interpreting symbolic forms, individuals incorporate them into their own understanding of themselves and others. They use them as a vehicle for reflection and self-reflection, as a basis for thinking about themselves, about others and about the world to which they belong. I shall use the term 'appropriation' to refer to this extended process of understanding and self-understanding. To appropriate a message is to take hold of its meaningful content and make it one's own.[32] It is to assimilate the message and incorporate it into one's life – a process that sometimes takes place effortlessly, and sometimes involves deliberate application. In appropriating a message we adapt it to our own lives and life contexts. We apply it to a set of circumstances which, in the case of media products, are generally different from the circumstances in which the message was produced.

The appropriation of symbolic forms – and, in particular, of the messages conveyed by media products – is a process that can extend well beyond the initial context and activity of reception. Media messages are commonly discussed by individuals in the course of reception and subsequent to it; they are thereby elaborated discursively and shared with a wider circle of individuals who may or may not have been involved in the initial process of reception. In this and other ways, media messages can be relayed beyond the initial context of reception and transformed through an ongoing process of telling and retelling, interpretation and reinterpretation, commentary, laughter and criticism. This process may take place in a variety of circumstances – in the home, on the telephone, in the workplace – and may involve a plurality of participants. It may provide a narrative framework within which individuals recount their thoughts, feelings and experiences, interweaving aspects of their own lives with the retelling of media messages and with their responses to the messages retold. Through this process of discursive elaboration, an individual's understanding of the messages conveyed by media products may itself be transformed, as the message is viewed from different angles, subjected to the comments and criticisms of others, and gradually woven into the symbolic fabric of everyday life.

In receiving and appropriating media messages, individuals are also involved in a process of self-formation and self-understanding – albeit in ways that are often implicit and not recognized as such. By taking hold of messages and routinely incorporating them into our lives, we are implicitly involved in constructing a sense of self, a sense of who we are and where we are situated in space and time. We are constantly shaping and reshaping our skills and stocks of knowledge, testing our feelings and tastes and expanding the horizons of our experience. We are actively fashioning a self *by means of* the messages and meaningful content supplied by media products (among other things). This process of self-fashioning is not a sudden, once-and-for-all event. It takes place slowly, imperceptibly, from day to day and year to year. It is a process in which some messages are retained and others are forgotten, in which some become a basis for action and reflection, or a topic of conversation among friends, while others slip away from one's memory, lost amidst the continuous flow of images and ideas.

To say that the appropriation of media messages has become a means of active self-fashioning in the modern world is not to say that it is the *only* means: clearly it is not. There are many other forms of social interaction, such as those between parents and children, between teachers and students and between peers, which continue to play a fundamental role in this regard. Early processes of socialization in the family and the school are in many ways decisive for the subsequent development of the individual and for his or her self-conception. But we must not lose sight of the fact that, in a world increasingly permeated by the products of the media industries, a major new arena has been created for the process of self-fashioning. It is an arena which is severed from the spatial and temporal constraints of face-to-face interaction and, given the accessibility of television and its global expansion, is increasingly available to individuals worldwide.

2

The Media and the Development of Modern Societies

Some of the distinctive features of the modern world are the outcome of a set of fundamental institutional transformations which began to take hold in Europe in the late Middle Ages and the early modern period. These transformations were complex and varied; they affected some regions of Europe, and subsequently some parts of the world, earlier and more profoundly than others. They were also contingent transformations, in the sense that they were dependent on specific historical conditions; had some of these conditions been different, they could, quite possibly, have yielded different results. But once these transformations were under way, they acquired a momentum of their own. New institutions appeared and expanded the range of their activities. Traditional practices were gradually eclipsed by new kinds of action, new conventions and new forms of association. The impact of these transformations was increasingly felt well beyond the expanding urban centres and emerging states of Europe. Through exploration, trade and colonization, other parts of the world were increasingly drawn into a process of institutional transformation which began in Europe, but which became increasingly global in scope.

What were the main lines of institutional transformation that were constitutive of the societies that emerged in early modern Europe? Thanks to the work of classical social thinkers such as Marx and Weber, as well as the results of more recent research by social historians and historical sociologists, some of the main lines of institutional transformation have become clear. In the first place, the emergence of modern societies involved a distinctive set of economic changes through which European feudalism was gradually transformed into a new system of capitalist production and exchange. Second, the development of modern societies was characterized by a distinctive process of political change through which the numerous political units of medieval Europe were gradually reduced in number and forged into an interlocking system of nation-states, each claiming sovereignty over a clearly defined territory and possessing a centralized system of taxation and administration. Third, it seems clear that war and the preparation for war played a crucial role in this process of political change; with the development of modern societies, military power was increasingly concentrated in the hands of nation-states which laid claim, as Max Weber once put it, to a monopoly of the legitimate use of force within a given territory.

These broad lines of institutional transformation seem relatively clear and have received a good deal of attention in the recent scholarly literature. What is much less clear, however, is whether the development of modern societies has been characterized by systematic transformations in what may be loosely called the 'cultural' domain. Here the legacy of classical social thinkers is less explicit and less helpful. Marx, in so far as he considered this matter at all, appeared to assume that the development of the capitalist mode of production would lead to a progressive demystification of the social world: the traditional values and beliefs which shrouded social relations in the past would be swept aside by the brute economic realities of capitalist production and exchange. Weber gave more attention to developments in the cultural domain, and he regarded these developments as more autonomous and more complex than Marx's writings suggested. But the themes which dominated Weber's account – the differentiation of spheres of value, the rationalization of action and the disenchantment of traditional world-views – have remained controversial and, in some respects, difficult to substantiate. Whether the development of modern societies has involved a distinctive process of cultural transformation is, it seems, uncertain.

In this chapter I shall argue that the uncertainty concerning the process of cultural transformation stems, to some extent, from the fact that social theorists and others have been looking in the wrong place for the signs of systematic cultural change. They have tried to detect broad changes in values and beliefs, in attitudes and orientations – in what some recent French historians would call *mentalités*. Such changes, in so far as they have occurred, are certainly interesting and important; but they are also, by their very nature, elusive, varied and extremely complex. Changes that occur in one region or class may not occur in another, or may occur in quite different ways, at quite different rates and with quite different consequences. Hence it becomes difficult to draw general conclusions about cultural change which stand a chance of being sustained in the face of varied and conflicting evidence. One need only consider the continuing debates over the secularization thesis – that is, the thesis that the development of modern industrial societies is accompanied by the decline in the role and relevance of religious belief – to convince oneself of the difficulty of trying to generalize about changes in values and beliefs.

The argument I shall develop in this chapter is that, by shifting the focus of attention, we can discern a broad transformation in the cultural domain which is both more systematic and more clear-cut. If we focus in the first instance not on values, attitudes and beliefs, but rather on symbolic forms and their modes of production and circulation in the social world, then we shall see that, with the advent of modern societies in the late medieval and early modern periods, a systematic cultural transformation began to take hold. By virtue of a series of technical innovations associated with printing and, subsequently, with the electrical codification of information, symbolic forms were produced, reproduced and circulated on a scale that was unprecedented. Patterns of communication and interaction began to change in profound and irreversible ways. These changes, which comprise what can loosely be called the 'mediazation of culture', had a clear institutional basis: namely, the development of media organizations, which first appeared in the second half of the fifteenth century and have expanded their activities ever since. By focusing on the activities and products of these organizations, and by examining the ways in which their products have been taken up and used by the individuals who received them, we can gain a firm hold on the cultural transformations associated with the rise of modern societies.

In this chapter I shall highlight some of the key aspects of the mediazation of culture from the late fifteenth century to the present day. I shall begin by examining in more detail the main lines of institutional transformation characteristic of modern societies. I shall then concentrate on the development of printing and the periodical press in early modern Europe, highlighting some of the ways in which these developments altered the pre-existing networks of communication and the established relations of power. In this context I shall consider some arguments of a more theoretical character concerning the impact of print in the early modern period. I shall conclude by highlighting some of the major transformations in the media industries since the early nineteenth century, in a way that will prepare the ground for subsequent chapters.

Some Institutional Dimensions of Modern Societies

How should we characterize the main institutional transformations which began to take place in Europe in the late Middle Ages and which have together shaped the contours of the modern world? In the previous chapter I distinguished four forms of power – economic, political, coercive and symbolic power – and related them to resources and institutions of various kinds. I now want to use this framework to analyse the institutional transformations associated with the rise of modern societies. I shall examine briefly the changing institutional forms of economic and political power. The institutional forms of coercive power will not be discussed in detail, but will be considered only in relation to the development of the modern state. I shall then focus on the social organization of symbolic power and on the ways in which it has changed over time.

Let us begin with the economy.[1] The early medieval economy was predominantly an agrarian economy based on small-scale productive units, such as the village and the manor. It was primarily a subsistence economy, although some surpluses were generated and extensive trading networks existed. Peasants were commonly tied to the land, which they tilled but did not own, and a portion of their output was appropriated by the manor lord. Gradually, from about the eleventh century on, trade began to expand significantly and towns grew in size and influence. Urban merchants, artisans and others were able to accumulate capital and use it for the purposes of increasing trade and commodity production. A new set of economic relations began to emerge, first in the towns and cities and then in the countryside, involving the increased use of money and extended networks of exchange. These new relations coexisted with traditional feudal relations for several centuries, as the European economy of the later Middle Ages underwent successive phases of expansion and contraction.

By 1450 a distinctive system of commodity production and exchange had emerged in Europe and was rapidly expanding, in terms of both output and geographical scope. The main characteristics of this new capitalist system are well known: as private individuals accumulated capital, they used it to provide the means and materials for commodity production, employing workers who were paid in wages; the final products were then sold at prices which exceeded the costs of production, enabling capitalists to generate a profit which they appropriated privately and, in some cases, reinvested in further production. By the end of the fifteenth century, capitalist enterprises were established in the major trading centres of Europe, and in the course of the sixteenth and seventeenth centuries they expanded their activities substantially. Trade within Europe increased and trading links were forged with other parts of the world, which, as Wallerstein and others have shown, were increasingly drawn into commercial relations with Europe. Cities such as Amsterdam, and later London, became major centres of capital accumulation and economic power within a network of commercial relations that were becoming global in scope.

The Industrial Revolution of the late eighteenth and early nineteenth centuries took place within the context of a capitalist economic system that had existed in Europe and elsewhere for several centuries. By introducing a range of new methods of production – including the use of power machinery, the ramified division of labour within a factory system, etc. – the Industrial Revolution greatly augmented the productive capacity of enterprises, ushering in the era of large-scale manufacturing industry. But these developments occurred within a set of property and productive relations that remained relatively stable. It was not until the twentieth century that attempts would be made, initially in the Soviet Union and subsequently in China and elsewhere, to develop large-scale manufacturing industry (as well as agricultural production) within a fundamentally different set of property and productive relations, in which economic institutions were increasingly subordinated to the centralized power of the state.

The modern state as we know it today – the 'nation-state' or 'national state' – is a cluster of institutions whose distinctive form emerged gradually from a lengthy process of state formation.[2] Medieval Europe was characterized by a large number of political units of varying size and strength, from relatively small city-states and urban federations to larger and more powerful kingdoms and principalities. In terms of political organization, medieval Europe was highly fragmented; as late as 1490 there were as many as 500 state-like entities in Europe. Five centuries later, the number of sovereign political units in Europe had been dramatically reduced, to around 25 states. The mechanisms by which this process of consolidation and centralization occurred have been well analysed by Charles Tilly.[3] There were, in Tilly's view, two key factors. On the one hand, rulers built up the means for exercising coercive power – primarily the means for waging war against external rivals and warding off external threats, but also the means for suppressing internal revolts and maintaining order within the territories over which they claimed jurisdiction. On the other hand, in order to build up the means for exercising coercive power, rulers had to develop ways of extracting resources, including men, equipment and capital, from their subject populations. These resources were rarely yielded willingly, and hence rulers had to develop increasingly effective means of taxation and administration, backed up by the ability to apply force if necessary. As the scale of military conflict increased, those states which could extract the resources to establish large standing armies, and to maintain them in a condition of war-readiness for extended periods of time, had a material advantage. They eventually became the key political units in an interlocking system of nation-states, each characterized by a centralized system of government and administration, each claiming sovereignty over a clearly defined territory, and each possessing the means to defend their claims by recourse to force if necessary.

While European states were consolidating their control over contiguous territories on the European continent, some of the major European powers were also expanding their spheres of influence overseas. Foreign territories provided additional sources of revenue for European states and were important trading partners for the capitalist firms and merchants based in Europe. As the economic importance of overseas territories grew, the major European powers devoted more of their resources to maintaining and expanding their spheres of influence and to warding off threats from rivals. Systems of colonial administration were installed in many of these territories, forming the basis for the subsequent development of political institutions which were modelled along European lines. The transformation of colonial territories into independent nation-states, with their own clearly defined boundaries and sovereign institutions, was a process that would be slow and faltering, that would come relatively late in the history of the nation-state (not until the mid-twentieth century in many cases), and that would be an endemic source of tension and conflict in the modern world.

The internal political organization of the emerging European states varied considerably over time, and from one region to another. In the period between the fifteenth and the eighteenth centuries, a form of absolutism, or absolute monarchy, emerged in France, Austria, Prussia, Spain and elsewhere.[4] Absolutism was characterized by the growing concentration of power in the hands of the monarch, who undertook to exercise this power in a relatively uniform way over the whole territory of the state. This task was facilitated by the development of a permanent centralized bureaucracy and a standing army, developments that were particularly marked in Prussia. The absolute monarch generally claimed to be the sole human source of law, unaccountable to representative assemblies and subject only to the law of God. But elsewhere in Europe – notably in England – the project of building an absolutist state never really took hold. For a variety of historical reasons, the English state developed into a form of constitutionalism in which the power of the monarch was tempered by a greater emphasis on the rule of law, the separation of powers and the role of opposition – both within and outside of Parliament. This emphasis, together with the dramatic political upheavals of the late eighteenth century and the growing pressure for political participation, helped to foster the development of the kind of liberal, representative and multiparty democracy characteristic of many twentieth-century states.

The formation of modern nation-states, whether in Europe or in other regions of the world, was interwoven in complex ways with the creation of symbols and sentiments of national identity. The establishment of a strong state generally preceded the formation of a strong sense of national identity within its boundaries – something which has, in any case, remained an elusive and deeply contested feature of modern political life. National identity could be roughly defined as a sense of belonging to a particular, territorially based nation or 'homeland', and of sharing a common set of rights, duties and traditions.[5] Since most modern states were formed through the forceful incorporation of diverse populations into discrete territorial units, a clear and pervasive sense of national identity was rarely present in the early phases of state-building. But the creation of a sense of national identity had advantages for political rulers: it could help to consolidate the nation-state, to counter tendencies towards fragmentation and to mobilize support for military and other aims. It could be argued, moreover, that the emergence of a sense of national identity – and indeed of national*ism*, understood as the channelling of national identity into the explicit pursuit of political objectives – was closely linked to the development of new means of communication which enabled symbols and ideas to be expressed and diffused in a common language. We shall return to this argument later. But first we must consider more carefully the nature of symbolic power and its transformation over time.

In what ways did the social organization of symbolic power change with the advent of modern societies in late medieval and early modern Europe? There are two changes which have been well discussed in the sociological and historical literature. One concerns the shifting role of religious institutions. In medieval Europe, the Roman Catholic Church was a central institution of symbolic power, holding a virtual monopoly on the production and diffusion of religious symbols and on the inculcation of religious belief. Following the collapse of the Roman Empire, the Church continued to provide a loose normative framework throughout Europe and established a system of monastic schools which specialized in teaching the skills of literacy and in transmitting sacred knowledge. In the early phases of European state formation, alliances were commonly forged between religious and political elites. Bishops and abbots helped rulers to control their domains, and rulers appealed to religious doctrine to sustain their authority and legitimate their rule.[6] The papacy also provided some degree of regulation and arbitration in interstate relations, helping to restrain some rulers and to maintain a balance of power. But as European states grew in strength and developed their own specialized systems of administration, the Church became increasingly marginal to the exercise of political power. Moreover, with the advent of Protestantism in the sixteenth century, the virtual monopoly of the Catholic Church was shattered. Religious authority became increasingly fragmented among a plurality of sects advocating distinctive lifestyles and claiming alternative paths of access to scriptural truth.

The fragmentation of religious authority and its declining hold on political power was paralleled by a second shift: the gradual expansion of systems of knowledge and learning that were essentially secular in character. The sixteenth century witnessed a significant development of sciences such as astronomy, botany and medicine. These emerging disciplines stimulated the formation of learned societies throughout Europe and found their way on to the curricula of the more liberal universities. As scientific knowledge was gradually freed from the hold of religious tradition, so too the system of education was prized apart from the Church. Schools and universities became increasingly oriented towards the transmission of a range of skills and forms of knowledge, of which scriptural knowledge was merely a part (and, in most cases, an increasingly diminishing one). Of course, access to the educational system was highly restricted throughout the early modern period; university students were almost exclusively the sons of urban elites, and a large proportion of the rural population remained illiterate. It was not until the nineteenth century that comprehensive systems of education were introduced by many European states, providing a set of nation-specific frameworks for the inculcation of a range of basic skills, such as literacy in a standardized national language.

There was, however, a third important shift in the social organization of symbolic power which has generally received less attention than the two just noted, even though it underpinned both to some extent: this was the shift from script to print and the subsequent development of the media industries. It is to this development that we now turn.

Communication, Commodification and the Advent of Printing

The rise of the media industries as new bases of symbolic power is a process that can be traced back to the second half of the fifteenth century. It was during this time that the techniques of printing, originally developed by Gutenberg, spread to urban centres throughout Europe. These techniques were exploited by printing presses organized, for the most part, as commercial enterprises. Their success and continued survival generally depended on their capacity to commodify symbolic forms effectively. The development of the early presses was thus part and parcel of the growth of a capitalist economy in late medieval and early modern Europe. At the same time, however, these presses became new bases of symbolic power which stood in ambivalent relationships with the political institutions of the emerging nation-states, on the one hand, and with those religious institutions which claimed a certain authority with regard to the exercise of symbolic power, on the other. The rise of the printing industry represented the emergence of new centres and networks of symbolic power which were generally outside the direct control of the Church and the state, but which the Church and the state sought to use to their advantage and, from time to time, to suppress.

The technical innovations which made possible the development of printing are well known and it will suffice to describe them very briefly here. The earliest forms of paper and printing were developed in China, well before they became widespread in the West.[7] Textiles were broken down into fibres, soaked in water and then matted into paper and dried. A writing brush made from hairs and ink made from lampblack were used to inscribe an elaborate system of ideographs involving several thousand characters. By the third century AD, paper was widely used throughout China for writing and other purposes. The techniques of paper manufacture gradually spread westward and, from the eighth century on, paper mills were established in Baghdad and Damascus. Merchants brought paper into Europe, although it was not until the thirteenth century that European paper production began on a significant scale. In the period 1268–76 the first Italian paper mill was established at Fabriano. Paper mills soon appeared in other Italian cities, including Bologna, Padua and Genoa, and Italy became a major source of supply for the rest of Europe. By the middle of the fourteenth century, paper was in use throughout Europe, providing a lightweight, smooth-textured and readily available medium of inscription which would prove ideal for the purposes of printing.

As with paper, the techniques of printing were originally developed in China. Block printing emerged gradually from processes of rubbing and stamping and was probably first used around 700 AD. Improved methods were introduced during the Sung dynasty (960–1280), including an early version of moveable type. The invention of moveable type is usually attributed to Pi Sheng who, during the period 1041–8, used clay to make characters which were hardened in fire.[8] The methods of printing by means of moveable type were developed further in Korea from the early thirteenth century on. The Koreans were the first to develop a form of moveable type made of metal, probably by adapting methods originally used for casting coins. Political authorities in Korea took a keen interest in type casting, printing and book manufacture; they established an Office of Publications which, by the fifteenth century, was responsible for a substantial output of printed materials. Although there is no direct evidence of the transfer of printing techniques from China and Korea to Europe, these methods may have spread with the diffusion of paper money, playing cards and books printed in China and with the gradual expansion of commercial and diplomatic contacts between East and West.[9] Block prints began to appear in Europe in the latter part of the fourteenth century, and block-printed books appeared in 1409. However, the developments commonly associated with Gutenberg differed from the original Chinese method in two key respects: the use of alphabetic type rather than ideographic characters; and the invention of the printing press.

Johann Gutenberg, a goldsmith from Mainz, began experimenting with printing around 1440.[10] Techniques of metal casting were well known in Europe by the beginning of the fifteenth century, but they had not been adapted to the purposes of printing. Gutenberg developed a method for the replica-casting of metal letters, so that large quantities of type could be produced for the composition of extended texts. He also adapted the traditional screw press, known in Europe since the first century AD, to the purposes of manufacturing printed texts. By virtue of this combination of techniques, a page of type could be composed, held together and handled as a single block; ink could then be applied to the block and paper pressed against it, in such a way that the paper took the imprint of the type. Although the technical details were subsequently refined in many ways, the basic principles of Gutenberg's press remained in use for more than three centuries.

By 1450 Gutenberg had developed his techniques far enough to exploit them commercially, and by 1455 several printing workshops were operating in Mainz. The techniques of printing spread rapidly, as printers carried their equipment and their skills from one town to another. By 1480 presses had been set up in more than a hundred towns and cities throughout Europe and a flourishing book trade had emerged. Cities in Germany and Italy became particularly important publishing centres, but presses were also established in France, The Netherlands, England, Spain and elsewhere. The output of these early presses was formidable. Febvre and Martin estimate that by the end of the fifteenth century at least 35,000 editions had been produced, amounting to at least 15 or 20 million copies in circulation.[11] At this time the population in the countries where printing developed was less than 100 million, and only a minority could read.

Most of the books – or 'incunabula', as they are sometimes called – produced by the early presses were in Latin, and a significant proportion (about 45 per cent) were religious in character.[12] These included many editions of the Scriptures (both in Latin and in the vernacular), as well as books used for church services and for private prayer, such as Books of Hours. The early presses also produced books of classical and medieval philosophy and theology, together with texts on law and scientific subjects, which were intended primarily for a university clientele. In producing these books, the early presses were building on and expanding a trade that had existed well before the advent of printing. Throughout the Middle Ages manuscript books had been produced by scribes working in monastic scriptoria as well as by copyists working in a putting-out system for lay stationers, who supplied books to university faculties and mendicant orders.[13] The early printers saw an existing market and developed a highly effective means of entering it. They produced printed books which initially looked very similar to copied manuscripts, and many booksellers sold both alongside one another. But gradually printing displaced the activities of scribes and copyists. Printed books acquired their own distinctive format and appearance, types and scripts became more uniform and the market for books expanded rapidly.

The early presses were, for the most part, commercial enterprises organized along capitalist lines. Printers had to raise sufficient capital to acquire the means of production – premises, presses, founts of type, etc. – and to purchase the paper and other raw materials necessary to produce books. Some of the early printers had enough assets to go into business on their own and operated effectively as publisher-printers, selecting material to print and taking the risks associated with it. Other printers required external financial backing. In some cases, they received backing from private financiers, publishers and booksellers, who chose the material to be printed and commissioned the printers; in other cases, they were commissioned by the Church or the state to produce liturgical texts and official publications. Most printing organizations remained relatively small-scale throughout the early modern period. In seventeenth-century Paris, for instance, most workshops had fewer than four presses and ten workmen.[14] But some larger organizations did emerge. Anton Koberger of Nuremberg developed a substantial publishing organization which, by the early sixteenth century, had 24 presses and about 100 workmen, as well as an extensive commercial network embracing the most important trading centres of Europe. Plantin of Antwerp formed a syndicate of publishers in 1563 and built up a large and powerful publishing organization, gaining a virtual monopoly on the sale of liturgical texts throughout the Spanish Habsburg Empire.[15]

The printing and publishing organizations that emerged in early modern Europe were cultural as well as economic institutions. This janus-faced character was reflected in the distinctive atmosphere of many of the early publishing houses, which were not only businesses but also meeting places for clerics, scholars and intellectuals. Moreover, the fact that printers and publishers were concerned with the commodification of symbolic forms meant that their relations with religious and political authorities were both enormously important and fraught with difficulties. The rise of the printing industry created new centres and networks of symbolic power which were based primarily on principles of commodity production, and which were therefore relatively independent of the political and symbolic power wielded by Church and state. Both Church and state sought to use this nascent industry for their own purposes, commissioning official documents, printed notices and regulations as well as works of a more extended kind. But their capacity to control the output of printers, and hence to maintain a firm grip on these new centres of symbolic power, was limited in various ways.

In the early years of printing, the Church strongly supported the development of the new methods of textual reproduction. The clergy commissioned printers to supply liturgical and theological works, and many monasteries invited printers into their premises. But the Church could not control the activities of printers and booksellers with the same degree of circumspection as it had exercised over the activities of scribes and copyists in the age of manuscripts. There were simply too many printing firms and outlets, capable of producing and distributing texts on too great a scale, for the Church to be able to exercise effective control. In the late fifteenth and early sixteenth centuries, numerous attempts were made by the Church – often acting in collaboration with secular authorities – to suppress printed material.[16] In 1485 Archbishop Berthold of Mainz asked the town council of Frankfurt to examine the books to be exhibited at the Lenten Fair and to assist the Church in suppressing pernicious works. In 1501 Pope Alexander VI tried to establish a more rigorous and comprehensive system of censorship, forbidding the printing of any book without the authorization of ecclesiastical powers. As the number of banned books increased, the Church eventually compiled an *Index librorum prohibitorum*; initially promulgated in 1559, the *Index* was continuously revised and updated and it remained in effect for some four hundred years. But while the interventions of religious and political authorities were numerous in the late fifteenth and sixteenth centuries, they were of limited success. Printers found countless ways to evade the censors, and books banned in one city or region were often printed in another and smuggled in by merchants and pedlars. Censorship stimulated a vigorous trade in contraband books.

The difficulties inherent in trying to control the trade in printed materials are well illustrated by the Reformation. That the new techniques of printing played a fundamental role in diffusing the ideas of Luther and other reformers cannot be doubted.[17] Luther's Ninety-Five Theses, initially posted on the door of the Augustinian church at Wittenberg on 31 October 1517, were soon translated into vernacular languages, printed as flysheets and distributed throughout Europe; it has been estimated that the theses were known throughout Germany in a fortnight and throughout Europe in a month.[18] Luther's sermons and tracts were published in numerous editions and were enormously popular. His pamphlet *To the Christian Nobility of the German Nation* was published on 18 August 1520 and had sold 4,000 copies within three weeks; by 1522, 13 separate editions had appeared.[19] It was not long before attempts were made in various cities and countries to suppress the literature associated with the Protestant revolt. The papacy condemned Luther's works, and monarchs issued edicts commanding that his books be burned. In France, for instance, a royal decree of 18 March 1521 ordered Parlement to ensure that no work was published which did not bear the imprint of the University of Paris, and on 13 June 1521 Parlement issued an embargo on the printing and sale of writings on scripture that had not first been approved by the University Faculty of Theology.[20] But these decrees and embargoes were of limited effect. Many printers migrated to cities just beyond the French frontier, such as Antwerp, Strasbourg and Basel, and printed material for clandestine export to France. Large quantities of material were produced and smuggled into France by merchants and pedlars. Illicit organizations emerged which specialized in the distribution of banned books. Renewed attempts were made, following the 'affaire des placards' in 1534, to crack down on the trade in forbidden works, and François I ordered a series of spectacular executions in which printers and booksellers were burned at the stake. The trade, however, continued. There were simply too many presses and too many ways of transporting books across frontiers for the trade to be effectively controlled by papal or royal decree.

If the medium of print contributed to the diffusion of Protestantism and the fragmentation of Christendom, it also had important consequences for other aspects of early modern European culture. Although a large proportion of the books produced by the early presses were religious in character, the works of classical authors – Virgil, Ovid, Cicero and others – were printed in multiple editions. The increasing availability of classical texts both facilitated and stimulated the revival of interest in antiquity, which had been under way among Italian literati since the twelfth century. The spread of Italian humanism to northern Europe no doubt owed a good deal to the intermediary role of printers, publishers and translators;[21] and the medium of print made it possible for scholars to try to fix and standardize the texts of antiquity, to an extent that would have been inconceivable when each text had to be copied individually by hand.[22] Scholars devoted themselves to the preparation of critical editions of classical works, which then became a basis for reproduction. Thanks to the reproductive and preservative powers of print, the work of the quattrocento humanists could become something more than a localized and ephemeral revival of interest in classical thought.

The medium of print also made it much easier to accumulate and diffuse data about the natural and social worlds, and to develop standardized systems of classification, representation and practice. Some of the early presses specialized in the production of texts on medicine, anatomy, botany, astronomy, geography, mathematics, etc., working closely with university professors and faculties in the preparation of scientific works. Printing created a new flow of data, charts, maps and theories which could be consulted, discussed and debated by scholars throughout Europe.[23] The early presses also printed many works of popular science, practical manuals and almanacs, which sold in large numbers. Almanacs contained, among other things, standardized tables for computing costs of goods, for converting weights, measures and systems of coinage, for calculating distances and travel times, etc.; they were used extensively by merchants and businessmen, providing them with a common framework for the conduct of trade beyond their immediate locales. Practical manuals and conduct-books offered guidance on a wide range of activities, from manners, morals and forms of speech to methods of business practice. Erasmus's *De Civilitate Morum Puerilium*, which fixed a code of manners and provided guidelines for the instruction of children, was enormously successful. First published in Basel in 1530, it is estimated that at least 47,000 copies of Erasmus's work were in circulation by 1600; it was translated into many vernacular languages, and many imitations and plagiarized versions appeared.[24]

Who read the books produced by the early presses? What was the social composition of the early reading public? The main customers of the books produced by the early presses were undoubtedly the educated urban elites, including the clergy, scholars and students, political elites and the rising commercial class. But it is likely that books were also available to, and read by, a substantial and growing proportion of urban craftsmen and tradesmen. Although evidence on rates of literacy in early modern Europe is fragmentary and inconclusive, there is some evidence to suggest that literacy rates were relatively high among certain groups of craftsmen, such as apothecaries, surgeons, printers, painters, musicians and metalworkers.[25] Books were available for sale in town shops and market stalls, and the smaller and cheaper books – like the chapbooks of the so-called 'Bibliothèque Bleue' – were almost certainly within the means of urban workers and craftsmen.[26] To what extent books were actually purchased and read by those individuals is difficult to determine with any degree of accuracy. Inventories of household goods left at death suggest that in early sixteenth-century France most artisans had no books in their possession when they died.[27] It is quite possible, however, that many individuals bought and read books and then sold them again, or borrowed books from others. Books could be resold relatively easily and – apart from works of reference like the Bible or the Books of Hours – there may have been little incentive for individuals of modest means to collect them.

Rates of literacy were relatively low among some sectors of the urban population, such as women, children and unskilled workers, and among the peasantry, which constituted the bulk of the population in early modern Europe. It does not follow, however, that individuals from these groups were untouched by the printed word. Chapbooks, almanacs and other printed materials were distributed throughout the countryside by pedlars, who carried their wares from village to village and offered them for sale.[28] Moreover, it is likely that on some occasions books were read aloud to groups of individuals who had gathered together for one reason or another. Such occasions may have included routine gatherings of family and friends, special feasts and festivals, as well as the meetings of special reading groups, like the secret Protestant assemblies which met to read and discuss the Bible.[29] Thanks to the practice of reading aloud, the audience for printed materials was considerably larger than the relatively small group of individuals who possessed the skills of literacy. Books and other texts were incorporated into popular traditions that were primarily oral in character, and only gradually did the printed word transform the content of traditions and their mode of transmission.

As the readership for printed books expanded in the course of the sixteenth century, a growing proportion of books were printed in vernacular languages rather than Latin. Printers, publishers and authors began to orient their production increasingly towards specific national populations who could read vernacular languages such as German, French and English.[30] The increasing use of vernacular languages stimulated attempts to render them more uniform. Many dictionaries and grammar books were produced with a view to standardizing spelling, vocabulary and grammar. National traditions of literature began to emerge and to acquire a distinctive character. Latin continued to be used as a scholarly and diplomatic language, and as the official language of the Catholic Church, throughout the sixteenth and seventeenth centuries. But by the late seventeenth century, in many linguistic contexts and in most parts of Europe, Latin had given way to a variety of national vernacular languages.[31] For a while French became a common language of scholarly and diplomatic exchange, although it never attained the preeminent position that Latin had occupied previously. It was not until the twentieth century that English would emerge as the new lingua franca of international – indeed global – communication.

The decline of Latin and the rise of national languages was a process propelled in part by the printing industry, but it had consequences that went well beyond the concerns of the industry as such. It was a process that was interwoven in complex ways with the changing position of the Church and with the growth and consolidation of nation-states. In so far as the Catholic Church continued to regard Latin as its official language and to forbid the use of vernaculars, a language barrier of ever greater dimensions developed between the Catholic clergy and lay populations. The clergy became more remote, the liturgy appeared more esoteric, and the authority of the Church – already dealt a severe blow by the success of Protestantism – became more vulnerable to criticism. On the other hand, in those countries that were predominantly Protestant in character, vernacular editions of the Bible and of other religious and liturgical texts played a crucial role in establishing a relatively uniform and generally accepted national language. Luther himself sought to abandon his own native dialect, that of Lower Saxony, and to fashion a language that would be readily intelligible throughout the German lands.

The growing importance of vernacular languages was also linked to the growth and consolidation of nation-states. In some cases the political authorities of early modern states actively favoured the process of linguistic unification, adopting a particular national language as the official language of state. For instance, in 1539, by the Edict of Villers-Cotterêts, François I established French as the official language of the courts of justice.[32] Regional languages and dialects continued to be spoken in the provinces and in contexts of daily life, but gradually they lost their institutional bases and became increasingly subordinated to the national language. Fluency in the national language became increasingly important as the means of interaction with state officials and as a means of access to the labour market.[33] Many regional dialects – especially those which remained primarily oral and were rarely used in print – declined in significance or disappeared. Moreover, as European states expanded their spheres of influence overseas, the official languages of the European powers became the dominant languages in other parts of the world, subordinating the languages of indigenous peoples to those of the colonizers. When decolonization gained momentum in the nineteenth and twentieth centuries, these dominant languages remained in many cases intact as the official languages of the newly formed nation-states.

It could be plausibly argued that the fixing of vernacular languages in print, and the promotion of some of these languages to the status of official languages of state, were important preconditions for the emergence of forms of national identity and nationalism in the modern world. This is the argument of Benedict Anderson, who maintains that the convergence of capitalism, the technology of print and the diversity of languages in late fifteenth- and sixteenth-century Europe led to the erosion of the sacred community of Christendom and to the emergence of a plurality of 'imagined communities' which subsequently became the bases for the formation of national consciousness.[34] As printers and publishers made increasing use of vernacular languages, they created unified fields of communication which were more diverse than Latin and less diverse than the multiplicity of spoken dialects. By reading vernacular texts, individuals gradually became aware of the fact that they belonged to a virtual community of fellow readers with whom they would never directly interact, but to whom they were connected via the medium of print. It is this virtual community of fellow readers that would eventually become, Anderson suggests, the imagined community of the nation.

This is an important and provocative argument, and it has had considerable impact on recent debates. It is certainly plausible to suggest that the formation of national communities, and of the distinctively modern sense of belonging to a particular, territorially based nation, was linked to the development of new systems of communication which enabled individuals to share symbols and beliefs expressed in a common language – that is, to share what might roughly be called a national tradition – even though these individuals may never have interacted directly. But there are problems with Anderson's argument. The main problem is that the precise nature of the alleged link between the development of printing and the rise of nationalism is never spelled out in detail. There is a considerable gulf – historically as well as conceptually – between the emergence of a plurality of reading publics in sixteenth-century Europe, on the one hand, and the emergence of various forms of national identity and nationalism in the nineteenth and twentieth centuries, on the other. If the early reading public was the embryo of the nationally imagined community, why did it take nearly three centuries for this embryo to mature?

Anderson recognizes, of course, that the development of print and other technical media of communication was at best a necessary condition for the emergence of national consciousness, not a sufficient condition. He devotes a good deal of attention to the struggles against colonialism which have played such an important role in shaping nationalist movements in the nineteenth and twentieth centuries. But the discussion of these later developments is not connected by Anderson in a clear and cogent way to the advent of what he calls 'print-capitalism' in early modern Europe. He sketches what is at best a loose and tentative connection; the causal links (if they exist) are not examined in any detail. As an account of the rise of nationalism, therefore, Anderson's argument is suggestive but not entirely persuasive. One is left with the impression that, while the development of printing may have played some (as yet rather imprecisely defined) role, the main explanation for the rise of nationalism is likely to be provided by other factors.

More generally, while Anderson's argument focuses our attention on the possible social and political consequences of changes in the nature of communication media in early modern Europe, it does not trace through these consequences in a convincing fashion. Partly this may be due to the fact that his overriding concern is to try to understand the phenomenon of nationalism rather than to examine the nature and impact of communication media as such. Hence he does not examine, for instance, the ways in which media products were used by individuals, the changing forms of action and interaction made possible by new media of communication and the ways in which the development of communication media gradually altered the nature of tradition and individuals' relation to it. These are some of the issues we shall explore in more detail in subsequent chapters.

The Rise of the Trade in News

There is another way in which the development of printing transformed the patterns of communication in early modern Europe: it gave rise to a variety of periodical publications which reported events and conveyed information of a political and commercial character. Prior to the advent of printing, a number of regularized networks of communication had been established throughout Europe. We can distinguish at least four distinct types of pre-print communication network. First, there was an extensive network of communication established and controlled by the Catholic Church. This network enabled the papacy in Rome to maintain contact with the clergy and political elites dispersed throughout the loosely knit realm of Christendom. Second, there were networks of communication established by the political authorities of states and principalities; these networks operated both within the territories of particular states, facilitating administration and pacification, and between states which maintained some form of diplomatic communication with one another. A third type of network was linked to the expansion of commercial activity. As trade and manufacturing increased, new networks of communication were established within the business community and between the major trading centres. Commercial and banking houses – like the Fugger family of Augsburg and the great merchant houses of Florence – built up extensive systems of communication and began to supply information to clients on a commercial basis. Finally, information was also transmitted to towns and villages via networks of merchants, pedlars and travelling entertainers, such as storytellers and ballad singers. As individuals gathered in market-places or taverns and interacted with merchants and travellers, they picked up news about events which took place in distant locales.

In the course of the fifteenth, sixteenth and seventeenth centuries, these networks of communication were affected by two key developments. In the first place, some states began to establish regular postal services which became increasingly available for general use. In France Louis XI established a royal post in 1464; private individuals could use the post by special permission and payment of a fee.[35] In central Europe Maximilian I developed an extensive postal network which linked the heartland of the Habsburg empire with cities throughout Europe. In 1490 he appointed Franz and Johann von Taxis as chief postmasters, thus establishing an imperial postal system that remained under the control of the von Taxis family for several centuries.[36] In England a royal post was established early in the reign of Henry VIII, and a postmaster was appointed around 1516, although the development of regular postal services for general public use did not occur until the early seventeenth century.[37] Gradually in the course of the seventeenth and eighteenth centuries, an integrated network of public postal communication emerged, providing common carrier services for both domestic and foreign post. Of course, by twentieth-century standards, postal communication in early modern Europe was very slow. Messages were transported by horse and carriage at a time when the roads in many parts of Europe were of poor quality. Mail rarely travelled at more than 10 miles per hour over extended distances. In the late eighteenth century, Edinburgh was still a journey of 60 hours from London, and it took 24 hours to travel from London to Manchester. It was not until the early nineteenth century, with the development of the railways, that the time required to transmit messages through the post was sharply reduced.

The second development which profoundly affected the established networks of communication in early modern Europe was the application of printing to the production and dissemination of news. Soon after the advent of printing in the mid-fifteenth century, a variety of printed information leaflets, posters and broadsheets began to appear. These were a mixture of official or semi-official statements of government decrees; polemical tracts; descriptions of particular events, such as military encounters or natural disasters; and sensationalized accounts of extraordinary or supernatural phenomena, like giants, comets and apparitions. These leaflets and news sheets were generally one-off or irregular publications. They were printed by the thousands and sold in the streets by hawkers and pedlars. They provided individuals with a valuable source of information about current and distant events.

Periodical publications of news and information began to appear in the second half of the sixteenth century, but the origins of the modern newspaper are usually traced to the first two decades of the seventeenth century, when regular journals of news began to appear on a weekly basis with some degree of reliability.[38] In 1609 weekly journals were published in several German cities, including Augsburg, Strasbourg and Wolfenbüttel, and there is some evidence to suggest that a weekly paper may have appeared somewhat earlier (1607) in Amsterdam. Printed weeklies – or 'corantos', as these early compilations of news were called at the time – soon appeared in other cities and languages. The cities located along the major European trading routes, such as Cologne, Frankfurt, Antwerp and Berlin, became early centres of newspaper production. The news which made up the corantos was often supplied by postmasters, who collected the news in their regions and then forwarded it to the major cities. A single individual could then assemble and edit the postmasters' reports, printing them in the form of a series of short paragraphs with details of the date and place of origin of the information. The weeklies could also be translated into other languages and sold in different cities and countries.

By 1620 Amsterdam had become the centre of a rapidly expanding trade in news. There was a growing public interest in the Thirty Years' War and this provided a major stimulus to the development of the fledgling newspaper industry. The first newspaper to appear in English was probably produced in Amsterdam in 1620 by the Dutch printer and map engraver Pieter van den Keere and exported to London.[39] Between 2 December 1620 and 18 September 1621, 15 issues of van den Keere's coranto appeared. Although it was not published weekly, it did appear fairly frequently and it provided regular coverage of the Thirty Years' War. The first coranto printed in England was probably produced by the London stationer Thomas Archer in 1621. Archer was subsequently imprisoned for publishing an unlicensed news sheet on the war in the Palatinate, but other English corantos and news pamphlets soon appeared.

Most of these early forms of newspaper were concerned primarily with foreign news, that is, with events which were taking place (or had taken place) in distant locales. The individuals who read these papers, or listened to them being read aloud by others, would learn of events taking place in distant parts of Europe – events they could not witness directly, in places they would never, in all likelihood, visit. Hence the circulation of the early forms of newspaper helped to create a sense of a world of events which lay beyond the individual's immediate milieu, but which had some relevance to, and potentially some bearing on, his or her life. Of course, the geographical scope of this world remained quite limited in the early seventeenth century: it rarely extended beyond the major cities and countries of Europe. Moreover, the circulation of the early newspapers was very low by present-day standards (one estimate puts the minimum print run of the early newspapers at 400 copies,[40] and in many cases it was probably not much more than that), although papers were no doubt read by more than one individual, and were commonly read aloud. But the importance of this new mode of information diffusion, through which printed reports of distant events were made available on a regular basis to an unlimited number of recipients, should not be underestimated.

While the early corantos were concerned mainly with foreign news, it was not long before newspapers began to devote more attention to domestic events. In England this development had to wait until 1640, when the government's strict control of the press began to weaken. Since 1586 a Star Chamber decree had established a comprehensive system of licensing and censorship (supplemented by a further decree of 1637), which limited the number of printers in England and subjected them to specific censors for each type of publication. But as the crisis between Charles I and Parliament deepened, it became increasingly difficult for the Crown to enforce its control of the press, and in July 1641 the Star Chamber was abolished. The crisis also stimulated a public demand for up-to-date news of domestic political affairs. Between mid-November 1641 and the end of December 1641 three domestic weekly newspapers appeared, each providing summaries of the proceedings of Parliament; and in the first three months of 1642 another eight newspapers appeared, though some did not last for long.[41] This was the beginning of a period of relatively uncontrolled and intensive publication of newspapers, newsbooks and pamphlets dealing with the events of the Civil War and the issues surrounding it. During most weeks of 1645, 14 newspapers were on sale in the streets of London, as well as a multitude of other pamphlets and political tracts. While strict controls were reimposed by Charles II after the restoration of the monarchy in 1660, the period between 1641 and the restoration was an important one in the history of the press. For it was during this time that periodical publications emerged as key players in the affairs of state, providing a continuous flow of information on current events and expressing a range of differing views – sometimes sharply conflicting views – on matters of public concern.

The development of a commercially based periodical press which was independent of state power, and yet was capable of providing information and critical commentary on issues of general concern, entered a new phase in eighteenth-century England. The system of licensing, which had been re-established by Charles II in 1662, fell into abeyance at the end of the seventeenth century and was followed by a spate of new periodical publications. The first daily newspaper in England, Samuel Buckley's *Daily Courant*, appeared in 1702 and was soon joined by others. A variety of more specialized periodicals appeared, some concentrating on entertainment and cultural events, some on financial and commercial news, and others on social and political commentary. The latter included a number of journals which popularized the genre of the political essay, like the *Tatler*, the *Spectator*, Nicholas Amhurst's *Craftsman*, Daniel Defoe's *Review* and Jonathan Swift's *Examiner*. By 1750 London had five well-established daily papers, six thrice-weeklies, five weeklies and several other cut-price periodicals, with a total circulation between them of around 100,000 copies per week.[42] The papers were distributed in the city by networks of hawkers and agents, as well as by a loose federation of coffee houses which acquired the major papers and made them available for their customers to read. Since many papers were read in public places like taverns and coffee houses, their readership was almost certainly much higher than their circulation – perhaps as much as ten times higher. London papers were also distributed to the provinces by rapidly improving stage-coach and postal services.

The political authorities sought to exercise some control over the proliferation of newspapers and periodicals by imposing special taxes, which would, it was thought, serve to restrict production and force the more marginal periodicals out of business, while at the same time raising additional revenue for the Crown. The Stamp Act of 1712 required newspaper proprietors to pay one penny for every printed sheet and one shilling for every advertisement. Subsequent Acts increased the amounts and broadened the basis for the application of the law. The Stamp Acts were bitterly opposed and became a rallying point in the struggle for the freedom of the press. It was not until the 1830s that the taxes were progressively reduced, and in the 1860s they were eventually abolished. Elsewhere in Europe the periodical press of the eighteenth century was controlled and censored with varying degrees of severity.[43] In the United Provinces the press remained relatively free, although it was discouraged from discussing local politics and was occasionally subjected to bouts of intensive censorship. In France a centralized and highly restrictive system of licensing, supervision and censorship existed until the Revolution; a brief post-revolutionary period of press freedom was finally brought to an end by Napoleon, who instituted a strict system of censorship and control. In the states and principalities of Germany and Italy the degree of official control varied from one state to another, but newspapers were generally allowed more leeway in reporting foreign news than in discussing domestic politics.

There is considerable force in the argument that the struggle for an independent press, capable of reporting and commenting on events with a minimum of state interference and control, played a key role in the development of the modern constitutional state. Some of the early liberal and liberal democratic thinkers, such as Jeremy Bentham, James Mill and John Stuart Mill, were fervent advocates of the liberty of the press. They saw the free expression of opinion through the organs of an independent press as a vital safeguard against the despotic use of state power.[44] It is significant that, following their successful war of independence against the British Crown, the American colonists incorporated the right of press freedom in the First Amendment to the Constitution. Similarly, the post-revolutionary French constitutions of 1791 and 1793, building on the Declaration des Droits de l'Homme of 1789, explicitly protected the freedom of expression (even if this freedom was subsequently abolished by Napoleon). Statutory guarantees of freedom of expression were eventually adopted by various European governments so that by the end of the nineteenth century the freedom of the press had become a constitutional feature of many Western states.

The Theory of the Public Sphere: A Preliminary Assessment

While the importance of an independent press was apparent to many of the early liberal and liberal-democratic thinkers, this is a theme which has, with a few exceptions, faded from view in the work of more recent social and political theorists. One exception is Habermas's early, path-breaking work, *The Structural Transformation of the Public Sphere*.[45] Habermas argues that the development of mercantile capitalism in the sixteenth century, together with the changing institutional forms of political power, created the conditions for the emergence of a new kind of public sphere in early modern Europe. In this context, the meaning of 'public authority' began to shift: it began to refer less to the domain of courtly life and increasingly to the activities of an emerging state system which had legally defined spheres of jurisdiction and a monopoly on the legitimate use of violence. At the same time, 'civil society' emerged as a domain of privatized economic relations which were established under the aegis of public authority. The 'private' realm thus comprised both the expanding domain of economic relations and the intimate sphere of personal relations which became increasingly disengaged from economic activity and anchored in the institution of the conjugal family. Between the realm of public authority or the state, on the one hand, and the private realm of civil society and personal relations, on the other, there emerged a new sphere of 'the public': a bourgeois public sphere which consisted of private individuals who came together to debate among themselves the regulation of civil society and the conduct of the state. This new public sphere was not part of the state but was, on the contrary, a sphere in which the activities of the state could be confronted and subjected to criticism. The medium of this confrontation was itself significant: it was the public use of reason, as articulated by private individuals engaged in argument that was *in principle* open and unconstrained.

In accounting for the emergence of the bourgeois public sphere, Habermas attributes particular importance to the rise of the periodical press. The critical journals and moral weeklies which began to appear in Europe in the late seventeenth and eighteenth centuries provided a new forum for the conduct of public debate. While these publications often originated as journals devoted to literary and cultural criticism, they increasingly became concerned with issues of more general social and political significance. Moreover, a variety of new centres of sociability appeared in the towns and cities of early modern Europe. These included the salons and coffee houses which, from around the mid-seventeenth century on, became places of discussion and milieux where educated elites could interact with one another and with the nobility on a more or less equal footing.

It was in England at the beginning of the eighteenth century that the most favourable conditions were created for the emergence of the bourgeois public sphere. Censorship and political control of the press were less stringent than in some other parts of Europe, and papers and journals proliferated. At the same time, coffee houses flourished; by the first decade of the eighteenth century, there were an estimated three thousand coffee houses in London alone, each with a core of regular clients. Many of the new periodicals were closely interwoven with the life of the coffee houses, as they were read and debated by individuals who came together to discuss the issues of the day.

Part of Habermas's argument is that the critical discussion stimulated by the periodical press eventually had a transformative impact on the institutional form of modern states. By being constantly called before the forum of the public, Parliament became increasingly open to scrutiny, eventually abandoning its right to prevent the publication of its proceedings. Parliament also became more responsive to the press and began to play a more constructive role in the formation and articulation of public opinion. These and other developments were of considerable significance; they are an enduring testimony to the political impact of the bourgeois public sphere and to the role it played in the shaping of Western states. But Habermas also argues that, in the specific form in which it existed in the eighteenth century, the bourgeois public sphere did not last for long. We shall return to this aspect of his account below.

Habermas's argument, sketched very briefly here, has the considerable merit of highlighting the broader political significance of the development of the periodical press in early modern Europe. The development of the press is treated not as a history set apart from broader social-historical processes, but rather as integral to them. There are, however, many difficulties with Habermas's account. In later chapters I shall examine in detail the conception of publicness which is implicit in this account and the normative issues which arise from it. Here I shall restrict myself to considering some of the historical problems.

(1) One of the criticisms most frequently made of Habermas's account is that, by focusing attention on the *bourgeois* public sphere, he tends to neglect the significance of other forms of public discourse and activity which existed in seventeenth-, eighteenth- and nineteenth-century Europe, forms which were not part of, and in some cases were excluded from or opposed to, the forms of bourgeois sociability.[46] The work of E. P. Thompson, Christopher Hill and others has highlighted the significance of a variety of popular social and political movements in the early modern period,[47] and it cannot be assumed that these movements were either derivative of, or organized along similar lines to, the activities which took place in the bourgeois public sphere. On the contrary, the relationship between the bourgeois public sphere and popular social movements was often a conflictual one.[48] Just as the emerging bourgeois public sphere defined itself in opposition to the traditional authority of royal power, so too it was confronted by the rise of popular movements which it sought to contain.

This is a forceful line of criticism and it is to Habermas's credit that, reflecting on these issues 30 years later,[49] he acknowledges the shortcomings of his earlier approach. Not only were popular social movements much more important in the early modern period than he had previously allowed, but it is also clear that they cannot be adequately understood as a mere 'variant' of the liberal model of the bourgeois public sphere, as he had somewhat hastily suggested.[50] A satisfactory account of popular social movements and popular cultural forms would require a more flexible approach, one which allows for the possibility that they may have a shape and dynamic of their own.

(2) In a similar vein, one can question Habermas's emphasis on the periodical press of the early eighteenth century. It is not difficult to see why Habermas focuses on this material: political periodicals like Defoe's *Review* and Swift's *Examiner* exemplified the kind of cultivated criticism and debate that Habermas wished to encapsulate in the idea of the public sphere. But these periodicals were by no means the first or the most common of the early forms of printed material. As we have seen, the seventeenth century – especially during the years of the English Civil War – was a time of intensive periodical publication; moreover, a wide range of other printed materials, from books and pamphlets to news sheets and placards, had been in circulation throughout Europe for at least two centuries before periodicals like the *Review* and the *Examiner* were founded. Habermas's grounds for excluding these earlier forms of printed material from the scope of his argument are not altogether clear.[51] Moreover, had Habermas paid more attention to other forms of printed material, he might have painted a somewhat different picture of the character of public life in the early modern period, one which placed less emphasis on the idea of gentlemen engaged in coffee-house debate and highlighted more sharply the commercial character of the early press and the somewhat scurrilous and sensationalist content of many of its products.

(3) A third problem with Habermas's argument concerns the restricted nature of the bourgeois public sphere. It is clear that Habermas regarded this model as an idealization of actual historical processes. Although the bourgeois public sphere was based on the principle of universal access, in practice it was restricted to those individuals who had the education and the financial means to participate in it. What does not emerge very clearly from Habermas's account, however, is the extent to which the bourgeois public sphere was not only restricted to educated and propertied elites, but was also a predominantly *male* preserve. Habermas was not unaware of the marginalization of women in the bourgeois public sphere and of the patriarchal character of the bourgeois family. But it could be argued very plausibly that, at the

time of writing *Structural Transformation*, he did not appreciate the full significance of this issue.

In recent years a number of feminist scholars have examined the gendered character of the public sphere and political discourse in the early modern period, and have brought sharply into focus a set of issues which remained rather blurred in Habermas's account.[52] Concentrating on France in the period from 1750 to 1850, Joan Landes argues that the exclusion of women from the public sphere was not simply a contingent historical circumstance, one of the many respects in which the public sphere in practice fell short of the ideal; rather, the exclusion of women was constitutive of the very notion of the public sphere. For the notion of the public sphere, as it was articulated in the political discourse of the time, was juxtaposed to the private sphere in a gender-specific way. The public sphere was generally understood as a domain of reason and universality in which men were uniquely well equipped to partici- pate, while women, being inclined (supposedly) to particularity and to mannered, frivolous talk, were commonly thought to be better suited to domestic life. Hence the masculine character of the bourgeois public sphere was not an incidental aspect: it was a fundamental feature of a public sphere which, in its very concep- tion, was shaped by a deeply rooted set of assumptions about gender differences.

Habermas has been swayed by the force of this line of argu- ment. Today he accepts that, while workers and peasants as well as women were largely excluded from the bourgeois public sphere, the exclusion of women needs to be thought about differently, precisely because this exclusion had, as Habermas now puts it, 'structuring significance'.[53] This shift in Habermas's approach is important, but the consequences it might have in practice for the theory and analysis of the public sphere are not spelled out in any detail by him.

(4) In historical terms, the weakest parts of Habermas's account are probably not the arguments concerned with the emergence of the bourgeois public sphere, but rather the arguments concerned with its alleged decline. Habermas argues that, while the bour- geois public sphere flourished in the propitious conditions of the eighteenth century, subsequent developments gradually led to its transformation and demise. The separation between the state and civil society – which had created an institutional space for the bourgeois public sphere – began to break down as states assumed

an increasingly interventionist character and took on more and more responsibility for managing the welfare of citizens, and as organized interest groups became increasingly assertive in the political process. At the same time, the institutions which once provided a forum for the bourgeois public sphere either died out or underwent radical change. The salons and coffee houses declined in significance, and the periodical press became part of a range of media institutions which were increasingly organized as large-scale commercial concerns. The commercialization of the media alters their character in a fundamental way: what was once an exemplary forum of rational-critical debate becomes just another domain of cultural consumption, and the bourgeois public sphere collapses into a sham world of image creation and opinion management. Public life takes on a quasi-feudal character. Sophisticated new media techniques are employed to endow public authority with the kind of aura and prestige which was once bestowed on royal figures by the staged publicity of feudal courts. This 'refeudalization of the public sphere' turns politics into a managed show in which leaders and parties seek, from time to time, the acclamatory assent of a depoliticized population. The mass of the population is excluded from public discussion and decision-making processes and is treated as a managed resource from which political leaders can elicit, with the aid of media techniques, sufficient assent to legitimate their political programmes.

Is there any substance to this thesis of the refeudalization of the public sphere? Certainly it has some prima facie plausibility. In the course of the twentieth century, and especially since the advent of television, the conduct of politics has become inseparable from public relations management (or from what I shall call, in a later chapter, 'the management of visibility'). But if we examine Habermas's argument more carefully, it is clear that there are serious weaknesses. Let me highlight two. In the first place, Habermas's argument tends to assume, in a very questionable way, that the recipients of media products are relatively passive consumers who are enthralled by the spectacle and easily manipulated by media techniques. In making this assumption, Habermas was betraying his debt to the work of Horkheimer and Adorno, whose theory of mass culture provided part of the inspiration for his own account. Today it is clear, however, that this argument exaggerates the passivity of individuals and takes far too much for granted concerning the process of reception. Assumptions of this kind have to be replaced by a more contextualized and hermeneutically sensitive account of the ways in which individuals receive media products, use them and incorporate them into their lives.

A second problem with Habermas's argument concerns his claim that the public sphere in modern societies has been 'refeudalized'. It is not difficult to see why Habermas made this claim: the showiness characteristic of mediated politics today and its concern to cultivate personal aura rather than to stimulate critical debate may seem, at least at first glance, to resemble the kind of 'representative publicness' typical of the Middle Ages. But the similarity is more apparent than real. As I shall endeavour to show in the following chapters, the development of communication media has created new forms of interaction, new kinds of visibility and new networks of information diffusion in the modern world, all of which have altered the symbolic character of social life so profoundly that any comparison between mediated politics today and the theatrical practices of feudal courts is superficial at best. Rather than comparing the mediated arena of the late twentieth century with a bygone age, we need to think again about what 'publicness' means today in a world permeated by new forms of communication and information diffusion, where individuals are able to interact with others and observe persons and events without ever encountering them in the same spatial-temporal locale.

While Habermas's argument concerning the fate of the public sphere is flawed in various ways, he was certainly right to call attention to the fact that the media industries underwent major changes in the course of the nineteenth and twentieth centuries. Habermas's account of these changes – one which emphasizes above all the growing commercialization of the media – is hardly satisfactory, and the implications he drew were questionable, as we have seen. But if one wishes to trace the impact of communication media, then an institutional analysis of the changing character of the media industries is essential.

The Growth of the Media Industries: An Overview

I want to conclude this chapter by highlighting some of the central trends in the development of the media industries since the early nineteenth century. I shall highlight three trends: (1) the transformation of media institutions into large-scale commercial concerns; (2) the globalization of communication; and (3) the development of electronically mediated forms of communication. My discussion of these trends will be brief. Some of the developments have been extensively documented elsewhere in the literature, and some of the issues raised by them will be pursued in more detail in later chapters.

(1) The transformation of media institutions into large-scale commercial concerns is a process that began in the early nineteenth century. Of course, the commercialization of media products was not a new phenomenon; the early presses, as we have seen, were primarily commercial organizations oriented towards the commodification of symbolic forms. But in the course of the nineteenth century the scale of commercialization increased significantly. This was due partly to a series of technical innovations in the printing industry, and partly to a gradual transformation in the financial basis of the media industries and their methods of economic valorization. Technical innovations, such as the development of Koenig's steam press and, subsequently, the rotary printing press, greatly increased the reproductive capacity of the printing industry. They enabled the production of newspapers and other printed materials to be subjected to a set of processes – including the use of power machinery, the ramified division of labour within a factory system, etc. – which were revolutionizing other spheres of commodity production. At the same time, many Western societies experienced substantial growth of urban populations and, during the second half of the nineteenth century, significant increases in rates of literacy, so that there was a steadily expanding market for printed materials.

As the printing industry became increasingly industrialized and the market expanded, the financial basis of the press began to change. Whereas the newspapers of the seventeenth and eighteenth centuries had been aimed primarily at a restricted, relatively well-off and well-educated sector of the population, the newspaper industry of the nineteenth and twentieth centuries became increasingly oriented towards a broader public. Technological developments and the abolition of taxes enabled prices to be reduced, and many newspapers adopted a lighter and livelier style of journalism, as well as a more vivid style of presentation, in order to attract a wider readership.[54] As the readership expanded, commercial advertising assumed an increasingly important role in the financial organization of the industry; newspapers became a vital medium for the sale of other goods and services, and their capacity to secure advertising revenue was directly linked to the size and profile of their readership. Newspapers – and to some extent other sectors of the press – increasingly became large-scale commercial ventures which required relatively large quantities of capital in order to be initiated and sustained in the face of increasingly intense competition. The traditional proprietor-publisher who owned one or two newspapers as a family concern gradually gave way to the development of large-scale, multi-newspaper and multimedia organizations.

The social and economic history of the media industries in the twentieth century is well documented and there is no need to describe it in detail here.[55] Processes of growth and consolidation have led to the increasing concentration of resources in many sectors of the industry, with fewer organizations commanding larger shares of the market. The degree of concentration is particularly striking in the newspaper industry (although by no means unique to it); by the early 1990s in Britain, for instance, four large media groups controlled around 92 per cent of the circulation of national daily newspapers and around 89 per cent of the circulation of Sunday papers.[56] Moreover, the processes of growth and consolidation are increasingly assuming a multimedia character as large corporations acquire extensive interests in various sectors of the media industries, from local and national newspapers to terrestrial and satellite television, from book and magazine publishing to film production and distribution. Faced with the economic power of large corporations, many smaller media organizations have been squeezed out of existence or forced into defensive mergers. But the growing concentration of resources has not eliminated all smaller organizations or stifled the development of new enterprises capable of exploiting technological innovations, catering for specialist markets and providing a range of information- and communication-related services. In many sectors of the media industries today, the dominance of large corporations coexists with a diverse array of smaller production and service organizations, many of which are interconnected through subcontracting and out-sourcing arrangements.[57]

Partly through mergers, takeovers and other forms of diversification, large-scale communication conglomerates have emerged and assumed an increasingly important role in the media domain.

Communication conglomerates are transnational, multimedia organizations which have interests in a variety of industries concerned with information and communication. Diversification on a global scale enables large corporations to expand in ways that avoid the restrictions on ownership which apply in many national contexts; it also enables corporations to benefit from certain kinds of cross-subsidization. Today the major communication conglomerates – such as Time Warner, the Bertelsmann group, Rupert Murdoch's News Corporation, Silvio Berlusconi's Fininvest – have become key players in the media industries. These huge concentrations of economic and symbolic power provide institutional bases for the production of information and symbolic content and its circulation on a global scale.

(2) The globalization of communication is a process whose origins can be traced back to the mid-nineteenth century. In earlier centuries, printed materials were commonly transported over large distances and across the boundaries of states, kingdoms and principalities. But in the course of the nineteenth century the international flow of information and communication assumed a much more extensive and organized form. The development of international news agencies based in the major commercial cities of Europe, together with the expansion of communication networks linking the peripheral regions of empires with their European centres, established the beginnings of a global system of communication and information processing which has become increasingly ramified and complex. I shall reserve the analysis of this system and its consequences for a later chapter.

(3) The uses of electrical energy for the purposes of communication were among the great discoveries of the nineteenth century. The key technical innovations are well known.[58] The first experiments with electromagnetic telegraphy were carried out in the 1830s in the United States, England and Germany, and the first viable telegraph systems were established in the 1840s. Electromagnetic transmission was successfully adapted for the purposes of conveying speech in the 1870s, paving the way for the development of telephone systems on a commercial scale. During the last decade of the nineteenth century Marconi and others began experimenting with the transmission of signals via electromagnetic waves, thereby dispensing with the need for conduction wires. In 1898 Marconi successfully transmitted signals across 23 km of

sea, and in 1899 he transmitted signals across the English Channel. The technology for transmitting speech via electromagnetic waves was developed during the first decade of the twentieth century by Fessenden and others. Following the First World War, Westinghouse in the United States and Marconi in England began experimenting with broadcasting – that is, the transmission of messages via electromagnetic waves to an indeterminate and potentially vast audience. The subsequent development of broadcasting systems – radio from the 1920s on, television from the late 1940s on – was rapid and pervasive.

The development and exploitation of these various technologies were interwoven in complex ways with economic, political and coercive power. Commercial, political and military interests played a vital role in the expansion of cable networks during the second half of the nineteenth century, as we shall see in a later chapter. Marconi's early experiments in wireless telegraphy were supported by the British Post Office, the Admiralty and the War Office, and his first commercial contracts were with the British navy. Recognizing the commercial potential and strategic significance of radio, the British, German and American governments and military establishments played an active role in its development.[59] The subsequent evolution of broadcasting systems took place within institutional frameworks which varied greatly from one national context to another and which generally represented some kind of settlement – subject to continuous review and renegotiation – between the commercial interests of the media industries, on the one hand, and the political concern to regulate, cultivate and control the new media, on the other.

The media environment bequeathed to us by the developments of the late nineteenth and early twentieth centuries is today very much in flux. Partly this is a result of the intensification of processes that were set in motion more than a century ago: the growth of communication conglomerates has continued and their predatory activities, in many contexts facilitated by the relaxation of government controls, have reached feverish pitch; and the processes of globalization have deepened, as they continue to draw far-flung parts of the globe into ever tighter and more complex webs of interdependency. But there are also new factors at work. Among these are the development of new forms of information processing based on digital systems of codification, and the gradual convergence of information and communication technology on a common digital system of transmission, processing and storage.[60] These developments are creating a new technical scenario in which information and symbolic content can be converted rapidly and with relative ease into different forms. They offer the possibility of much greater flexibility, both in the handling of information and in its transmission. We shall explore some of the implications of these developments – as well as some of the overly optimistic claims associated with them – in later chapters. But first I want to look back over the ground covered in this chapter and try to elaborate a different way of thinking about the developments we have traced.

3

The Rise of Mediated Interaction

For most of human history, most forms of social interaction have been face-to-face. Individuals interacted with one another primarily by coming together and exchanging symbolic forms, or engaging in other kinds of action, within a shared physical locale. Traditions were primarily oral in character and depended for their survival on a continuous process of renewal, through storytelling and related activities, in contexts of face-to-face interaction. Hence traditions were somewhat open-ended in terms of their content, since the process of renewal was a series of creative acts in which individuals reiterated, as best they could, utterances and actions which were impressed in their memory or conduct – in much the same way as a medieval minstrel would reinvent a story each time it was told. Traditions were also relatively restricted in terms of their geographical reach, since their transmission was dependent on face-to-face interaction and on the physical movement of individuals from one locale to another.

How did the development of communication media affect traditional patterns of social interaction? How should we understand the social impact of the growing diffusion of media products from the late fifteenth century on? In order to answer these questions, we have to see that the development of new media of communication does not consist simply in the establishment of new networks for the transmission of information between individuals whose basic social relationships remain intact. Rather, the development of communication media creates *new* forms of action and interaction and *new* kinds of social relationships – forms which are quite different from the kind of face-to-face interaction which has prevailed for most of human history. It also brings about a complex reordering of patterns of human interaction across space and time. With the development of communication media, social interaction is separated from physical locale, so that individuals can interact with one another even though they do not share a common spatial-temporal setting. The use of communication media thus gives rise to new forms of interaction which are extended in space (and perhaps also in time), and which display a range of characteristics that differentiate them from face-to-face interaction. The use of communication media also gives rise to new forms of 'action at a distance' which enable individuals to act for others who are dispersed in space and time, as well as enabling individuals to act in response to actions and events taking place in distant locales.

In this chapter I shall seek to develop a conceptual framework for the analysis of the forms of action and interaction created by the media. I shall begin by distinguishing three forms of interaction and analysing their main characteristics. I shall then focus on the type of interactional situation created by the 'mass media' and, taking the example of television, I shall examine its features in some detail. In the final two sections I shall explore some of the forms of action at a distance to which the use of communication media has given rise.

Three Types of Interaction

In order to explore the kinds of interactional situation created by the use of communication media, it is helpful to distinguish between three forms or types of interaction – what I shall call 'face-to-face interaction', 'mediated interaction' and 'mediated quasi-interaction'. Face-to-face interaction takes place in a *context of co-presence*; the participants in the interaction are immediately present to one another and share a common spatial-temporal reference system. Hence participants can use deictic expressions ('here', 'now', 'this', 'that', etc.) and assume that they will be understood. If the referent of a demonstrative pronoun is unclear, the speaker can remove the ambiguity by pointing to the object in question. Face-to-face interaction is also *dialogical* in character, in the sense that it generally involves a two-way flow of information and communication; recipients can respond (at least in principle) to producers, and producers are also recipients of messages addressed to them by the addressees of their own remarks. A further characteristic of face-to-face interaction is that the participants commonly employ a *multiplicity of symbolic cues* in order to convey messages and to interpret messages conveyed by others. Words can be supplemented by winks and gestures, frowns and smiles, changes in intonation and so on. Participants in face-to-face interaction are constantly and routinely engaged in comparing the various symbolic cues employed by speakers, using them to reduce ambiguity and to refine their understanding of the message. If participants detect inconsistencies, or cues that do not tally with one another, this can become a source of trouble which may threaten the continuation of the interaction and cast doubt on the sincerity of the speaker.

Face-to-face interaction can be contrasted with 'mediated interaction', by which I mean forms of interaction such as letter writing, telephone conversations and so on. Mediated interaction involves the use of a technical medium (paper, electrical wires, electromagnetic waves, etc.) which enables information or symbolic content to be transmitted to individuals who are remote in space, in time, or in both. Mediated interaction is stretched across space and time, and it thereby acquires a number of characteristics which differentiate it from face-to-face interaction. Whereas face-to-face interaction takes place in a context of co-presence, the participants in mediated interaction are located in contexts which are spatially and/or temporally distinct. The participants do not share the same spatial-temporal reference system and cannot assume that others will understand the deictic expressions they use. Hence participants must always consider how much contextual information should be included in the exchange – for example, by putting the place and date at the top of a letter, or by identifying oneself at the beginning of a telephone conversation.

Mediated interaction also involves a certain narrowing of the range of symbolic cues which are available to participants. Communication by means of letters, for instance, deprives the participants of a range of cues associated with physical co-presence (gestures, facial expressions, intonation, etc.), while other symbolic cues (those linked to writing) are accentuated. Similarly, communication by means of telephone deprives the participants of the visual cues associated with face-to-face interaction while preserving and accentuating the oral cues. By narrowing the range of symbolic cues, mediated interaction provides participants with fewer symbolic devices for the reduction of ambiguity. Hence mediated interaction acquires a somewhat more open-ended character than face-to-face interaction. As the range of symbolic cues is narrowed, individuals have to fall back more and more on their own resources in order to interpret the messages conveyed.

Let us now consider the third form of interaction – what I have called 'mediated quasi-interaction'. I use this term to refer to the kinds of social relations established by the media of mass communication (books, newspapers, radio, television, etc.).[1] Like mediated interaction, this third form of interaction involves the extended availability of information and symbolic content in space and/or time – in other words, mediated quasi-interaction is stretched across space and time. In many cases it also involves a certain narrowing of the range of symbolic cues by comparison with face-to-face interaction. However, there are two key respects in which mediated quasi-interaction differs from both face-to-face interaction and mediated interaction. In the first place, the participants in face-to-face interaction and mediated interaction are oriented towards specific others, for whom they produce actions, utterances, etc.; but in the case of mediated quasi-interaction, symbolic forms are produced for an indefinite range of potential recipients. Second, whereas face-to-face interaction and mediated interaction are dialogical, mediated quasi-interaction is monological in character, in the sense that the flow of communication is predominantly one-way. The reader of a book, for instance, is primarily the recipient of a symbolic form whose producer does not require (and generally does not receive) a direct and immediate response.[2]

Since mediated quasi-interaction is monological in character and involves the production of symbolic forms for an indefinite range of potential recipients, it is best regarded as a kind of quasi-interaction. It does not have the degree of reciprocity and interpersonal specificity of other forms of interaction, whether mediated or face-to-face. But mediated quasi-interaction is, none the less, a form of interaction. It creates a certain kind of social situation in which individuals are linked together in a process of communication and symbolic exchange. It is a structured situation in which some individuals are engaged primarily in producing symbolic forms for others who are not physically present, while others are involved primarily in receiving symbolic forms produced by others to whom they cannot respond, but with whom they can form bonds of friendship, affection or loyalty.

Table 3.1 summarizes some of the similarities and differences between the three types of interaction. The table shows that both mediated interaction and mediated quasi-interaction differ from face-to-face interaction in terms of their space-time constitution and the range of available symbolic cues. But mediated quasi-interaction differs from mediated interaction in terms of its action orientation and its monological character.

In distinguishing between these three types of interaction, I do not wish to suggest that specific interactional situations will always concur neatly with one of the three types. On the contrary, many of the interactions which develop in the flow of day-to-day life may involve a mixture of different forms of interaction – they have, in other words, a hybrid character. For example, individuals

Table 3.1 Types of interaction

Interactional characteristics	Face-to-face interaction	Mediated interaction	Mediated quasi-interaction
Space-time constitution	Context of co-presence; shared spatial-temporal reference system	Separation of contexts; extended availability in time and space	Separation of contexts; extended availability in time and space
Range of symbolic cues	Multiplicity of symbolic cues	Narrowing of the range of symbolic cues	Narrowing of the range of symbolic cues
Action orientation	Oriented towards specific others	Oriented towards specific others	Oriented towards an indefinite range of potential recipients
Dialogical/ monological	Dialogical	Dialogical	Monological

may have a discussion with others in the room while they are watching television, thus combining face-to-face interaction and mediated quasi-interaction in the same interactional situation. Similarly, a television programme may involve face-to-face interaction between members of a panel and members of a studio audience, although the relation between these individuals taken together and the diverse recipients of the TV programme remains a form of mediated quasi-interaction. It would be easy to adduce more complex variations (for example, some individuals phone in questions to members of a studio panel, whose responses are heard or seen by listeners or viewers, and so on). One of the merits of the analytical framework outlined above is that it enables us to separate out the different types of interaction involved in complex situations of this kind. It enables us to analyse these situations with some degree of rigour and precision, and thereby to avoid some of the misunderstandings that could arise from a hasty characterization of the interactional situations created by the media. (We shall consider some of these misunderstandings later.)

A further qualification should be added at this stage: in distinguishing three types of interaction, I do not want to suggest that these are the only possible types, or that this typology will suffice for all possible scenarios. I do not wish to preclude the possibility that new forms of interaction might be created by, for example, the development of new communication technologies which allow for a greater degree of input from recipients.[3] The analytical framework outlined above is intended as a heuristic device whose value should be judged by its usefulness; one can leave open the possibility that a more elaborate analytical framework might be required for specific purposes.

Later in the chapter I shall use this analytical framework to examine some of the interactional features of the social relationships established by the media. But first I want to show how, used historically, this framework can help us to assess the significance of the development of new media of communication from the mid-fifteenth century on. Prior to the early modern period in Europe, and until quite recently in some other parts of the world, the exchange of information and symbolic content was, for most people, a process that took place exclusively within the context of face-to-face situations. Forms of mediated interaction and quasi-interaction did exist, but they were restricted to a relatively small sector of the population. To participate in mediated interaction or quasi-interaction required special skills – such as the capacity to write or read – which were largely the preserve of political, com-

mercial or ecclesiastical elites. However, with the rise of the printing industry in fifteenth- and sixteenth-century Europe and its
subsequent development in other parts of the world, and with the
emergence of various types of electronic media in the nineteenth
and twentieth centuries, face-to-face interaction has been increasingly supplemented by forms of mediated interaction and quasi-
interaction. To an ever increasing extent, the exchange of
information and symbolic content in the social world takes place
in contexts of mediated interaction and quasi-interaction, rather
than in contexts of face-to-face interaction between individuals
who share a common locale.

The historical rise of mediated interaction and quasi-interaction
has not necessarily been at the expense of face-to-face interaction.
In some cases, the diffusion of media products has provided a
stimulus for interaction in face-to-face situations – in the way, as
we have seen, that books in early modern Europe were commonly
read aloud to individuals who had gathered together to hear the
written word. Indeed, many books in the sixteenth and seventeenth centuries were composed with a view to being read aloud:
they were addressed to the ear as well as the eye, and were thus
produced with the aim of being re-embedded in contexts of face-
to-face interaction.[4] But the growing importance of mediated
interaction and quasi-interaction, and the gradual development of
new forms of reception and appropriation (such as the development of reading as a silent, solitary practice[5]), do mean that social
life in the modern world is increasingly made up of forms of
interaction which are not face-to-face in character. With the rise of
mediated interaction and quasi-interaction, the 'interaction mix'
of social life has changed. Individuals are increasingly likely to
acquire information and symbolic content from sources other
than the persons with whom they interact directly in their day-to-
day lives. The creation and renewal of traditions are processes that
become increasingly bound up with mediated symbolic exchange.
In subsequent chapters we shall explore some of the consequences
of this transformation.

The Social Organization of Mediated Quasi-interaction

So far I have been concerned to distinguish between several forms
of interaction and to describe some of their general characteristics.

In this section I want to focus on mediated quasi-interaction and to examine its features in more detail. It is helpful to begin by introducing a further distinction – this time drawn from the work of Goffman.[6] Any action or performance takes place within a particular interactive framework which involves certain assumptions and conventions as well as the physical features of the setting (spatial layout, furniture, equipment, dress, etc.). An individual acting within this framework will to some extent adapt his or her behaviour to it, seeking to project a self-image which is more or less compatible with the framework and with the impression that the individual wishes to convey. The action framework, and the features that are accentuated by the individuals acting within it, comprise what Goffman calls the 'front region'.[7] Actions and aspects of self which are felt to be inappropriate, or which might discredit the image that the person is seeking to project, are suppressed and reserved for other settings and encounters – for settings that may be described as 'back regions' relative to the front region in which the action takes place. In back regions individuals often act in ways that knowingly contradict the images they seek to project in front regions. In back regions they relax and allow themselves to lower their guard – that is, they no longer require themselves to monitor their own actions with the same high level of reflexivity generally deployed while acting in front regions.

The distinction between front region and back regions is seldom clear-cut, and individuals are constantly involved in adapting their behaviour to shifting boundaries. In some cases the back regions may simply be located around the periphery of a front region, in such a way that actors can withdraw from the main performance with relative ease; but in these cases there is always a risk that the back-region behaviour may be seen or overheard. The fuzziness of boundaries between regions can be minimized by erecting physical boundaries. In restaurants, for example, the kitchens are generally separated from the dining areas by corridors or swinging doors; and many business premises have reception areas which are set apart from the working areas, and from which the working areas cannot be seen. The passage between front region and back regions is often strictly controlled, since back-region behaviour might compromise the impression that individuals or organizations wish to cultivate.

The distinction between front region and back region is typical of many action contexts, irrespective of whether they involve the use of a technical medium of communication. But the use of communication media can have a quite profound impact on the nature of front and back regions and the relation between them. Since mediated interaction generally involves a separation of the contexts within which the participants are situated, it establishes an interactive framework that consists of two or more front regions which are separated in space and perhaps also in time. Each of these front regions has its own back regions, and each participant in the mediated interaction must seek to manage the boundary between them. In the course of a telephone conversation, for example, an individual may seek to suppress noises which arise from the physical locale in which he or she is speaking – the sound of a television, the comments or laughter of a friend or colleague, etc. – as such noises may be regarded as back-region behaviour relative to the mediated interaction. By locating the telephone in a special room, or in a space that can be sequestered by closing doors, the risk of interference from back-region behaviour can be greatly reduced.

In the case of technically mediated quasi-interaction, the interactive framework is fragmented in a way that distinguishes it from the kind of mediated interaction which occurs in a telephone conversation. Symbolic forms are produced in one context (what I shall call the 'interactive framework of production') and received in a multiplicity of other contexts (the 'interactive frameworks of reception'). Each of these contexts is characterized by its own regions and regional demarcations. Since the flow of communication is predominantly one-way, the front region of the framework of production is typically available to the recipients and is therefore a front region relative to the frameworks of reception. But the reverse does not hold: that is, the regions in the reception sphere do not directly impinge on the framework of production, and hence are not, strictly speaking, front regions and back regions relative to this framework.

The interactive framework of reception may serve not only as a setting for the quasi-interaction mediated by the television or other technical forms, but also as a setting for face-to-face interaction which bears some affinity to the activity of reception. Individuals watching television or listening to music, for instance, may interact with one another while they participate in the activity of reception. In such cases, the extent to which the activity of reception provides the principal focus of the face-to-face interaction will vary from one instance to another. The conversational content of the face-to-face interaction may be determined largely by the activity of reception, as when individuals are involved in commenting on the messages or images received. In other cases, the activity of reception may be largely peripheral to the face-to-face interaction, and the reception of mediated symbolic forms may be little more than background music or noise for a conversation that takes place face-to-face.

Of course, individuals who engage in interaction, whether mediated or face-to-face, are always drawing on skills and accumulated resources of various kinds. Their action is always part of a structured field of interaction which both creates and limits the range of opportunities available to them. But in the cases of mediated interaction and quasi-interaction, the fields of interaction acquire an additional complexity, since they are now stretched across extended reaches of space (and perhaps also of time), and since the participants may be situated in contexts which are quite diverse in terms of their institutional and structural characteristics.

Figures 3.1, 3.2 and 3.3 summarize and illustrate some of the differences in the social organization of face-to-face interaction, mediated interaction and mediated quasi-interaction. We can develop this account further by considering an example of mediated quasi-interaction and comparing it with face-to-face interaction. There are, of course, many different kinds of mediated quasi-interaction, and their characteristics differ in certain respects, depending on the nature of the technical medium, the typical mode of appropriation, and so on. Here I shall focus on the example of television and examine some of its interactional features.

One of the technical achievements of television is that it is able to employ a wide range of symbolic cues, of both an audio and a visual kind. Whereas most other technical media restrict the range of symbolic cues to a single type of symbolic form (such as the spoken or the written word), television has a symbolic richness which endows the television experience with some of the features of face-to-face interaction: the communicators can be seen as well as heard, they move through time and space in much the same way as participants in everyday social interaction, and so on. Nevertheless, the range of symbolic cues available to the television viewer is different from, and in some respects narrower than, the range available to the participants in face-to-face interaction. It is different because the television focuses the recipients' attention on

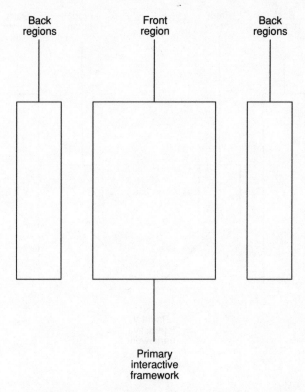

Figure 3.1 The social organization of face-to-face interaction

certain features at the expense of others and is able to employ a range of techniques (flashbacks, voice-overs, the use of archival material, etc.) which are not characteristic of face-to-face interaction. But in some respects television also narrows the range of symbolic cues. While television is much richer in symbolic terms than many other technical media, there are none the less a range of symbolic cues that cannot be transmitted by it, such as those associated with smell or touch. Moreover, the participants in the quasi-interaction created by television are deprived of the kinds of continuous and immediate feedback which are characteristic of face-to-face interaction, and which interactional participants routinely incorporate into the reflexive monitoring of their conduct.

Like all forms of mediated interaction and quasi-interaction, television involves the separation of the contexts of production and reception, so that the messages transmitted by it have ex-

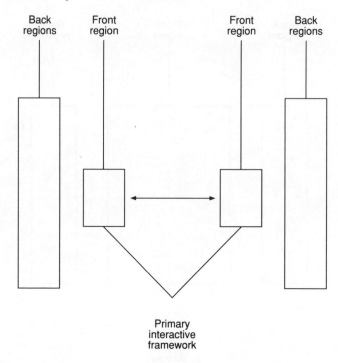

Figure 3.2 The social organization of technically mediated interaction

tended availability in space and time. But the implications of this extended availability are somewhat different in the case of television than in other types of mediated quasi-interaction, precisely because the individuals who communicate through television can be seen to act within a specific spatial-temporal context. In order to examine these issues further, it is helpful to distinguish between three sets of space-time coordinates. First, there are the space-time coordinates of the context of production – that is, of the context within which the communicators act and interact with one another. Second, there are the space-time coordinates of the televisual message itself. These coordinates may or may not coincide with those characteristic of the context of production; the coordinates can be altered, obscured or entirely redefined by editing and other techniques. Third, there are the space-time coordinates of the diverse contexts of reception. The quasi-interaction created by television involves a continuous process of splicing together these three sets of coordinates, a process that I shall

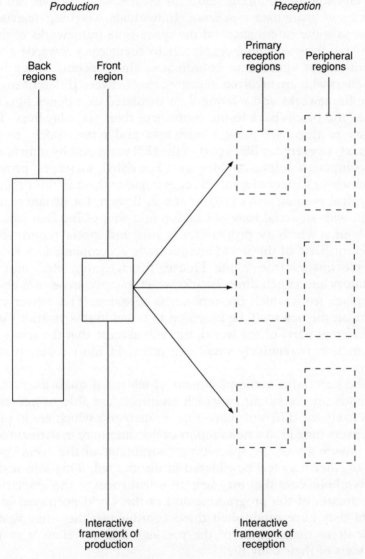

Figure 3.3 The social organization of mediated quasi-interaction

describe as 'space-time interpolation'. In receiving televisual messages, individuals routinely orient themselves towards space-time coordinates which differ from those characteristic of their contexts of reception, and interpolate mediated space-time coordinates into the spatial-temporal frameworks of their everyday lives.

Televisual quasi-interaction thus creates what we can call *discontinuous space-time experience*. Individuals watching television must to some extent suspend the space-time frameworks of their everyday lives and temporarily orient themselves towards a different set of space-time coordinates; they become space-time travellers who are involved in negotiating between different space-time frameworks and relating their mediated experience of other times and places back to the contexts of their everyday lives. The ability to negotiate these frameworks and return safely to the contexts of everyday life is part of the skill possessed by individuals as competent television viewers. Televisual messages provide them with a variety of symbolic cues to guide them in this process. A typical evening news programme in Britain, for instance, may begin with an aerial view of London or a shot of Big Ben striking the hour at which the programme begins; and special reports from different parts of the world are generally accompanied by recognizable images (the White House, the Kremlin, etc.) and by prefatory and concluding remarks which remove any doubt about the place from which the reporter is speaking. The viewer who turns on the news will be prepared to travel in this vicarious way to different parts of the world, but will assume that the temporal disjunction is relatively small (no more, in most cases, than a day).

The successful accomplishment of televisual quasi-interaction depends on the extent to which recipients are able to negotiate effectively the different space-time frameworks which are in play. If viewers tune in to a news report or documentary midstream and are unsure about the space-time coordinates of the events portrayed, they may feel bewildered or disoriented. They will search for symbolic cues that may help to orient them to the space-time coordinates of the programme and of the world portrayed in it. Until they have established these coordinates, they may find it difficult to make sense of the message and to relate it to the contexts of their daily life.

In examining the spatial and temporal characteristics of televisual quasi-interaction, I have used the example of watching news. It is clear that watching news, and other programmes that seek to present or portray actual persons or events, involves a certain type of space-time interpolation, precisely because the persons or events are generally assumed by viewers to exist in real space and real time – albeit in a space and a time which is non-contiguous and non-contemporaneous with the space-time coordinates of the contexts of reception. This interpolation of space-time regions which are presumed to be real can be distinguished from the kinds of interpolation involved in watching programmes which viewers know or believe to be fictional in character. In such cases viewers typically orient themselves towards specific sets of space-time coordinates, guided once again by a variety of symbolic cues (such as the title of a programme or series – *Dallas, Miami Vice, LA Law, NYPD Blue,* etc.); but viewers typically suspend the assumption that these coordinates correspond to real space and real time. They interpolate a space-time that is presumed to be imaginary, although it may also be presumed to bear a fictive relation to a real place and a real time (for instance, Dallas, Texas). In a later chapter I shall consider in more detail the ways in which individuals experience the various worlds that are presented to them through television and other media. Here I wish only to call attention to the fact that watching television presupposes a kind of space-time interpolation which involves imaginary as well as real space-time, and that viewers are continuously and routinely engaged in negotiating the boundaries between them.

Televisual quasi-interaction can be analysed, therefore, in terms of the intersection of different planes of space-time coordinates. Unlike face-to-face interaction, in which the space-time coordinates of the participants are the same or very similar, televisual quasi-interaction involves different sets of space-time coordinates which must be spliced together by recipients. Competent viewers are skilled space-time interpolators: they know which symbolic cues to look for, and they use these cues skilfully to orient themselves toward the space-time coordinates of the message and of the world portrayed therein. Their experience of space and time is no longer restricted by the physical movement of their bodies through space and time, or by their face-to-face interaction with others in a shared locale. Their experience of space and time becomes increasingly discontinuous, as they are able to move between worlds, both real and imaginary, at the flick of a switch. And yet, despite this increased mobility, the space-time framework of the context of reception remains the 'anchor frame' for most viewers, since their life projects are rooted primarily in the practical contexts of their day-to-day lives. (We shall return to this theme in chapter 7.)

Let us now turn our attention to another aspect of television: its monological character. Like all forms of mediated quasi-interaction, television involves a predominantly one-way flow of messages from producers to recipients. The messages that are exchanged in the televisual quasi-interaction are produced overwhelmingly by one set of participants and transmitted to an indefinite range of recipients, who themselves have relatively little opportunity to contribute directly to the course and content of the quasi-interaction. There are, of course, some avenues of intervention open to recipients. They can telephone or write to television companies to express their approval or disapproval of particular programmes. They can form pressure groups in an attempt to influence programming schedules. Some channels have 'right to reply' programmes which enable a small number of selected viewers to express their opinions. But, in practice, these avenues of recipient intervention are used by relatively few individuals. For the vast majority of recipients the only way in which they intervene in the quasi-interaction is by deciding whether to initiate it by turning on the TV, to continue it by leaving it on and paying some degree of attention to it, or to close it down by ignoring it, changing channels or turning it off.

The structural asymmetry between producers and receivers is not the only consequence of the monological character of television. By virtue of its monological character and the separation of contexts associated with it, televisual quasi-interaction (and the relationships formed therein) is severed from the reflexive monitoring of others' responses which is a routine and constant feature of face-to-face interaction. In face-to-face situations, the interlocutors are able (and are generally obliged) to take account of the ways in which others respond to what they say, and to modify their subsequent actions and utterances in the light of these responses. If, for instance, the person to whom one is speaking fails to give off the signs which indicate that he or she is following what is being said (a lack of eye contact, the absence of an affirming 'yes' or 'uh-huh', etc.), then the speaker may interrupt the narrative with a probe designed specifically to elicit a response ('Are you listening to me?') or with an elliptical probe which enables the speaker to determine whether the other is following without making the doubt explicit. In so far as mediated interaction (such as a telephone conversation) is dialogical, it too involves the reflexive monitoring of others' responses, although the symbolic mechanisms and cues which are available to participants for this purpose are generally more restricted than they are in face-to-face interaction. (Verbal indications of recipient response, such as 'yes' and 'uh-huh', are particularly important in telephone conversations, precisely because of the absence of visual cues.)[8]

In mediated quasi-interaction in general, and televisual quasi-interaction in particular, the reflexive monitoring of others' responses is not a constitutive feature of the interaction as such. Moreover, the absence of reflexive monitoring of others' responses is a characteristic of quasi-interaction of which the participants – producers as well as recipients – are aware, and which they routinely incorporate into their own modes of participation. It is a characteristic which is both enabling and constraining for participants, a source of interactional creativity and liberty as well as a source of uncertainty, inaction and trouble. From the viewpoint of the producers, it enables them to determine the course and content of the quasi-interaction without having to take account of recipient response. This gives the producers much more liberty than they would typically have in face-to-face interaction. They do not have to pay attention to the recipients and try to determine whether they are following what is being said, and they do not have to respond to the interventions of others. But the absence of reflexive monitoring of others' responses is also a potential source of uncertainty and trouble for producers, since they are deprived of the kinds of continuous and immediate feedback which would enable them to determine whether and how their messages are being received and understood. One way of countering this uncertainty is to turn the production process into a face-to-face interaction, as in chat shows and panel discussions, a strategy to which we shall return below.

From the viewpoint of recipients, the absence of reflexive monitoring of others' responses means that recipients are at liberty to determine the degree of attention they pay to the producers. They can direct their attention towards or away from the producers at will, and they are under no obligation to display the signs of understanding which are constituent features of face-to-face and mediated interaction. They can respond to the producers and their messages in any way they wish (with laughter or abuse, with pleasure or pain, with interest, apathy or total disregard), and do so without disrupting the quasi-interaction or offending the producers. In this sense, the recipients are much less constrained in the nature and extent of their participation in the quasi-interaction than are the interlocutors in a face-to-face situation. On the other hand, unlike the latter, the responses of the recipients do not directly and immediately affect the content of the quasi-interaction. The recipients can control the nature and extent of their participation and can use the quasi-interaction to suit their own needs and purposes, but they have relatively little power to intervene in the quasi-interaction and determine its course and content.

I have used the term 'participation' to describe the involvement of individuals in televisual quasi-interaction. But it is clear that, by virtue of the absence of reflexive monitoring of others' responses and the structural asymmetry of producers and receivers, the kind of participation characteristic of quasi-interaction is quite different from that which occurs in face-to-face situations. While face-to-face situations commonly involve significant differentials of power and resources, nevertheless they are characterized by fundamental forms of reflexivity and reciprocity which are absent from televisual quasi-interaction. The participants in face-to-face interaction routinely monitor the responses of others, and routinely provide signs which assure others of their participation. The participants can *in principle* intervene in and contribute to the conversation, even if in practice they do not. Since televisual quasi-interaction lacks these fundamental forms of reflexivity and reciprocity, it would be more accurate to describe the involvement of producers and recipients as a kind of 'quasi-participation'. Neither producers nor recipients are under any mutual obligation to take account of the responses of the other; and the position of the recipients is such that their responses could not, in any case, be taken into account by the producers as a constitutive feature of the quasi-interaction.

Let us now consider in more detail the nature of the social relationship established through mediated quasi-interaction. As a result of the structural asymmetry and symbolic richness of television, some of the producers (namely, those located in the front region of the production framework) are available to recipients in a unique and distinctive way – they have what one could describe as 'tele-visibility'. The distinctive feature of tele-visibility is that it combines audio-visual presence with spatial-temporal distance. Hence the producers are present to the recipients but absent from the context of reception. This distinctive combination of presence and absence is constitutive of the relationship that recipients form with producers. The persons that recipients come to know through television are 'personalities' (or 'personae'[9]) whose traits are defined largely within the front region of the production sphere (supplemented by refinements and elaborations in related media, such as newspapers and magazines). These personalities are constructed at a distance, and the relationship established between personalities and recipients is quite different from the kinds of relationships formed in face-to-face interaction. For recipients, the producers are personalities with whom they can sympathize or empathize, whom they can like or dislike, detest or revere; but the traits of these personalities cannot normally be refined or controverted by the kind of dialogical interaction characteristic of face-to-face interaction. Hence TV personalities can acquire an 'aura' which is sustained in part by the distance that separates personalities from viewers. In exceptional circumstances this distance may be bridged – as, for example, when viewers meet a television celebrity, or when individuals encounter a political leader known to them only through the media. But the odd and somewhat awkward character of such encounters attests to the fact that the relationship established through television is one which does not normally involve the sharing of a common locale.

For producers, the relationship established with recipients is also a peculiar one. Recipients are, for the most part, anonymous and invisible spectators of a performance to which they cannot contribute directly, but without whom the performance would not exist. Tele-visibility is not reciprocal with regard to producers and recipients. Producers can be seen and heard, but they can neither see nor hear the recipients; recipients, by contrast, can see and hear producers, but can be neither seen nor heard by them. While producers are in a position to determine the course and content of the performance, they are nevertheless dependent on recipients for their continued existence as performers. Hence producers relate to recipients not as co-present partners in a dialogue (for they cannot be that), but rather as anonymous spectators who can be pleased or persuaded, entertained or informed, whose attention can be held or lost and whose spectatorship is the *sine qua non* of their own existence as producers. While recipients depend on producers for the content of the performance which they witness when they turn on the television, producers in turn depend on recipients for their willingness to watch and for the support afforded by their spectatorship. The relationship between producers and recipients is a bond of mutual dependence, though the nature of the dependence varies in each case.

Later we shall return to the nature of the social relationship established between producers and recipients, exploring in particular the distinctive bonds of intimacy that may be formed through mediated quasi-interaction. In the remaining sections of this chapter I want to focus in turn on the sphere of production and the sphere of reception, examining in more detail the kinds of action that take place in each.

Action at a Distance (1): Acting for Distant Others

The development of communication media not only creates new forms of interaction, it also gives rise to new kinds of action which have distinctive characteristics and consequences. The most general characteristic of these new kinds of action is that they are oriented towards or responsive to actions or other persons who are situated in contexts that are spatially (and perhaps also temporally) remote. In other words, the development of communication media has given rise to new kinds of 'action at a distance' which have become increasingly common in the modern world. Whereas in earlier societies actions and their consequences were generally restricted to contexts of face-to-face interaction and their immediate environs, today it is common for individuals to orient their actions towards others who do not share the same spatial-temporal locale, or for their actions to have consequences which spill well beyond their immediate locales.

The growing significance of action at a distance is not only linked to the development of new communication media. A whole range of technological innovations – from gunpowder to nuclear fission, from electricity to information technology – have extended the reach of human action in space and time, sometimes in unforeseen and unforeseeable ways. But the development of communication media has created new kinds of action at a distance which have distinctive characteristics. Here I shall restrict myself once again to the medium of television and examine some of the forms of action made possible by it.

Consider first the context of production. Although recipients are not physically present in the production sphere and do not directly contribute to the course and content of the performance, producers typically orient their behaviour towards recipients. The recipient orientation of producers' behaviour is partly constitutive of the action itself, although this can occur in various ways. Here I shall distinguish and examine briefly four forms of acting for distant others – what I shall call 'recipient address', 'mediated everyday activity', 'media events' and 'fictionalized action'.

The most straightforward type of acting for distant others is *recipient address*, which can be either direct or indirect. Direct recipient address occurs when producers face the camera and speak to it, so that viewers have the impression of being spoken to. The speech of the producer is a monologue addressed to an indefinite number of absent recipients. An example of direct recipient address is the traditional news broadcast, where the broadcaster faces the camera and reads a text that is carefully prepared in advance. Direct recipient address is a somewhat austere form of action and is seldom used today in an unmodified form. The individual news broadcaster has in many cases been replaced by a pair or team of broadcasters who can, from time to time, engage in conversation among themselves in order to break up the monotony of a monologue addressed to absent others. Vivid film footage is used to engage the attention of viewers and provide them with visual alternatives to the 'talking head'. The front region of the broadcasting set has also been modified in various ways. In some cases, for example, the wall behind the newsreader has been replaced by a glass barrier, so that viewers can see a range of newsroom activity in the background. The construction of a glass barrier is a way of redrawing the boundary between front-region and back-region behaviour in the production sphere. It enables viewers to see (but not to hear, apart from the occasional sound of a muffled telephone) a limited range of activity which was traditionally treated as back-region behaviour, and it uses this expanded visibility as a way of countering the visual blandness of direct recipient address.

The reading of the news is a routine form of direct recipient address: it is scheduled to take place at a fixed time and on a regular basis, and recipients can integrate it into the temporal flow of their daily lives. But there are also exceptional forms of direct recipient address, such as a presidential or prime ministerial address to the nation. The very existence of such an address is an extraordinary phenomenon which attests to extraordinary circumstances – a nation in the midst or on the verge of war, for example, or a government engulfed by scandal. The extraordinary circumstances often endow the occasion with a solemn character: it is an occasion on which the pre-eminent political leader chooses to bypass the normal channels of information diffusion and address directly the people on whose support he or she ultimately depends. It is also an occasion on which the leader may seek to outmanoeuvre the opposition he or she faces in the more restricted political field of professional representatives; by appealing over the heads of the professionals, leaders can seek to marginalize their opposition and to portray it as petty, vindictive or obstructionist. As a direct presentation to the people, a presidential or prime ministerial address has an essentially personal character. Hence the leader and the production team must take great care to strike the right balance between solemnity and intimacy. This balance will be reflected in the speech, which is likely to combine, for instance, the pronouncement of general principles and lofty ideals with the use of personal pronouns ('I', 'you', 'we', etc.) and the recounting of personal experience. Given the personal character of the address, impassioned discourse and fiery rhetoric would be out of place; a calmer and more informal conversational style, woven together with carefully constructed moments of self-disclosure, is a more suitable form of speech.[10] The balance between solemnity and intimacy will also be reflected in the design of the front region. The set will often include a recognizable symbol of national identity, such as a flag standing discreetly in the corner or a suitable portrait hanging on the wall; but the leader may also be seated in a room which could reasonably be construed as a study or as part of a private domestic space, with additional cosiness created by a fire burning in the background. In some cases the leader may include members of his or her family in the front region, thereby creating a kind of familial intimacy which may facilitate the attempt to communicate personal matters in a public way or public matters in a personal way.

We can distinguish these forms of recipient address, both of which are direct, from indirect recipient address. The latter occurs when the front region of the production sphere becomes a site for face-to-face interaction among producers who, in interacting with one another, indirectly address a range of absent recipients. Although the producers must orient themselves towards the others who are in their immediate vicinity, they know that they are simultaneously addressing distant others and they take this into account, as best they can, in the way they present and express themselves. By transforming the front region into a site of face-to-face interaction, indirect recipient address enables producers to replace monologue with dialogue and to remove some of the uncertainty associated with mediated quasi-interaction. The face-to-face situation allows the speakers to adopt a more conversational style and enables them to monitor reflexively the responses of others. At the same time, however, indirect recipient address creates a situation in which the audience is split between co-present participants and absent viewers, giving rise to the possibility of tension or conflict between modes of address which are well tailored to one kind of audience but ill-suited to the other.

There are many examples of indirect recipient address: televised interviews, press conferences, chat shows, panel discussions (with or without a studio audience), televised party conferences, televised proceedings of Parliament or of special committees of inquiry, and so on.[11] If we consider for a moment the example of an interview with a prominent political leader like the US President, we can see that this situation differs in important ways from direct recipient address. The occurrence of the interview is certainly an important event which is likely to be preceded and succeeded by a good deal of media commentary, but the occasion lacks the kind of solemnity characteristic of a presidential address to the nation. It is an important event but not an extraordinary one and, unlike the presidential address, it does not presuppose a set of extraordinary circumstances with regard to which it can be seen as a magisterial response. Since the interview is a face-to-face dialogue conducted in a conversational style, it has a degree of informality which is lacking from the presidential address. The interlocutors address their questions and comments to one another, and are able to monitor reflexively the other's responses, clarifying points that have not been understood, etc. At the same time, they know they are addressing indirectly a range of absent recipients. Unlike, for example, a speech to a public gathering or a conference which happens to be televised, the televised interview is conducted solely for the purposes of being received by absent viewers. Hence the questions and comments, while directed towards the co-present interlocutor, must be constructed with this absent audience in mind.

The televised interview is a face-to-face interaction that takes place in the front region of a mediated quasi-interaction, and part of the art of skilful interviewing is to know how to combine effectively the action orientations relevant to each. If, for example, the President concentrates exclusively on the face-to-face interaction and seeks to engage in detail with the interviewer, he runs the risk of appearing combative or pedantic and of losing some of the aura that stems in part from his ability to stand aloof from the messy details of political life. If, on the other hand, the President largely disregards the face-to-face interaction and concentrates his efforts on trying to express what he wants to convey to the absent recipients, then he is likely to be perceived as dodging the questions. To manage the interview successfully, the President must achieve an effective balance between these two action orientations – an outcome which, thanks to the dialogical and open-ended character of face-to-face interaction, cannot be guaranteed in advance.

The interview has a degree of informality that can be used to the President's advantage. It enables him to appear before a significant proportion of the population and to communicate his views in a conversational style, eschewing the solemnity of a formal address. At the same time, however, the interview carries serious risks which the President must seek carefully to avoid. The interview enables the President to appear comfortably in command of the issues, capable of responding to probing questions with a casual fluency that attests to a leader firmly in control; but it also carries the risk that the President may appear incompetent, abrasive, ill-informed or simply very dull. A slip of the tongue, an ill-judged remark, an inaccurate statistic, an unclear or convoluted reply: all are potential sources of trouble for a leader who takes the risk of engaging in mediated quasi-interaction through the relatively open-ended process of a face-to-face encounter. There are, of course, certain ways to minimize these risks (or to limit the damage if a blunder occurs): a leader can, for example, ask to see the questions in advance, prepare the replies in some detail, and above all choose the interviewer carefully. But the risks that distinguish the interview (or, in somewhat different ways, the press conference) from the presidential address cannot be eliminated completely.

Let us consider briefly another example of indirect recipient address, the TV chat show.[12] The front region of the TV chat show is generally organized differently from the front region of an interview with a political leader. In the case of the chat show, the interlocutors are generally seated in a more informal setting, which helps to create a degree of casualness and intimacy that is lacking from most political interviews. Moreover, the chat show often includes a studio audience which provides the interlocutors with a set of responses (laughter, cheers, clapping, etc.) and enables the interlocutors to monitor the reception of their actions and remarks. The studio audience occupies a peculiar position. The members of this audience are part of a face-to-face interaction that takes place primarily between the chat show host and the guest; members of the audience may occasionally be called on or invited to participate directly in the interaction, but their role is generally restricted to that of co-present recipients who can respond in certain conventional and non-discursive ways. With regard to the mediated quasi-interaction of which the chat show is part, the studio audience is situated in the front region of the production sphere, but the relation between the studio audience and viewers at home is distinctive and complex. For viewers, the studio audience is part of an interaction which they can see and hear but in which they cannot directly participate. But the studio audience, in so far as its members are spectators of an interaction to which they can contribute very little, also provides the viewers with a set of model responses with which they may empathize or sympathize (laughter, approval, etc.). Hence, by conducting the chat show in the presence of a studio audience, the producers can pursue two interactional aims simultaneously: they can provide the interlocutors with a set of co-present recipients whose responses will enable them to monitor, to some extent, the impact of their actions and utterances; and they can provide the absent recipients (the viewers) with a set of model responses which may serve as a stimulus for their own responsive action – although the extent to which the model does act as a stimulus is not, given the nature of the quasi-interaction, a matter that the producers can monitor or control.

I now want to consider a different kind of acting for distant others, what I have described as *mediated everyday activity*. The distinctive feature of this type of action is that it is part of, or presented as part of, the actual flow of conduct in day-to-day life. Hence the front region of the production sphere is the setting for a series of actions or interactions which are part of the everyday life of the individuals who perform or participate in them. But the fact that these actions or interactions are filmed or taped and then transmitted to a range of absent recipients, and hence are also part of a mediated quasi-interaction, may affect the nature of the action or interaction itself, as well as its subsequent course. Indeed the very possibility of being filmed and made visible to television viewers may transform the ways in which individuals act and interact in the contexts of daily life.

In order to examine further this type of action, it is helpful once again to distinguish several subtypes. Consider first the case of everyday action which is filmed and transmitted in such a way that the actors themselves are unaware that they are being filmed. Since the actors are not aware that they are part of a mediated quasi-interaction, it is unlikely that they are orienting their behaviour towards absent recipients: their action becomes, in other words, a form of mediated everyday activity with no recipient address. An example would be an everyday setting or event, such as a street scene or a public demonstration, which is filmed in a way that is sufficiently discreet to avoid detection by the participants. But mediated everyday activity with no recipient address is a kind of limiting case; it does occur, but it is probably less common than it might at first seem. For even if participants are unaware that they are being filmed as and when they act, they may be aware of the possibility that they could be filmed and may alter their behaviour accordingly. So, for example, soldiers patrolling the streets of Northern Ireland or the Israeli-occupied West Bank may not always know when they are in the lens of a distant camera; but they do know that they could be at almost any time, and they are therefore likely to adjust their behaviour to take account of this possibility.

Consider next the type of mediated everyday activity which involves indirect recipient address. This is the kind of action that occurs when individuals pursue their day-to-day conduct while knowing that it is being (or might be) filmed, recorded and transmitted to absent recipients. The individuals must, at least to some extent, orient their behaviour towards the others in their immediate social milieu; for if they do not, the action will lose its mundane character and the interaction will break down. But the individuals know that their action is (or may be) part of a mediated quasi-interaction, and hence they also orient their behaviour, simultaneously and indirectly, towards the absent recipients. For example, the participants in a major international conference or a meeting of heads of state may know that the proceedings will be filmed and transmitted to a wide audience, which will include recipients in their own country on whose support they may depend. Hence, while they must orient their behaviour towards the other members of the conference in order to participate effectively in it, they must also take account of the possibility that their actions and utterances will be seen and heard by a much wider range of recipients, and their conduct will therefore be shaped by this dual orientation.

Mediated everyday activity can also involve direct recipient address. In this type of activity, the orientation to absent recipients is a principal constitutive feature of the action itself. An example would be the hijacking of an aeroplane or the taking of a hostage by a paramilitary group. The members of the group know that their action will receive a high degree of media coverage, and part of the purpose of their action is to call the attention of absent others to their cause. They may also hope that, by seizing individuals and holding them in a way that is visible to a large number of ordinary people, they can exercise pressure indirectly on governments or political leaders. This is, of course, a risky strategy, and they may well fail to achieve their political aim. But there can be no doubt that part of the very point of actions such as hijackings and hostage-takings is to achieve a degree of visibility in a global political arena where the ability to be seen and heard is linked to the capacity to attract a television camera.

There is another type of mediated everyday action which deserves consideration: what we could call simulated everyday activity. This occurs when individuals pretend to engage in ordinary action or interaction solely for the purpose of being filmed, that is, solely to create a televisable event. An example: the behaviour of military or paramilitary personnel who fire several rounds into the air or shoot at a distant enemy apparently in their sights in order to create the impression of military conflict occurring then and there. While this activity is simulated, it is distinct from fictionalized action, precisely because it takes place in a real-life context and is presented as if it were real. The individuals involved in producing simulated everyday activity cannot give any indication that their action is anything other than real, for if they did, the action would fail to achieve its aim.

Media events are a third form of acting for distant others. Following Dayan and Katz, we can use the term 'media events' to refer to those great, exceptional occasions which are planned in advance, which are broadcast live and which interrupt the normal flow of events.[13] Unlike everyday mediated activity, media events are carefully pre-planned and rehearsed. Although they are generally organized by institutions other than the media, they are conceived of as media events, and hence media institutions are invariably involved in the planning process. They are also announced well in advance so that as the event approaches there is a gradual build-up of expectations. The event itself is broadcast live and is often carried by several channels, networks and media. They interrupt the normal schedules and the normal flow of everyday life. They are exceptional occasions: they break with routine, they create an atmosphere of high expectation, and they command the attention of millions.

Examples of media events include great occasions of state like coronations and royal weddings, the inauguration of a new president, and state funerals; major sporting events like the Olympic Games or the World Cup; and great moments of conquest or reconciliation, like the landing on the moon, the signing of the Camp David accord as a step towards peace in the Middle East, or the freeing of Nelson Mandela in South Africa. On all such occasions the media are there in force; and while the individuals participating in these events must concentrate on what they are doing in the specific locales in which they are acting, they know that their actions are part of events which have a much broader significance, precisely because they are being broadcast live and endowed with the character of the exceptional event.[14]

We can distinguish media events from a fourth form of acting for distant others, which we can call *fictionalized action*. A good deal of the output of television production is explicitly fictional in character: it is the construction of a story which is fully scripted and which is acted out by individuals who know they are acting (in the sense of playing a part), and who are generally perceived as such by absent recipients. Here individuals are acting in a way that is very similar to the kind of acting that takes place in the theatre: they are playing a part, speaking the words of a character whom they must construct and convincingly portray, but whom they know to be something other than themselves. But while fictionalized action for television is similar to playing a theatrical part, it differs from the latter in exactly the way that mediated quasi-interaction differs from face-to-face interaction: it is action for distant others, and hence it lacks the presence of an audience and the kinds of recipient response (laughter, clapping, etc.) which are characteristic of the theatre.

While fictionalized action can be distinguished from other forms of acting for distant others, it is clear that in the actual practice of television production the distinction between fictionalized and non-fictionalized action may sometimes be difficult to draw. The material which comprises most interviews, news reports and documentaries is edited and integrated into an audio-visual construct which differs in certain respects from the events as they actually occurred. Many mediated actions or events are performed or constructed for the purpose (at least in part) of being televised, and hence they are reflexively shaped by the orientation towards an absent audience. Moreover, there are some programmes which seek explicitly to blur the boundaries between fiction and non-fiction, such as 'drama-documentaries' which use actors and a partly fictionalized plot to tell a story that is allegedly real. The blurred and shifting boundary between fiction and non-fiction in the sphere of television is a phenomenon which raises interesting issues, but here it is not the main focus of my concern. Rather, my aim has been to explore some of the ways in which individuals, embedded in relations of mediated quasi-interaction, are able to act for others who are situated in distant locales.

Action at a Distance (2): Responsive Action in Distant Contexts

Just as the development of communication media creates new forms of acting for distant others, so too it gives rise to new kinds of 'responsive action' which take place in contexts far removed from the contexts of production. Thanks to the space-time distanciation generated by the media, individuals can receive and respond to actions and events which take place in distant locales. At the same time, responsive action is severed from the dialogical character of face-to-face interaction and can unfold in ways that are difficult to monitor and control, giving rise to a new kind of mediated indeterminacy which can have large-scale consequences. In order to pursue these issues further, we must examine in more detail the social organization of receptive activities.

Like all kinds of action, the reception of media products takes place in particular spatial-temporal contexts. What is unique about receptive activity is that (a) the spatial-temporal context of reception does not overlap with that of production, and (b) there are multiple reception contexts which do not overlap with one another. While reception contexts do not overlap in space (and may not coincide in time), nevertheless they may share certain characteristics, depending on the nature of the technical medium deployed. In the case of television, for instance, the primary reception region is often (though by no means always) a particular room in a private domestic residence. This primary region is often separated from peripheral regions in the same residence by means of physical barriers such as walls and doors. The relation between primary and peripheral regions in a context of reception is not the same, however, as the relation between front and back regions in the production sphere or in a face-to-face interaction. For recipients do not participate in the televisual quasi-interaction in the same way as producers, and hence they do not need to manage their self-presentation with regard to the quasi-interaction in the same way. If certain areas and forms of behaviour are excluded from the quasi-interaction of recipients, this is done for other reasons – for example, to minimize interruption or interference, or to manage the presentation of self in the face-to-face interaction that takes place among recipients within the primary reception region.

Since recipients cannot generally respond directly to producers, their forms of responsive action are not part of the quasi-interaction as such. In responding to the actions or utterances of producers, they generally do so as a contribution to *other* interactions of which they are part, such as the interaction among recipients who have gathered together in front of a television. In this way media messages acquire what I shall describe as 'discursive elaboration': they are elaborated, refined, criticized, praised and commented on by recipients who take the messages received as the subject matter of discussions with one another and with others. The process of discursive elaboration may involve individuals who were not party to the mediated quasi-interaction – in the way, for instance, that individuals may describe what they saw on television to friends who did not watch the programme. Hence media messages may acquire an additional audience of secondary recipients who did not themselves participate in the mediated quasi-interaction, but who assimilate some version of the message through face-to-face interaction with the primary recipients.

In a world characterized by multiple forms of media transmission, it is also common for media messages to be taken up by media organizations and incorporated into new media messages, a process that can be described as 'extended mediazation'. There is a relatively high degree of self-referentiality within the media, in the sense that media messages commonly refer to other media messages or to events reported therein. For example, a morning newspaper may report what a government minister said in a television interview the day before, an interview during which the minister was commenting on a reported incident, and so on. An individual who did not see the interview or hear the earlier report of the incident will have other opportunities to learn about them, either through other mediated quasi-interactions or through face-to-face interactions with individuals who did. Moreover, those individuals who did see the interview or hear the earlier report will have the opportunity to review their understanding of the incident or of the minister's comments by reading the newspaper report, or by discussing the various events and messages with others.

Figure 3.4 illustrates some of the ways in which the process of receiving media messages may extend beyond the initial activity of reception within the primary reception region. I use the term 'appropriation' to refer to the extended process of receiving messages. As I explained in an earlier chapter, 'to appropriate' is 'to make one's own' something which is alien or strange; it is to find a way of relating to it and incorporating it into one's life. In so doing individuals draw on their background knowledge, their acquired skills and dispositions and the resources available to them. These social attributes are key elements in a process of appropriation that begins with the initial reception of media messages but extends well beyond it, involving other contexts, other individuals, other messages interwoven with those initially received.

While the diverse contexts of reception may have certain common characteristics, it is important to emphasize that the social

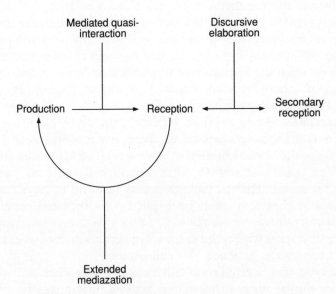

Figure 3.4 The extension of reception processes

attributes which individuals bring to these contexts are not everywhere the same. Since mediated quasi-interaction makes messages available to an indefinite range of recipients who are
far-flung in space (and perhaps also in time), the diversity of social
attributes which individuals bring to bear on the reception process
is likely to be much greater than that found in face-to-face interaction. Moreover, in the case of face-to-face interaction, differences in the social attributes of the interlocutors will be reflected
in the interaction – in the way, for instance, that some individuals
participate actively and effortlessly in a conversation while others
hesitate or remain silent. In the case of mediated quasi-interaction, by contrast, differences in the social attributes of recipients
are not reflected in the quasi-interaction as such (except in so far
as producers seek to take these differences into account – for
example, by using language which will be intelligible and accept-
able to a wide range of recipients). Social differences among
recipients affect primarily the ways in which they relate to the
messages they receive, how they understand them, appreciate
them, discuss them and integrate them into their lives. Hence the
appropriation of media messages must be seen as an ongoing and
socially differentiated process that depends on the content of the
messages received, the discursive elaboration of the messages
among recipients and others and the social attributes of the individuals who receive them.

The reception and appropriation of media messages are ways of
acting in response to others who are spatially and temporally
remote. It involves individuals in a set of activities (watching,
listening, reading, discussing, etc.) which are stimulated by the
actions of others who are situated in distant locales. In many
cases, these responsive activities will unfold in ways that are varied
and unrelated to one another, reflecting the diversity of the contexts in which the messages are received. But it is also clear that in
some cases the actions of distant others, relayed via media such as
television, can give rise to what I shall call *concerted forms of
responsive action*. That is, recipients may respond in ways that are
similar and that may even be explicitly coordinated, either by
some aspect of the media message or by a relatively independent
agency operating within the contexts of reception. Let us examine
some of the ways in which this can occur.

One type of concerted responsive action arises when individuals
react in similar ways to mediated actions, utterances or events,
although the individuals are situated in diverse contexts and there

is no communication or coordination between them. We can regard this as concerted but uncoordinated responsive action. An example would be the actions of individuals who hear through the media that the sales tax will be increased on a certain date and respond by purchasing consumer goods before that date, resulting in a surge in retail sales. This outcome is the result of the discrete and largely uncoordinated actions of individuals who respond in similar ways to an item of reported news. In practice, however, most concerted actions of this kind generally involve some degree of coordination which stems from a combination of discursive elaboration and extended mediazation. The recipients of media messages commonly discuss these messages with others in their immediate social milieu, and the views and actions of others may influence their own behaviour. Moreover, some degree of coordination may be provided by the media, which may, for instance, encourage individuals to purchase goods by predicting or speculating about a surge in retail sales, or by reporting a surge in sales that is already under way (a mediated version of the bandwagon effect). In such cases, concerted responsive action is to some extent the unintended outcome of a media message or of the ongoing commentary on the responses to a media message.

We can distinguish this type of concerted action from another type which occurs when individuals respond in similar ways to symbolic devices that are explicitly intended to coordinate recipient response. The importance of these devices stems in part from the peculiar nature of mediated quasi-interaction. Unlike the interlocutors in a face-to-face situation, the producers of media messages are not in a position to monitor directly the responses of recipients and to modify their action in the light of this feedback. Moreover, since recipients do not share a common locale, they are not in a position to monitor the responses of other recipients (except those with whom they directly interact) and to modify their behaviour accordingly. In these circumstances, producers may employ a range of symbolic devices whose aim is to elicit similar responses among absent recipients – what I shall call 'intended mechanisms for the coordination of recipient response'. A well-known example of such mechanisms is the use of prerecorded laughter sequences in TV sitcoms. By simulating audience responses at key points in the narrative flow, the prerecorded laughter sequences serve as audio cues intended to initiate similar responsive action among absent recipients. A live studio audience can also be used as a mechanism for coordinating recipient response, as we noted earlier. If a live audience is included in the front region of the production sphere, recipients can see how others (albeit carefully selected others) respond to the principal communicators and may even feel that they are part of a collective audience whose responses they broadly share.

Of course, the use of mechanisms intended to coordinate recipient response may not always give rise to concerted responsive action. The very structure of mediated quasi-interaction is such that producers cannot monitor directly the ways in which their messages are received, and cannot take remedial action to secure the desired response. The responsive action of recipients may be guided by the message but it is not controlled or determined by it, precisely because the responsive action of recipients is not part of the reciprocal interaction with producers but is a new set of actions belonging to a diverse set of contexts in which a great variety of abilities, expectations and priorities are brought to bear on the messages received.

Let us now consider a third form of concerted responsive action, that which acquires some degree of organization and coordination within the contexts of reception. Here we are dealing with forms of collective action which are stimulated and nourished by mediated images, actions and utterances. These forms of collective action can vary from relatively diffuse clusters of individuals acting in similar or partly convergent ways, on the one hand, to well-organized social movements with clearly articulated goals, on the other. In most cases these forms of collective action draw support from a variety of sources; the role of the media is one among a set of elements which give rise to and sustain the concerted actions of individuals. But there can be little doubt that in some cases the media have played (and continue to play) a very important role and that, if mediated images and information had not been available to recipients, the forms of collective action would not have developed in the way, to the extent and with the speed that they did.

It seems likely, for example, that the extensive and vivid coverage of the Vietnam War was at least partially responsible for the strength and concerted character of the anti-war movement.[15] The Vietnam War was the first major American military involvement overseas which was covered in detail by television. The vivid images of napalm attacks, wounded soldiers and civilians, screaming children and frightened refugees, as well as reports of US military setbacks and rising death tolls, fuelled the controversy in the United States concerning the legitimacy of the intervention and provided individuals with readily available grounds for protest. In the light of the Vietnam experience, it is not surprising that military establishments in the United States and elsewhere have sought to exercise much tighter control over the media coverage of armed conflicts and skirmishes. During the Gulf War, the military authorities imposed tough guidelines on journalists, and access to the front was strictly controlled.[16] Reports compiled and transmitted by one of the few Western correspondents remaining in Baghdad – Peter Arnett of CNN – were denounced by the Bush Administration. The considerable effort invested in seeking to control the media representation of the war is testimony to the fact that, in the age of the media and especially television, wars must be fought on two fronts: on the battlefield and in the home, where images of the battlefield and its costs are made available to the individuals on whose support the war effort ultimately depends. While political and military authorities may justify their attempts to control the media on the grounds of battlefield logic (such as the need to prevent disclosures which would put the lives of soldiers at risk), they are well aware that much more is at stake. They know that mediated images and information have the potential to stimulate forms of responsive action, criticism and dissent which may weaken the war effort.[17]

The revolutionary upheavals in Eastern Europe in 1989 provide another example of the ways in which media messages can stimulate and nourish collective action by individuals located in distant contexts. There were, of course, many factors that contributed to the extraordinary events which occurred during the last three months of 1989. These events were the cumulative outcome of many years of economic impoverishment and oppressive political control, and they were precipitated by, among other things, the new political thinking introduced by Gorbachev. But it seems unlikely that the revolutionary upheavals of 1989 would have occurred as they did – with breathtaking speed and with similar results in different countries – in the absence of extensive and continuous media coverage.[18] Not only did television provide individuals in Eastern Europe with a flow of images of the West, portraying life conditions which contrasted sharply with their own, but it also provided Eastern Europeans with a virtually instantaneous account of what was happening in neighbouring countries, as well as in neighbouring cities or locales in their own countries. East Germans had long been able to receive West

German television, and the images of refugees crowding into embassies in Prague and Budapest, and eventually being escorted to the West and greeted as heroes, could hardly fail to have an explosive impact in East Germany. When the Berlin Wall fell on the night of 9 November, the images of young people celebrating beneath the Brandenburg Gates and hacking at the wall with pickaxes were transmitted live around the world.

In Czechoslovakia the pressure for political change mounted throughout October and November. When the mass demonstration in Prague on 17 November was brutally suppressed by police, foreign television crews were on hand to film the events and the footage was subsequently screened, amid much controversy, within Czechoslovakia itself. Even in Romania, where the national media were strictly controlled by the state, individuals were able to learn about the dramatic changes taking place elsewhere in Eastern Europe, and elsewhere in their own country, by tuning in to radio and TV broadcasts from the Soviet Union, Hungary and Yugoslavia. As conflict intensified within Romania, control of the means of television broadcasting became a crucial stake in the battle. When the Ceauşescus were finally arrested, tried by military tribunal and executed by firing squad, their crumpled bodies were filmed beneath a bullet-riddled wall and transmitted via television to an astonished audience in Romania and throughout the world.

These examples illustrate some of the ways in which the development of communication media, and especially television, has introduced a new and fundamentally important element into social and political life. By providing individuals with images of, and information about, events that take place in locales beyond their immediate social milieux, the media may stimulate or intensify forms of collective action which may be difficult to control with the established mechanisms of power. It seems likely that the concerted action displayed in the streets of Leipzig, Berlin, Prague, Timişoara, Bucharest and elsewhere in Eastern Europe was, to some extent, action stimulated by the activities of distant others whose aims and aspirations, successes and failures, had been relayed via the media. Moreover, given the nature of modern electronic media and the availability of satellite relays, images and information can be transmitted across vast distances with very little time delay. Individuals in Bucharest can know something about what is happening in Timişoara as quickly – even more quickly – than individuals in Timişoara, and the events unfolding in Romania can be watched more or less as they unfold by millions of viewers around the world. Hence the actions and reactions which are stimulated by the media can be linked together closely in time while separated in space, thus comprising a chain of events which can transcend the boundaries of particular nation-states and rapidly slip out of control.

The phenomenon of concerted responsive action highlights the fact that the media are not simply involved in reporting on a social world which would, as it were, continue quite the same without them. Rather, the media are actively involved in constituting the social world. By making images and information available to individuals located in distant locales, the media shape and influence the course of events and, indeed, create events that would not have existed in their absence. Moreover, the individuals involved in these events may be well aware of the constitutive role of the media. They know that what they say on radio or television will be heard by thousands or millions of others who may respond in concerted ways to what is said. They know that, by watching television or listening to the radio, they can learn something – however partial – about what is happening beyond their immediate social milieux, and they can use this information to guide their own action. They know that, by controlling the flow of images and information, the media can play a crucial role in controlling the flow of events.

These examples of concerted responsive action also highlight the fact that, while any particular instance of mediated quasi-interaction generally involves a one-way flow of information or communication, in the actual circumstances of social life the patterns of information flow are often much more complicated. For in actual circumstances there is often a plurality of sources and channels of communication, so that individuals may find themselves in the position of being both producers and recipients. So, for instance, a political leader who appears on television from time to time may also routinely watch television, read newspapers, etc. Similarly, individuals who are normally recipients of media products may act in ways which become televisable events, and which in turn elicit televisable responses from others. In this way the media come to form part of the very field of interaction within which different individuals and groups pursue their aims and objectives. This media-constituted field of interaction is not like a face-to-face situation in which the interlocutors confront one another directly and engage in dialogical conversation. Rather it is a new kind of field in which face-to-face interaction, mediated interaction and mediated quasi-interaction intersect with one another in complex ways. It is a field in which the participants use the technical means at their disposal to communicate to distant others who may or may not watch or listen to them, and in which individuals plan their courses of action partly on the basis of the images and information they receive through the media. Of course, within this mediated field of interaction there are some individuals who have much more opportunity to use the media to their advantage than others, much more opportunity to appear within the front regions of the production spheres and to communicate to distant others. But, as the upheavals in Eastern Europe attest, this advantage does not always give individuals the ability to control the course of events. Given the fact that there are multiple channels of transnational communication which particular governments may find difficult to restrict, and given the fact that the reception of media messages is in any case a relatively independent process that producers cannot completely control, the mediated field of interaction is a field in which relations of power can shift quickly, dramatically and in unpredictable ways. The development of the media has helped to create a world in which fields of interaction can become global in scale and the pace of social change can be accelerated by the speed of information flows.

The growth of multiple channels of communication and information flow has thus contributed significantly to the complexity and unpredictability of an already exceedingly complex world. By creating a variety of forms of action at a distance, enabling individuals to act for distant others and enabling others to respond in uncontrollable ways to actions and events taking place in distant locales, the development of the media has given rise to new kinds of interconnectedness and indeterminacy in the modern world, phenomena whose characteristics and consequences we are far from understanding fully. In a later chapter I shall address some of the normative implications of these developments. But first I want to explore some related themes in more detail.

4

The Transformation of Visibility

Today we are accustomed to thinking of the individuals who appear before us on our television screens as belonging to a public world which is open for all to see. We may feel some degree of familiarity with the personalities and political leaders who appear regularly on television and in other media. We may come to think of them as associates or even as friends, and we may refer to them on a first-name basis. But we know that in appearing before us they are appearing also before thousands or millions of others, they are available to and observable by many individuals other than ourselves. And we know that, while we may regularly see and hear the personalities and political leaders who appear on our television screens, it is very unlikely that we shall ever encounter them in the course of our day-to-day lives.

These considerations are an index of the gulf that separates our world today from the world that existed a few hundred years ago. Prior to the development of the media (and especially electronic media such as radio and television), how many people were ever able to see or hear the individuals who held positions of political power? When the only available form of interaction for most people was face-to-face, how many would ever interact with the political leaders who ruled them? And how, in turn, could political leaders appear before anything other than a relatively small number of individuals who happened to be gathered together in the same locale? Prior to the development of the media, political leaders were invisible to most of the people over whom they ruled, and they could restrict the activity of managing their self-presentation to the relatively closed circles of the assembly or the court. But today it is no longer possible to restrict the activity of self-presentation in this way. Whether they wish to or not, political leaders today must be prepared to adapt their activities to a new kind of visibility which works in new ways and on an altogether different scale. And they ignore this new visibility at their peril.

In this chapter I want to explore this transformation in the nature of visibility and the changing relation between visibility and power. I shall try to show that this transformation is part of a broader shift in the nature of the public sphere. I shall therefore pick up and pursue, in a rather different direction, some issues that were raised in chapters 1 and 2. I shall begin by reconsidering the distinction between the public and the private. By differentiating between two senses of the public–private dichotomy (section 1), we can reassess the ways in which the development of the media transformed the nature of publicness (section 2) and retrace the changing historical relations between power and visibility (section 3). While the transformation in the nature of publicness has created new opportunities for political leaders, it has also created new risks; and in the final section we shall explore some of the new sources of trouble, from gaffes to scandals, which are an ever-present risk to the exercise of power in an age of mediated visibility.

The Public and the Private

The distinction between the public and the private has a long history in Western social and political thought.[1] It can be traced back to the philosophical debates of classical Greece concerning the life of the polis, in which citizens came together to discuss issues of common interest and to forge a social order oriented towards the common good. The explicit formulation of the distinction probably stems from the early development of Roman law, which separated public from private law, and from the Roman conception of the *res publica*. However, in the late medieval and early modern periods, the public–private distinction began to acquire new meanings, partly in relation to the institutional transformations that were taking place at that time. As old institutions changed and new institutions began to appear, the terms 'public' and 'private' were used in new ways and, to some extent, redefined by changes in the object domains to which they referred.

If we focus on the development of Western societies since the late medieval period, we can distinguish two basic senses of the public–private dichotomy. These two basic senses do not, of course, exhaust the meanings of these polysemous terms, but they do highlight some of the most important ways in which the terms have been used since the late Middle Ages.

The first sense of the dichotomy has to do with the relation between, on the one hand, the domain of institutionalized political power which was increasingly vested in the hands of a sovereign state and, on the other hand, the domains of economic activity and personal relations which fell outside direct political control. Thus, from the mid-sixteenth century on, 'public' came increasingly to mean activity or authority that was related to or derived from the state, while 'private' referred to those activities or spheres of life that were excluded or separated from it. This sense of the dichotomy partially overlaps with a distinction that was to become increasingly prominent in the writings of legal and political theorists in the course of the eighteenth and nineteenth centuries – namely, the distinction between state and civil society. The term 'civil society' was used in a great variety of ways by early modern thinkers, ways that were often inconsistent with one another.[2] The most common use of the term today is one which is indebted primarily to Hegel, or rather to a certain interpretation of Hegel's philosophy of law, according to which civil society is construed as a sphere of private individuals, organizations and classes which are regulated by civil law and formally distinct from the state. Hence the domain of the private could be said to include civil society in this sense, as well as the sphere of personal relations centred primarily, though not exclusively, on the family.

Of course, this broad distinction between the public and the private was never rigid or clear-cut in the historical development of modern societies. The emergence of capitalist economic organizations was a process that took place within a set of legal and political frameworks that were established and continuously modified by states. The activities of states, in turn, were influenced and constrained in various ways by the development of the economy – in particular, by their capacity to raise revenue through taxation. Moreover, since the late nineteenth century, the boundaries between the public and the private have become increasingly blurred. States have adopted an increasingly interventionist role, pursuing policies aimed at regulating economic activity and offsetting the negative consequences of economic growth. Private individuals have come together to form organizations and pressure groups aimed at influencing government policy. Indeed, the very boundary between the public and the private has become a key stake in political debates as successive governments seek to redefine the scope of state activity by expanding public services and investment or, alternatively, by removing concerns from the public sector through privatization.

Some aspects of this broad distinction between the public and the private, as it developed in Western societies in the course of the nineteenth and twentieth centuries, are summarized in figure 4.1. The private domain includes privately owned economic organizations operating in a market economy and oriented to some degree towards profit realization, as well as a range of personal and familial relations which may be informal or formally sanctioned through law (for instance, by marriage). The public domain includes a range of state and quasi-state institutions, from legislative and judicial bodies to the police, military and secret services, from the civil service to a variety of welfare organizations; it also includes state-owned economic organizations, such as nationalized industries and state-owned public utilities. Between the private and public domains, various intermediate organizations

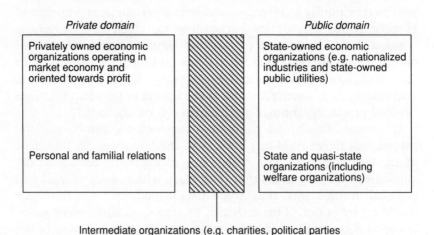

Figure 4.1 Private and public domains in contemporary Western societies

have emerged and flourished in recent years. These organizations are neither owned by the state nor lodged wholly within the private domain. They include, for example, non-profit-making charities like Oxfam or the Save the Children Fund; mutual benefit associations, such as clubs and trade associations; political parties and pressure groups which seek to articulate particular viewpoints; and economic organizations which are owned and operated on a cooperative basis.[3] These intermediate organizations are non-state private institutions in terms of their legal status, but they are legally and operationally distinct from privately owned economic organizations oriented towards profit realization.

We can, however, distinguish a second basic sense of the public–private dichotomy as it has emerged in Western social and political discourse. According to this sense, 'public' means 'open' or 'available to the public'.[4] What is public, in this sense, is what is visible or observable, what is performed in front of spectators, what is open for all or many to see or hear or hear about. What is private, by contrast, is what is hidden from view, what is said or done in privacy or secrecy or among a restricted circle of people. In this sense, the public–private dichotomy has to do with *publicness versus privacy*, with *openness versus secrecy*, with *visibility versus invisibility*. A public act is a visible act, performed openly so that anyone can see; a private act is invisible, an act performed secretly and behind closed doors.

This second sense of the dichotomy does not coincide with the first, but historically there is a complex and shifting relation between forms of government and the visibility or invisibility of power. In the classical Greek city-states, where citizens assembled in a common place to put forward proposals, debate issues and make decisions, the exercise of political power was relatively visible: the interventions and arguments of the participants could be seen and heard by those who had gathered together, and all citizens had an equal right to make their opinions heard. The assembly constituted a distinctive kind of public sphere in which the publicness (or visibility) of power was based on the capacity of individuals to engage in debate with one another in a common locale and to come to collective decisions through a show of hands or by a similar procedure. (Occasionally ballots were taken using pieces of pottery, but it seems likely that votes were usually estimated in only an approximate way.)[5] Of course, the classical Greek assembly was a public sphere to which access was quite restricted: only Athenian men over the age of 20 were allowed to participate, and women, slaves and 'metics' (non-citizen residents), among others, were excluded. But the assembly did illustrate the fact that ancient democracy, as a form of government, implied a certain commitment to the visibility of power, a commitment that was often lacking in other systems of rule.

In the traditional monarchical states of medieval and early modern Europe, the affairs of state were conducted in the relatively closed circles of the court, in ways that were largely invisible to most of the subject population. When kings, princes and lords appeared before their subjects, they did so in order to affirm their power publicly (visibly), not to render public (visible) the grounds on which their decisions and policies were based. Their public appearances were carefully staged events, full of pomp and ceremony, in which the aura of the monarch was both manifested and affirmed. Publicness was concerned, not with the exercise of power, but with its exaltation. In the early theoretical writings on the *raison d'état*, the privacy of decision-making processes was commonly justified by recourse to the *arcana imperii* – that is, the doctrine of state secrecy, which held that the power of the prince is more effective and true to its aim if it is hidden from the gaze of the people and, like divine will, invisible.[6] The invisibility of power was assured institutionally by the fact that decision-making processes took place in a closed space, the secret cabinet, and by the fact that the decisions themselves were only occasionally and selectively made public.

With the development of the modern constitutional state, the invisibility of power was limited in certain ways. The secret cabinet was replaced or supplemented by a range of institutions that were more open and accountable in character; important political decisions and matters of policy were subjected to debate within parliamentary bodies; and citizens were provided with certain basic rights, in some cases formally recognized in law, which guaranteed, among other things, their freedom of expression and association. The doctrine of *arcana imperii* was transformed into the modern principle of official secrecy and restricted in its application to those issues regarded as vital to the security and stability of the state.

In these and other respects, power was rendered more visible and decision-making processes became more public, although this broad trend was neither uniform nor complete. Those in positions of power found new ways of maintaining secrecy and new grounds

for doing so. New forms of invisible power and hidden government – from the inscrutable activities of security services and
paramilitary organizations to the wheeling and dealing of politicians behind closed doors – were invented. Limiting the invisibility of power has not rendered power fully visible: on the contrary,
the exercise of power in modern societies remains in many ways
shrouded in secrecy and hidden from the public gaze.

Publics without Places: The Rise of Mediated Publicness

Against the backcloth of these distinctions, I now want to consider
the ways in which the development of new media of communication – beginning with print, but including the more recent electronic media – has reconstituted the boundaries between public
and private life. How should we understand the impact of the
media on the nature of publicness and on the relation between
power and visibility?

Prior to the development of the media, the publicness of individuals or events was linked to the sharing of a common locale. An
event became a public event by being staged before a plurality of
individuals who were physically present at its occurrence – in the
manner, for instance, of a public execution in medieval Europe,
performed before a group of spectators who had gathered together
in the market square. I shall describe this as the 'traditional
publicness of co-presence'. This traditional kind of publicness
drew on, and was constituted by, the richness of symbolic cues
characteristic of face-to-face interaction. It was a publicness which
involved sight as well as sound, visual appearance as well as the
spoken word: the public event was a spectacle which, for those
relatively few individuals who happened to be present at its occurrence, could be seen, heard, perhaps even smelled or felt in some
way. Moreover, since the publicness of co-presence involves the
gathering together of individuals in a common locale, it is essentially dialogical in character. The individuals who speak or perform on such an occasion do so before others who can in principle
contribute to the event, whether by speaking or by displaying
other kinds of spectator behaviour (booing, hissing, clapping,
cheering, etc.), even if in practice they do not.

The development of the media has created new forms of

publicness which are quite different from the traditional publicness of co-presence. The fundamental feature of these new forms
is that, with the extension of availability made possible by the
media, the publicness of individuals, actions or events is no longer
linked to the sharing of a common locale. An action or event can
be made public by being recorded and transmitted to others who
are not physically present at the time and place of its occurrence.
Actions or events can acquire a publicness which is independent
of their capacity to be seen or heard directly by a plurality of co-
present individuals. The development of the media has thus given
rise to new forms of 'mediated publicness' which have assumed an
increasingly important role in the modern world. These new
forms have not entirely displaced the role of the traditional
publicness of co-presence. The traditional form remains an important feature of modern societies, as attested to by the continued importance of public meetings, mass demonstrations,
political debates in the face-to-face settings of parliaments and so
on. But as new media of communication became more pervasive,
the new forms of publicness began to supplement, and gradually
to extend, transform and displace, the traditional form of publicness. Let us consider briefly some phases of this development
and some of the forms of mediated publicness characteristic
of it.

The rise of printing in early modern Europe created a new form
of publicness which was linked to the characteristics of the printed
word and to its modes of production, diffusion and appropriation.
Like all forms of mediated publicness, the form created by the
printed word was severed from the sharing of a common locale:
with the advent of printing, actions or events could be endowed
with publicness in the absence of co-present individuals. Hence
the printed word was used from the outset both as a medium for
official proclamations by representatives of the state and as a
medium through which opposition groups could highlight actions
and events that might otherwise have passed unnoticed: both were
means of constituting phenomena as public for individuals who
were not physically present at their occurrence. These individuals
comprised a collectivity – a *reading public* – which was not localized in space and time. The reading public was not a community
in the traditional sense of a group of individuals who interact with
one another in face-to-face encounters. Rather, it was a *public
without a place* and it was defined, not by the existence or possibility of face-to-face interaction among its members, but rather by

the fact that its members had access to the kind of publicness made possible by the printed word.

Of course, some members of the reading public did interact with one another in common locales. Reading societies, clubs, coffee houses and other milieux provided places where individuals could meet and discuss what they had read, as Habermas has shown. But it would be misleading to suggest that these particular characteristics of the reception and appropriation of printed materials in early modern Europe were definitive of the kind of publicness made possible by print. For the publicness of the printed word extended well beyond the specific locales in which some printed materials, such as literary works and political periodicals, were discussed by some of their recipients, and the reading public did not coincide with the relatively select group of individuals who met in these locales to discuss what they had read.

The publicness created by print was not only severed from the sharing of a common locale: it was also disconnected from the kind of dialogical exchange characteristic of face-to-face conversation. With the advent of printing, the act of making something public was separated in principle from the dialogical exchange of speech-acts and became increasingly dependent on access to the means of producing and transmitting the printed word. Similarly, the act of witnessing or learning about public actions or events was separated in principle from the role of a potential participant in a face-to-face interaction. One could now learn about actions or events by reading about them, and the activity of reading neither required nor generally allowed the reader to communicate his or her views to the individuals involved in producing the original action or event. In other words, the relation between the producers of written materials and their recipients was fundamentally a relation of mediated quasi-interaction, and the kind of publicness created by the printed word was defined in part by this relation.

While I have emphasized the distinction between the traditional publicness of co-presence and the new form of publicness brought about by print, it is also important to recognize that in the historical conditions of early modern Europe these two forms of publicness overlapped in complex ways. Some actions or events which were performed or occurred in contexts of co-presence were given extended availability by being recorded or described in print. The actions or events thus acquired a new kind of publicness which not only supplemented the publicness of co-presence, but which also gradually transformed it, in so far as individuals acting in contexts of co-presence increasingly oriented their behaviour towards others who were part of a reading public. Moreover, while the relation between the producers of written materials and their recipients was non-dialogical in character, the process of reception was interwoven with various forms of dialogical communication. As we noted in previous chapters, books and pamphlets were commonly read aloud to individuals who had gathered together to hear the written word. The publicness created by the written word was thus made available, in contexts of co-presence, to individuals who did not possess the necessary skills (the capacity to read) which would give them direct access to it. Only gradually did the practice of reading aloud give way to the kind of reading practice which is common today – namely, the practice of reading with the eyes only and without moving the lips, of reading silently and on one's own. Only gradually, therefore, did the new form of publicness created by the printed word become dissociated from the conversational interaction which characterized many contexts of reception.

There was another respect in which the new form of publicness differed from the traditional publicness of co-presence: it attenuated the link between the publicness of an action or event and the sense perception of it. In contexts of co-presence, publicness is linked not only to the dialogical exchange of speech-acts among individuals who share a common locale, but also to the capacity of individuals to see and hear one another, to see and hear the actions or events which, by occurring or being performed in front of co-present others, acquire a public status. The others are spectators who bear witness to the occurrence of the action or event; by seeing and hearing it they can attest to its existence. The publicness of the action or event is thus rooted in the sense perception of co-present others.

With the advent of print, however, the link between publicness and sense perception was transformed. An action or event could now acquire a public status for others who were not present at the place of its occurrence, and who were not able to see or hear it. The link between publicness and visibility was thus attenuated: an action or event did not have to be literally seen by the individuals for whom it was a public action or event. Moreover, the individuals performing public actions or participating in public events could no longer see those individuals for whom the actions or events were, or would become, public phenomena. They had to act *blindly*, in the sense that the reading public was not within their field of vision. But the link between publicness and visibility, while significantly attenuated, was not eliminated: it was projected through the prism of print. For the practice of reading involved the use of sight; and printed materials commonly incorporated visual illustrations, produced by means of woodcuts, lithographs and similar techniques, to supplement the printed word.

So far I have been concerned to identify some of the characteristics of the form of mediated publicness created by print, and to distinguish this form from the traditional publicness of co-presence. But how should we think about the forms of publicness created by other kinds of mediated communication? How has the nature of publicness been transformed by the development of electronically based media in the twentieth century? Let us focus our attention on television: what are the characteristics of the form of mediated publicness created by TV?

As with print and other media, television severs publicness from the sharing of a common locale and from the dialogical communication characteristic of face-to-face interaction. But television, by virtue of the visual richness of its symbolic cues, establishes a new and distinctive relation between publicness and visibility. Like cinema, television places particular emphasis on the sense of vision; audio cues are combined with visual cues to produce a complex audio-visual image. Television thus enables recipients to see persons, actions and events as well as to hear the spoken word and other sounds. The publicness of persons, actions and events is reconnected with the capacity for them to be seen or heard by others. In the age of television, visibility in the narrow sense of vision – the capacity to be seen with the eyes – is elevated to a new level of historical significance.

In renewing the link between publicness and visibility, the new form of publicness created by television is somewhat similar to the traditional publicness of co-presence. But there are important differences. In the first place, the actions and events which are visible on television are visible to a much greater range of individuals who are located in diverse and dispersed contexts. Indeed, the factor of difference is so great – televised images are today visible to millions on a global scale, as opposed to the hundreds or possibly thousands that can witness an event in a context of co-presence – that it would be quite misleading to suggest that politics in the age of television is similar to the kind of theatrical practice characteristic of feudal courts. The showiness characteristic of many political events which appear on our TV screens today may bear a superficial similarity to courtly practices of the past. But the conditions under which political leaders today must seek to present themselves and manage their visibility are radically different from anything faced by the kings, lords and princes of the Middle Ages.

There is a second respect in which the form of publicness created by television differs from the traditional publicness of co-presence: television creates a field of vision which is altogether different from the field of vision which individuals have in their day-to-day encounters with others. The televisual field is, of course, much more extensive in scope, enabling individuals to see phenomena which are far removed from the locales of their day-to-day lives. It is also a field which is focused in ways that lie largely beyond their control. For the viewer is not free to choose the angle of vision, and has relatively little control over the selection of visible material. But the very fact that individuals are able to see phenomena which are far removed from the contexts of their daily lives, however much the fields of vision may be managed and controlled by those involved in the production of television messages, is something that distinguishes the kind of publicness created by television from that which existed previously.

A third difference concerns what we could call the 'directionality' of vision. In face-to-face contexts, individuals are in principle visible to one another. Even in large gatherings where a speaker is addressing an audience of thousands, the spectators are visible to the speaker, who is seen by them. In the case of television, however, the direction of vision is essentially one-way. The individuals who appear on the television screen can be seen by viewers whom they cannot see; the viewers, in turn, can see the individuals who appear before them, but the viewers remain invisible to the latter. The kind of publicness created by television is thus characterized by a fundamental contrast between producers and recipients in terms of their visibility and invisibility, their capacity to see and to be seen.

The development of television has thus created a new form of publicness, involving a distinctive kind of visibility, which is quite different from the traditional publicness of co-presence. It also differs in certain respects from the form of mediated publicness created by the written word. If we bear in mind the distinctions between these various forms of publicness, we can avoid the confusion that stems from the attempt to use a single model of public life to assess the kinds of publicness created by new media of communication. To gauge the significance of this confusion, let us return for a moment to Habermas's arguments concerning the emergence and transformation of the bourgeois public sphere.

In accounting for the rise of the bourgeois public sphere, Habermas attributes, as we have seen, a significant role to print. The printed word, expressed above all in the critical moral weeklies and political periodicals of the early eighteenth century, played a crucial role in stimulating debate among private individuals. But if we reread Habermas's work carefully, we will find, I think, that Habermas was not interested in print as such, in the distinctive characteristics of this communication medium and in the kinds of social relations established by it. His way of thinking about print was shaped by a model of communication based on the spoken word: the periodical press was part of a conversation begun and continued in the shared locales of bourgeois sociability. The press was interwoven so closely with the life of clubs and coffee houses that it was inseparable from it: 'One and the same discussion transposed into a different medium was continued in order to re-enter, via reading, the original conversational medium.'[7] So while the press played a crucial role in the formation of the bourgeois public sphere, the latter was conceptualized by Habermas not in relation to print, but in relation to the face-to-face conversations stimulated by it. In this respect, Habermas's account of the bourgeois public sphere bears the imprint of the classical Greek conception of public life: the salons, clubs and coffee houses of Paris and London were the equivalent, in the context of early modern Europe, of the assemblies and market places of ancient Greece. As in ancient Greece, so too in early modern Europe, the public sphere was constituted above all in speech, in the weighing up of different arguments, opinions and points of view in the dialogical exchange of spoken words in a shared locale.

It is not difficult to see why, with this conception of the public sphere in mind, Habermas was inclined to interpret the impact of newer communication media like radio and television in largely negative terms. It was not only because the media industries had become more commercialized and harnessed to particular interests; it was also because the kind of communication situation they created, in which the reception of media products had become a form of privatized appropriation, was a far cry from the dialogical exchange that took place among individuals who gathered together in the clubs and coffee houses of early modern Europe.[8] Habermas recognizes, of course, that radio and television create new forms of conversation – the TV chat shows, panel discussions, and so on. But these new forms of conversation, he argues, are in no way comparable to the critical-rational debate that was constitutive of the bourgeois public sphere. 'Today the conversation itself is administered,'[9] and active debate among informed citizens has been replaced by the privatized appropriation of a conversation carried out in their name.

However, we shall not arrive at a satisfactory understanding of the nature of public life in the modern world if we remain wedded to a conception of publicness which is essentially spatial and dialogical in character, and which obliges us to interpret the ever-growing role of mediated communication as a historical fall from grace. In adhering to the traditional notion of publicness as co-presence, Habermas has deprived himself of the means of understanding the new forms of publicness created by the media: he views them through the lens of the traditional model, whereas it is precisely this traditional model that has been displaced.[10] With the development of the new media of communication – beginning with print, but including the more recent forms of electronic communication – the phenomenon of publicness has become detached from the idea of a dialogical conversation in a shared locale. It has become despatialized and non-dialogical, and it is increasingly linked to the distinctive kind of visibility produced by, and achievable through, the media (especially television).

If the approach developed here enables us to avoid the problems inherent in Habermas's account, it also gives us a critical perspective on the work of another influential social theorist – Michel Foucault. Unlike Habermas, Foucault did not discuss directly the nature of the media and their impact on modern societies. But Foucault did develop, in *Discipline and Punish* and elsewhere, a distinctive argument about the organization of power in modern societies and the changing relation between power and visibility.[11] The argument, succinctly put, is this. The societies of the ancient world and of the ancien régime were societies of spectacle: the exercise of power was linked to the public manifestation of the strength and superiority of the sovereign. It was a regime of power in which a few were made visible to many, and in which the visibility of the few was used as a means of exercising power over the many – in the way, for instance, that a public execution in the market square became a spectacle in which a sovereign power took its revenge, reaffirming the glory of the king through the destruction of a rebellious subject. But from the sixteenth century on, the spectacular manifestation of power gave way to new forms of discipline and surveillance which increasingly infiltrated different spheres of life. The army, the school, the prison, the hospital: these and other institutions increasingly employed the more subtle mechanisms of power based on training, disciplining, observing, recording. The spread of these mechanisms gradually gave rise to a kind of 'disciplinary society' in which the visibility of the few by the many has been replaced by the visibility of the many by the few, and in which the spectacular display of sovereign power has been replaced by the normalizing power of the gaze.

Foucault uses a striking image to characterize this new relation between power and visibility: the Panopticon. In 1791 Jeremy Bentham published a blueprint for the ideal penitentiary, which he called the Panopticon.[12] Bentham envisaged a circular building with an observation tower at the centre. The walls of the building were lined with cells, each separated from one another by walls. The cells would have two windows: one on the inside, facing the observation tower, and one on the outside, allowing light to pass through the cell. By virtue of this unique architectural structure, a single supervisor in the central tower could subject a multiplicity of inmates to continuous surveillance. Each inmate, securely confined in a cell, is permanently visible; each action can be seen and monitored by a supervisor who remains unseen. Moreover, since the inmates know that their actions are always visible even if they are not being observed at every moment, they will adapt their behaviour accordingly and always act as if they were being observed. They are subjected to a state of permanent visibility which ensures the automatic functioning of power.

Foucault regards the Panopticon not merely as an ingenious if somewhat idiosyncratic piece of late eighteenth-century architectural design, but as a generalizable model for the organization of power relations in modern societies. This model – what he calls 'panopticism' – provided an effective alternative to earlier forms of exercising power. Gradually it supplemented and replaced earlier forms so that, in more and more spheres of social life, individuals were increasingly subjected to the kinds of discipline and surveillance that were so effectively employed in the prison. Increasingly individuals are caught up in a new system of power in which visibility is a means of control. They are no longer witnesses to a grand spectacle that unfolds before them but rather objects of the multiple, intersecting gazes which, through the daily exercise of surveillance, dispense with the need for spectacle.

In developing this argument Foucault has called attention to an

important set of issues which bear directly on the social organization of power. His analysis of the rise of the prison, and of the
ways in which methods of discipline and surveillance differ from
traditional forms of punishment and social control, is brilliantly
insightful. But his suggestion that the Panopticon provides a
generalizable model for the exercise of power in modern societies
is much less convincing. Of course, there are some organizations
in modern societies which rely on methods of surveillance: the
police, the military and the security services, above all, but also
some other agencies of the state and some private organizations
which are concerned with the routine gathering of information.
Moreover, it is clear that communication media have been used
for the purposes of surveillance; one need only retrace the role of
the military in the development of new communication technologies to assure oneself on this point.[13] But the significance of
surveillance can be exaggerated; and it would be quite misleading
to focus our attention exclusively on activities of surveillance while
neglecting the new forms of publicness created by the media.

If Foucault had considered the role of communication media
more carefully, he might have seen that they establish a relation
between power and visibility which is quite different from that
implicit in the model of the Panopticon. Whereas the Panopticon
renders many people visible to a few and enables power to be
exercised over the many by subjecting them to a state of permanent visibility, the development of communication media provides
a means by which many people can gather information about a
few and, at the same time, a few can appear before many; thanks
to the media, it is primarily those who exercise power, rather than
those over whom power is exercised, who are subjected to a
certain kind of visibility. But this new kind of mediated visibility is
very different from the type of spectacle that Foucault discerned
in the ancient world and the ancien régime. For the visibility of
individuals and actions is now severed from the sharing of a
common locale, and hence dissociated from the conditions and
constraints of face-to-face interaction.

The Management of Visibility

The changing nature of publicness – from the traditional
publicness of co-presence to the various forms of mediated

publicness prevalent today – has profoundly altered the conditions under which political power is exercised. We can begin to unfold the political implications of this transformation by considering the ways in which those who exercise political power seek to manage their visibility before others. There is nothing new about the concern of political rulers or leaders to construct their self-images and to control their self-presentation: the management of visibility is an ancient political art. But the development of communication media, and therewith the transformation in the nature of visibility, have changed the rules by which this art is practised.

Prior to the development of print and other forms of media, political rulers could generally restrict the activity of managing visibility to the relatively closed circles of the assembly or the court. Visibility required co-presence: one could be visible only to those who shared the same spatial-temporal locale. Hence emperors, kings, princes, lords and other power-holders could concentrate their efforts on managing their self-presentation before those with whom they interacted in face-to-face situations. Their audiences consisted primarily of members of ruling elites or of individuals who participated in the social life of the court: it was these individuals, above all, with whom they interacted in their day-to-day lives and to whom they directed their public behaviour.

There were occasions when rulers appeared before wider audiences comprising, among others, some of the subjects over whom they ruled. These occasions included major public events such as coronations, royal funerals and victory marches. The pomp and ceremony of such occasions, the extravagance of the apparel and surroundings, the aloofness of a figure who could be seen but not heard or touched or confronted as an equal: all enabled the ruler to maintain some distance from his subjects while enabling them temporarily to see and celebrate his existence in a context of co-presence. The maintenance of distance attested to the sacredness of power. The ruler was above – both literally and symbolically – the subjects over whom he ruled, and his existence was both mortal and divine.[14]

For most individuals in ancient or medieval societies, however, the most powerful rulers were rarely if ever seen. Individuals who lived in rural areas or in the peripheral regions of an empire or kingdom would rarely have the opportunity to see the emperor or king in flesh and blood. Apart from royal progresses, which were transient and relatively infrequent, most public appearances of the monarch took place in the political centre – in the halls and courts of the palace or in the streets and squares of the capital city.[15] In peripheral regions, individuals might routinely participate in festivals celebrating the monarch's existence without ever seeing him in person. During the first few centuries AD, for instance, cults of the Roman emperor flourished in the cities of Asia Minor, and imperial festivals were popular occasions for celebration. But these cults and festivals were established and sustained largely in the absence of the emperor himself – indeed, no emperor visited Asia Minor during the whole of the first century AD.[16] An individual who participated in a provincial festival might see an assortment of local priests and dignitaries draped in purple, and perhaps a few delegates from neighbouring cities, but would be very unlikely to see the emperor himself.

With the development of new means of communication, such as the early forms of print, political rulers had to concern themselves increasingly with their self-presentation before audiences which were not physically present. The new means of communication were used by them not only as a vehicle for promulgating official decrees, but also as a medium for fabricating a self-image which could be conveyed to others in distant locales. Monarchs in early modern Europe, such as Louis XIV of France or Philip IV of Spain, were well versed in the arts of image-making.[17] Their images were constructed and celebrated not only in traditional media, such as paint, bronze, stone and tapestry, but also in the newer media of print, including woodcuts, etchings, engravings, pamphlets and periodicals. Under the reign of Louis XIV, for example, periodicals like the *Gazette de France*, published twice a week, and the *Mercure Galant*, published monthly, devoted regular space to the actions of the king.[18] While the monarchies of early modern Europe were primarily court-based societies in which activities of self-presentation were centred in places designed for this purpose (the Louvre, Versailles, etc.), nevertheless the image of monarchs, and accounts of their activities, did achieve extended availability through print. But print was also a medium in which others could construct images and accounts which diverged from the self-images that rulers sought to present. Pamphlets were produced in which monarchs were described as vain, arrogant, unscrupulous and unjust, and satirical images were widely circulated. Print afforded extended reach not only for those who sought to celebrate the image of the king, but also for those who sought to detract from it.

In the course of the nineteenth and twentieth centuries, the task of managing the visibility of political leaders through the media has assumed an ever greater significance. While there are some similarities with the kinds of strategies employed by rulers such as Louis XIV, the social and political conditions of managing visibility in the late twentieth century are quite different from those which prevailed in early modern Europe. Three differences are particularly important. First, since the early nineteenth century there has been a massive expansion in the size of audiences capable of receiving mediated messages. Hence those concerned with the management of visibility now have to contend with a range of recipients which is far greater – in terms both of number and geographical spread – than anything confronted by political leaders in early modern Europe. Second, the development of television has re-emphasized the importance of visibility in the narrow sense of vision (that is, capable of being seen with the eyes), though visibility is now detached from the sharing of a common locale. Hence the visual appearance of political leaders – the way they dress, groom themselves, carry themselves, etc. – becomes an important feature of their self-presentation before audiences who are remote in space and who can see without being seen. Moreover, television enables individuals to appear before distant audiences in ways which are effectively 'live', thus heightening the degree of vigilance and reflexive monitoring required by political leaders and those entrusted with managing their visibility.

A third important difference concerns the relatively autonomous development of political systems which in many Western societies have increasingly assumed the form of liberal democracies in which organized political parties compete at regular intervals, in accordance with certain rules, with the aim of securing a sufficient proportion of the popular vote to install them in power. Since the early development of modern democratic systems, the press played a crucial role as a principal forum within which this competition took place, a role which, in the late twentieth century, has been increasingly taken over by television. Today the careful presentation of self before distant others whose allegiance must be constantly nourished, and whose support is vitally required from time to time, is not so much an option as an imperative for actual or aspiring political leaders and their parties. In the social and political conditions of the late twentieth century, politicians in liberal-democratic societies have little choice but to submit to the law of compulsory visibility. To renounce the management of visibility through the media would be either an act of political suicide or an expression of bad faith by someone who was so accustomed to the art of self-presentation, or so well placed in an organization that practised the art to good effect, that he or she could claim to do without it.

While the management of visibility through the media is an unavoidable feature of modern politics, the strategies employed by politicians, parties and governments vary greatly, as does the extent to which this task is turned into a concerted and self-conscious activity. Nixon was one of the first US presidential candidates who made a systematic attempt to use television to his advantage. After losing the 1960 election to Kennedy, during which he had come off badly in a much-discussed televised debate, Nixon decided that he had no alternative but to use television as a means of forging a new image and presenting it to the electorate. He fought the 1968 election with the help of a team of media advisers who were familiar with the techniques of advertising and well attuned to the political uses of television.[19] Through spot commercials and carefully arranged panel discussions, they sought to construct an image of Nixon as a statesman-like leader seeking to communicate with the people, while at the same time shielding him from the damage that could be caused by the uncontrolled questioning of journalists.

The management of visibility through the media is an activity pursued not only in the politically intensive periods of election campaigns, it is also a day-to-day part of the very business of governing. For the conduct of government requires a continuous process of decision-making concerning what is to be made public, to whom and how. The task of making and executing these decisions may be handed over in part to a team of specialized personnel who are responsible for managing the relation between the government and the media. Consider, for example, some of the strategies typically employed by the Reagan administration during the early 1980s.[20] The principal architects of Reagan's public relations approach – Michael Deaver and David Gergen – were convinced of the political importance of television and of the need to manage continuously the relation to the press. Gergen had worked for Nixon and had seen how, in the case of Watergate, a belligerent and overly secretive approach could backfire catastrophically. Deaver, Gergen and their colleagues therefore sought to cultivate a symbiotic relation with the media, providing the TV networks with a continuous programme of well-managed photo opportunities and well-illustrated stories to fill their broadcasting schedules.

While trying to satisfy the demand for new images and stories, the Deaver–Gergen team also sought strictly to control access to the President himself and to keep him away from the front line. Gergen devised the 'lightning-rod theory' of the relation between the President and the press: you only have one President and he has to be kept out of harm's way, but you have plenty of others who can be put forward to take the flak when the news is bad. As Gergen put it, 'One of the most destructive aspects of the Carter administration is that they continually let him go out there and be the point man, on everything! A lot of our strategy has to do with *not* having the President out answering questions every day.'[21] Hence the number of presidential press conferences was reduced and the President was increasingly isolated from reporters. Deaver and Gergen concentrated their efforts on projecting positive images of the President and cultivating amicable relations with the press while putting forward others, such as White House spokesman Larry Speakes, to deal with awkward questions from reporters.

There was another reason why Deaver and Gergen thought it important to keep Reagan away from the front line: they were worried about the 'gaffe problem'. Placed in front of reporters and given the task of responding live to questions, Reagan had a disconcerting tendency to utter statements that were ill-informed, simple-minded or quite simply wrong. This tendency threatened to undermine the attempt to present Reagan as a decisive and accomplished leader. 'The gaffe question went directly to the question of competence,' explained Gergen. 'If you had [Reagan portrayed as] both unfair and incompetent, you were in trouble.'[22] In order to defuse this problem, the Deaver–Gergen team pursued a two-pronged strategy. On the one hand, they went on the offensive and increased the opportunities for Reagan to appear before television viewers, on the assumption that his personal charm would outweigh the risks associated with incompetence and factual error. Thus they moved his press conferences from the afternoon to the evening, when they could be seen on prime-time television. On the other hand, they tightened the controls around the President and tried to limit the occasions when he might be called on to make an off-the-cuff remark. In spring 1982, for instance, Deaver tried to prevent reporters from asking questions during photo opportunities, a restriction which, while initially denounced by the networks, eventually met with some success.

Although there were occasional confrontations, the success of the Reagan administration's PR strategy depended on the cultivation of amicable relations with the major media institutions. Special efforts were made by Deaver, Gergen and their colleagues to win over the news organizations and keep them on their side, while the news organizations in turn tended to oblige so long as there was a continuous flow of vivid images and interesting stories. Hertsgaard describes this as a 'subtle form of media complicity' in which journalists became, in effect, uncritical mouthpieces for the Reagan administration.[23] While Hertsgaard's argument may be somewhat overstated, he is surely right to stress that, in societies where the media are not under the direct control of the state, the task of managing the visibility of political leaders is generally pursued in ways that are indirect, relying less on overt censorship than on mutual cooperation, carefully controlled access and the self-censorship of news organizations which have something to gain from adopting a conciliatory stance. That this kind of cosy collaboration between the managers of visibility and the purveyors of news represents something less than one might legitimately expect of media organizations in a democratic society is a consideration to which we shall return.

The Limits of Control: Gaffes, Scandals and Other Sources of Trouble

So far I have been concerned to analyse some of the ways in which individuals seek to employ the means of communication at their disposal in order to manage their visibility before others – and especially others, in the modern age of television, who are spatially (and perhaps also temporally) remote. But mediated visibility is a double-edged sword. While new media of communication have created new opportunities for the management of visibility, enabling political leaders to appear before their subjects in a way and on a scale that never existed before, they have also created new risks. The mediated arena of modern politics is open and accessible in a way that traditional assemblies and courts were not. Moreover, given the nature of the media, the messages produced by political leaders may be received and understood in ways that cannot be directly monitored and controlled. Hence the visibility created by the media may become the source of a new and distinctive kind of *fragility*. However much political leaders may seek to manage their visibility, they cannot completely control it; the phenomenon of visibility may slip from their grasp and, on occasion, work against them.

The inability to control the phenomenon of visibility completely is a constant source of trouble for political leaders. They must be on their guard continuously and employ a high degree of reflexivity to monitor their actions and utterances, since an indiscreet act or ill-judged remark can, if recorded and relayed to millions of viewers, have disastrous consequences. We can explore these issues further by focusing on several different sources of trouble. I shall distinguish four types of occurrence and consider some examples of each: the gaffe and the outburst; the performance that backfires; the leak; and the scandal. These four types of occurrence do not comprise an exhaustive list of sources of trouble. Moreover, they are not mutually exclusive: in certain circumstances they may overlap, in the way for instance that a leak may develop into a scandal. But by distinguishing these four types of occurrence and analysing some of the conditions and consequences of each, we can begin to explore a range of phenomena which have yet to be analysed in a systematic and thorough fashion.[24]

Gaffes and outbursts are among the most common sources of trouble for political leaders. They represent a failure on the part of the individual fully to control his or her behaviour, and they thereby attest to an individual who is not fully in command of the situation or of his or her own feelings, actions or utterances. Of course, gaffes and outbursts occur relatively frequently in contexts of everyday social interaction, and no doubt they were quite common within the circles of ruling elites in the past. What is new today is not the occurrence of gaffes and outbursts among political leaders, but rather the fact that, with the new means of electronic communication (and especially television), the gaffes and outbursts can be recorded live, seen and heard by millions, and replayed countless times before an ever-widening circle of recipients. Hence the gaffe and the outburst become public displays of incompetence and lack of self-control before audiences which are unprecedented in scale and capable of viewing (and reviewing) the event in detail. Moreover, such displays can have consequences both for the actions of distant others and for the careers of the individuals who have the misfortune of being seen to perform them.

I have already commented on Reagan's proneness to commit gaffes and on how his PR managers tried, with some success, to limit the negative consequences of these public displays of incompetence. But Reagan, while perhaps more gaffe-prone than other leaders, was by no means unique in this regard. In the 1976 primary campaign, President Ford displayed his unfamiliarity with Mexican food when, on a campaign rally in San Antonio, Texas, he was served with hot tamales by his hosts. As television cameras focused on his mouth, he proceeded to bite into the tamale; but the symbolic act of consumption was immediately aborted because he had failed to remove the corn husk in which the tamale was wrapped. The gaffe was relayed throughout the country on prime-time news broadcasts and featured on the front pages of many newspapers.[25]

While gaffes among political leaders are fairly common, outbursts are less so. Gaffes arise when leaders are not in command of the situation in which they find themselves or the material with which they are dealing; outbursts arise when leaders are not in control of themselves. The example of Senator Edward Muskie is well known. A leading candidate for the Democratic presidential nomination in 1972, Muskie appeared on the steps of the *Manchester Union Leader* on 26 February, in near blizzard conditions, in order to condemn a vicious attack the paper had made on his wife. Muskie called the newspaper's publisher 'a liar' and 'a gutless coward' and then, as he read the headline attacking his wife, his voice faltered and he broke down in tears. The outburst was recorded and repeatedly broadcast on television. Charges of weakness and emotionalism ensued, especially from Republican quarters, and Muskie's campaign rapidly lost momentum.[26]

Gaffes and outbursts do not always have destructive consequences. Many political leaders are able to limit the damage, and some (such as Reagan) may have teams of assistants who include damage limitation among their tasks. But other political figures – especially those with less political clout and less professional expertise at their disposal – may find it difficult to shake off the negative images created by well-publicized gaffes. Former Vice-President Dan Quayle's image was thoroughly tarnished by a series of gaffes, including his much-discussed attempt to correct the spelling of 'potato(e)'.[27] And it seems likely that the political career of Edwina Currie, who was a junior minister of health in Margaret Thatcher's government, suffered irreparable damage from her unfortunate remarks about eggs.[28]

The conditions of the performance that backfires are somewhat different from those of the gaffe or the outburst. In the case of the performance that backfires, the performing individual may be in complete control of his or her behaviour. The problem stems not from incompetence or loss of control, but rather from a misjudgement concerning the ways in which the performance would be received and understood by the people who watch and listen to it. As a result of this misjudgement, a message intended to have a certain effect may produce quite the opposite, and thus backfire on the producer. Moreover, since the recipients are not physically present at the place of production, the performing individual is generally unable to monitor their responses and adjust his or her behaviour accordingly. Hence the individual is deprived of the kind of feedback that would otherwise enable him or her to mitigate the negative consequences of a performance that was in the process of backfiring.

The risk of backfire is all the greater when there is a wide divergence of interests, values and beliefs between the performing individual and the main recipients. A striking example of this was the attempt by Saddam Hussein, in the run-up to the Gulf War, to use television as a means of showing the West that the foreigners held in Iraq were being treated in a courteous and hospitable way. On 24 August 1990 Saddam Hussein staged a press conference with a group of British hostages and their children. Dressed in civilian clothes, he fondled the children, asked them if they were getting enough food and exercise, and praised their role in preventing war. While apparently intended to reassure viewers in the West and to place further pressure on Western governments to desist from military action, the press conference was seen by many in Britain and elsewhere as a shameful manipulation of foreign nationals who were being held against their will.

Let us now consider two types of occurrence – the leak and the scandal – which are quite different from those considered so far. Both the leak and the scandal can be understood as a breakdown in the attempt to manage the relation between front-region and back-region behaviour. Information or behaviour that individuals want to withhold or conceal – that is, to reserve for a back region of private behaviour or covert activity – is suddenly thrust into the public domain and made visible to a large number of recipients.

The information or behaviour is generally such that, by being made visible in this way, it compromises or potentially undermines the public image that the individual or administration wishes to project, or the course of action they wish to pursue. Hence leaks and scandals are generally accompanied by defensive measures aimed at limiting the damage that could be caused by uncontrolled disclosures of sensitive information or private behaviour.

The phenomenon of the leak is more restricted in scope than that of the scandal. A leak is an intentional disclosure of information on the part of an insider who chooses to make public something which he or she knows to be reserved for a back region. The insider knows that his or her action may cause trouble for others, and knows that, if he or she is identified as the source of the leak, serious sanctions could be imposed. But these risks are accepted as part of the price to be paid in order to make public something which, in the insider's view, should be part of the public domain. The leak in this sense can be distinguished from the quasi-official release of information by a government body or agency: this type of disclosure is not so much a leak as a device used by government officials to manage the boundaries between the visible and the invisible.

Leaks can give rise to scandals or contribute to their formation, but scandals can also arise in other ways. The term 'scandal' is a common and widely used term which dates back to the late sixteenth century. While the original uses of the term often had a religious overtone (conduct which was an offence to religious sensibilities), gradually the term acquired a more general connotation and was used to express a sense of indignation or moral outrage. Scandalous behaviour was conduct that brought disgrace or offended the sense of decency. The term retains this connotation today, but the conditions under which scandalous activities occur have changed in certain respects. Of course, scandals occur in many spheres of life; but the scandals that erupt in the political sphere, and that figure so prominently today, are generally linked to breakdowns in the management of visibility through the media. Scandal is an occupational hazard of politics in the age of mediated visibility.

The scandals which receive so much attention today – not only the great scandals like Watergate and the Iran–Contra affair, but also the smaller-scale scandals which erupt with an almost numbing frequency in the press – can be partly understood in terms of the shifting boundaries between the public and the private.²⁹ These scandals arise when activities hitherto kept hidden or secret, and which could be carried out only in so far as they were kept hidden or secret, are suddenly disclosed or made visible through the media. The secrecy of the activity is essential to its existence: if the individuals performing the activity had openly declared what they intended to do, they would not have been able to follow through with their plans. Moreover, the public disclosure, generally through the media, of the hitherto secret or concealed activity is constitutive of its character as a scandal. This disclosure makes visible an activity which could not have been conducted openly and which, on becoming visible, gives rise to the kind of public outcry which constitutes the scandal.

Scandals generally presuppose sets of norms or expectations which are contravened or transgressed by the activities in question, and with reference to which the activities, once disclosed, are denounced. These norms and expectations vary from one social-historical context to another. Hence what counts as scandalous, and the extent of damage that it can cause to an individual or administration, will depend on the prevailing norms and expectations: bribery and embezzlement among government officials or extramarital affairs among members of the political elite do not have the same significance everywhere and at all times. What made the disclosure of Cecil Parkinson's affair with his secretary so damaging for the Conservative government in general, and for Parkinson's political career in particular, was the fact that it occurred at a time when Margaret Thatcher and her associates were attempting to build a political programme around the theme of a return to traditional values, among which the sacredness of the nuclear family was regarded as paramount. For Thatcher's erstwhile party chairman to be exposed as the man who made his secretary pregnant, and whose wife and family had to suffer the consequences, could hardly be seen, in that context, as anything other than scandalously hypocritical.³⁰

In the case of scandals which threaten to undermine support for political leaders or governments, attempts are generally made, as soon as the scandal begins to break out, to circumscribe the source of the trouble, to downplay its potentially damaging implications and to prevent senior officials from becoming implicated in the affair. These exercises in damage limitation are an integral part of the management of visibility: they are the normal responses of individuals and organizations whose strategies of visibility management have broken down. Indeed, it is not uncommon for individuals planning covert operations to build in arrangements which would limit the damage in the event that the operation is exposed. Such arrangements appear to have been in place, for instance, well before the Iran–Contra operation became headline news in November 1986. In his testimony to the select committees of the House of Representatives and the Senate, Oliver North admitted that CIA Director William Casey had informed him that he was probably not sufficiently senior to carry the blame and that his superior, Rear Admiral John Poindexter, might also have to take the fall.[31] Poindexter, in turn, told the committees that he had sought to provide the President with 'future deniability' of knowledge about the Iran–Contra operation. Whether Reagan knew about the operation or not, it is clear that those involved had fully appreciated the importance of insulating the President in the event that the operation became public.

The gaffe and the outburst, the performance that backfires, the leak and the scandal: all are occurrences which indicate that, however much individuals may seek to manage their visibility through the media, they cannot completely control it, and that they are vulnerable to new kinds of risk which stem from this double-edged character of mediated visibility. One of the reasons why it is so difficult to control the phenomenon of mediated visibility is the sheer proliferation of the means of producing and transmitting mediated messages in the world today. It is, of course, true that the means of production and transmission are organized in certain ways and that there is a significant degree of concentration in the media industries, as we saw earlier. It is also no doubt true that many media organizations are a good deal less inquisitive and less eager to probe the unseemly side of political life than some of the latter-day champions of the free press would suggest. But these considerations should not blind us to the fact that, with the growing proliferation of the means of producing and transmitting mediated messages, it is increasingly difficult for political leaders (and their PR teams) to control the visibility of themselves and of the actions and events they initiate or produce. It is increasingly difficult for them to throw a veil of secrecy around themselves and around particular domains of action, and to ensure that these domains will remain invisible or become accessible only in carefully predetermined ways. The exercise of political power today thus takes place in an arena which is increasingly *open to view*: however hard political leaders may try to restrict the visibility of themselves or of particular actions or events, they know they run the risk that they, or the actions or events for which they are responsible, may be shown and seen in ways they did not intend, and hence they must reckon with the permanent possibility of uncontrolled visibility.

We have yet to understand the full significance and long-term consequences of these aspects of mediated visibility. On the one hand, the rise of mediated visibility may make it more difficult for those who exercise political power to do so secretively, furtively, behind closed doors. Hence it may, under certain institutional conditions, render the exercise of political power more open and accountable to the members of an electorate. But, on the other hand, the uncontrollable character of mediated visibility also gives rise to a new kind of *fragility* in the political sphere. Governments racked by scandal, political leaders struggling to limit the damage caused by leaks and disclosures of various kinds: these are not the conditions under which decisive political leadership can readily be shown. They are, on the contrary, the conditions which may lead to weakened government and political paralysis, and which may nourish the suspicion and cynicism which many people feel towards politicians and established political institutions. They are also the conditions which could, perhaps, provide fertile ground for the growth of a new kind of demagoguery: the sudden rise to power of a figure who is seemingly untouched by the scandals and murky dealings of professional politicians and their clientele, and whose appeal is rooted in part in a pervasive sense of disaffection and distrust.

The possible consequences of mediated visibility are certainly important and in need of further study. But if we wish to understand the full significance of this phenomenon, we must situate it in a broader context. For the exercise of political power today is increasingly open to view, not only in the sphere of domestic politics but on a global scale. Actions such as military interventions in the Gulf or the suppression of demonstrations in China, South Africa or the West Bank are actions which take place in a new kind of mediated global arena: they are visible, observable, capable of being witnessed simultaneously and repeatedly by millions of individuals around the world. Even in cases where intense efforts are made to restrict visibility (as with the Gulf War), there is always the possibility that images will be transmitted which portray events in a different light (as was the case, for instance, with some of the reports from the CNN team which remained in

Baghdad and which, while operating under Iraqi censorship, fell outside the controls imposed by the coalition military command). The exercise of political power is thus subjected to a kind of *global scrutiny* which simply did not exist before. Given the possibility of such scrutiny, political actions carry unprecedented risks and may expose a regime to international condemnation and to economic and political isolation, as in the case of China following the Tiananmen Square massacre, or Iraq following the invasion of Kuwait.

What is global scrutiny? I use this term to refer to the regime of visibility created by an increasingly globalized system of communication in which television plays a central role. This system enables recipients to see individuals who are situated in other parts of the world, and to see them in a non-reciprocal way (that is, without themselves being seen). It enables recipients to witness events which take place in distant locales, and to witness them virtually simultaneously (that is, as and when they occur). Of course, recipients are not in full control of their own field of vision; they are not free to look in one direction or another and to focus on different individuals or objects, as they can in face-to-face situations. The field of vision is structured by the media organizations and by the processes of filming, reporting, editing, syndicating, transmitting, etc., which constitute part of the routine activity of these organizations. But the creation of global fields of vision, however structured they may be, represents a significant historical development. For it means not only that political leaders must now act in an arena which is in principle open to view on a global scale, but also that recipients are able to see and experience distant individuals and events in a way that was simply not possible before. In a later chapter we shall explore the implications of this development for the nature of experience and the self. But first we must examine more carefully the process of globalization which has created these new fields of vision.

5

The Globalization of Communication

One of the salient features of communication in the modern world is that it takes place on a scale that is increasingly global. Messages are transmitted across large distances with relative ease, so that individuals have access to information and communication which originates from distant sources. Moreover, with the uncoupling of space and time brought about by electronic media, the access to messages stemming from spatially remote sources can be instantaneous (or virtually so). Distance has been eclipsed by proliferating networks of electronic communication. Individuals can interact with one another, or can act within frameworks of mediated quasi-interaction, even though they are situated, in terms of the practical contexts of their day-to-day lives, in different parts of the world.

The reordering of space and time brought about by the development of the media is part of a broader set of processes which have transformed (and are still transforming) the modern world. These processes are commonly described today as 'globalization'. The term is not a precise one, and it is used in differing ways in the literature.[1] In the most general sense, it refers to the growing interconnectedness of different parts of the world, a process which gives rise to complex forms of interaction and interdependency. Defined in this way, 'globalization' may seem indistinguishable from related terms such as 'internationalization' and 'transnationalization', and these terms are often used interchangeably in the literature. But while these various notions refer to phenomena that are closely connected, the process of globalization, as I shall understand it here, involves more than the expansion of activities beyond the boundaries of particular nation-states. Globalization arises only when (a) activities take place in an arena which is global or nearly so (rather than merely regional, for example); (b) activities are organized, planned or coordinated on a global scale; and (c) activities involve some degree of reciprocity and interdependency, such that localized activities situated in different parts of the world are shaped by one another. One can speak of globalization in this sense only when the growing interconnectedness of different regions and locales becomes systematic and reciprocal to some degree, and only when the scope of interconnectedness is effectively global.

Understood in this sense, the process of globalization is a distinctive feature of the modern world, and it is a process that has intensified significantly in recent decades. But globalization is by no means a new phenomenon. Its origins can be traced back to the expansion of trade in the late Middle Ages and early modern period.[2] Prior to the late Middle Ages, most trade was local in character; the long-distance trade that did exist, such as the trade in spices and silk, was small in volume and restricted to a tiny fraction of the population. During the late fifteenth and early sixteenth centuries, however, the nature, volume and geographical extent of trade increased dramatically. Regular trading relations were established between Europe and other parts of the world, and a small number of European maritime nations – including Spain, The Netherlands and England – formed the core of an emerging world economy.

While the origins of globalization can be traced back to the expansion of trade in the late fifteenth and early sixteenth centuries, it was in the seventeenth, eighteenth and nineteenth centuries that the process of globalization gradually took hold and acquired many of the characteristics that it displays today. The consolidation of colonial power coupled with the development of industrialization created a new pattern of world trade based on an emerging international division of labour. Core countries imported raw materials from the colonies and exported manufactured goods throughout the world. Industrial production became increasingly important as a source of economic and political power for core countries, while peripheral regions became increasingly dependent on the most powerful colonial states. The fortunes of the core countries fluctuated: initially Britain took the lead, but was later overtaken by the United States, Germany and

Japan. The development of the global system was sporadic and uneven; it reflected fluctuations in economic activity and fundamental asymmetries in the distribution of power.

There can be no doubt that the organization of economic activity and concentrations of economic power have played a crucial role in the process of globalization. But all forms of power – economic, political, coercive and symbolic – have both contributed to and been affected by this process. If one retraces the process of globalization, one finds that these various forms of power overlap with one another in complex ways, sometimes reinforcing and sometimes conflicting with one another, creating a shifting interplay of forms of power. In this chapter I shall focus primarily on the social organization of symbolic power and the ways in which it has contributed to and been transformed by the process of globalization. But this will necessarily involve some discussion of economic, political and coercive power as well.

I shall begin by retracing the emergence of globalization in the sphere of communication. When did it begin? How did it develop? What forms did it assume? In the second section I shall analyse some of the structured characteristics of globalized processes of communication in the world today. I shall then examine the legacy of what is probably the most important theoretical interpretation of the globalization of communication and its consequences – the theory of cultural imperialism. In the final section I shall develop an alternative view which, while recognizing the structured character of global communication flows, places particular emphasis on the complex, creative interface between the globalized diffusion of media products and their localized appropriation.

The Emergence of Global Communication Networks

The practice of transmitting messages across extended stretches of space is not new. We have seen that elaborate networks of postal communication were established by political authorities in the Roman Empire and by political, ecclesiastical and commercial elites in medieval Europe. With the development of printing in the late fifteenth century, books, pamphlets and other printed materials were circulated well beyond the locales of their production, frequently crossing the frontiers of the emerging nation-states. Moreover, as European powers developed trading relations with other parts of the world, communication channels were established between Europe and those regions of the world that were drawn increasingly into the spheres of European colonial expansion.

It was only in the nineteenth century, however, that communication networks were systematically organized on a global scale. It was in the nineteenth century, therefore, that the globalization of communication took hold. This was partly due to the development of new technologies which enabled communication to be dissociated from physical transportation. But it was also linked directly to economic, political and military considerations. I shall examine the beginnings of the globalization of communication by focusing on three key developments of the late nineteenth and early twentieth centuries: (1) the development of underwater cable systems by the European imperial powers; (2) the establishment of international news agencies and their division of the world into exclusive spheres of operation; and (3) the formation of international organizations concerned with the allocation of the electromagnetic spectrum.

(1) The telegraph was the first medium of communication which successfully exploited the communication potential of electricity. Experiments with early forms of telegraphy took place in the late eighteenth and early nineteenth centuries, but the first electromagnetic telegraphs were developed in the 1830s. In 1831 Joseph Henry of Albany, New York, succeeded in transmitting signals over a mile-long circuit, and by 1837 usable systems had been developed by Cooke and Wheatstone in England and Morse in the United States. The system devised by Cooke and Wheatstone, which used needles that could be read visually, was initially installed along the railway between Paddington and West Drayton in July 1839. But Morse's system, which used a dot–dash code for the transmission of messages, eventually proved to be the most successful. In 1843 Morse built his first practical telegraph line between Washington and Baltimore with funds provided by the US Congress. Subsequently the telegraph industry developed rapidly in the United States and in Europe, stimulated by demand from the railways, the press, and the business and financial sectors.

The early telegraph systems were land-based and therefore

restricted in terms of their geographical scope. It was not until the 1850s that reliable methods of underwater telegraphy were developed. The early submarine cables were generally made of copper wire coated with gutta percha, a natural insulating material made from the sap of a Malayan tree.[3] In 1851–2 submarine cables were successfully laid across the English Channel and between England and Ireland. In 1857–8 the first attempt was made to lay a cable across the Atlantic Ocean, though it ended in failure. The first attempts to link Britain with India were similarly unsuccessful. In 1864, however, a submarine cable was successfully laid between Karachi and the Persian Gulf; the line was then connected by land-based cables to Constantinople and Europe. By 1865 a telegraph link between Britain and India was complete. A year later, a transatlantic cable was successfully laid.

Following these early successes, the submarine cable industry developed rapidly. In the early 1870s, cables were laid throughout South-East Asia, so that Europe was linked to China and Australia. Cables were also laid between Europe and South America, and along the coasts of Africa. Most of the cables were produced, laid and operated by private companies, although these companies often received substantial financial assistance from governments. London was the centre of this expanding communication network and was the principal source of finance for the international submarine cable business. By 1900, approximately 190,000 miles of submarine cable had been laid throughout the world. British firms owned 72 per cent of these cables, and a substantial proportion were owned by one firm – the Eastern and Associated Companies founded by the Manchester merchant John Pender, who had been involved in the submarine cable industry since the 1860s.

The early submarine cable networks were used primarily for commercial and business purposes, although political and military concerns also played an important role in their development. As leaders of the most extensive empire of the late nineteenth century, British officials were well aware of the strategic value of rapid communications. The British Admiralty and the Colonial, War and Foreign Offices placed pressure on the government to construct additional submarine cables which did not cross non-British territories, and which would therefore be less vulnerable in times of crisis. One such cable was laid between Britain and the Cape of Good Hope in 1899–1901, and was used during the Boer War. This line was subsequently extended to Mauritius, Ceylon,

Singapore and Australia, thereby connecting Britain to South-East Asia and Australia via a route which avoided the Middle East.

The submarine cable networks developed in the second half of the nineteenth century thus constituted the first global system of communication in which the capacity to transmit messages was clearly separated from the time-consuming processes of transportation. Individuals located in the major urban centres of Europe and North America acquired the means to communicate almost instantaneously with other parts of the world. The contrast with earlier forms of transport-based communication was dramatic. Up to the 1830s, a letter posted in England took five to eight months to reach India; and due to monsoons in the Indian Ocean, it could take two years for a reply to be received.[4] In the 1870s, a telegram could reach Bombay in five hours, and the answer could be back on the same day. And in 1924, at the British Empire Exhibition, King George V sent himself a telegram which circled the globe on all-British lines in 80 seconds. Rapid communication on a global scale – albeit along routes that reflected the organization of economic and political power – was a reality.

(2) A second development of the nineteenth century which was of considerable significance for the formation of global communication networks was the establishment of international news agencies. The significance of news agencies in this context was threefold. First, the agencies were concerned with the systematic gathering and dissemination of news and other information over large territories – primarily in Europe to begin with, but soon extending to other parts of the world. Second, after an initial period of competitive rivalry, the major news agencies eventually agreed to divide up the world into mutually exclusive spheres of operation, thus creating a multilateral ordering of communication networks which was effectively global in scope. Third, the news agencies worked closely with the press, providing newspapers with stories, extracts and information which could be printed and diffused to a wide audience. Hence the news agencies were tied into networks of communication which, via print (and later radio and television), would reach a significant and growing proportion of the population.

The first news agency was established in Paris by Charles Havas in 1835.[5] A wealthy entrepreneur, Havas acquired what was primarily a translating office, the *Correspondance Garnier*, and turned it into an agency which collected extracts from various European papers and delivered them daily to the French press. By 1840 the agency catered for clients in London and Brussels as well, supplying news by coach and by means of a regular pigeon service. In the late 1840s, rival news-gathering services were set up in London by Paul Julius Reuter and in Berlin by Bernard Wolff. The agencies took advantage of the development of telegraph cable systems, which made it possible to transmit information over ever-greater distances at great speed. Competition among the three agencies intensified in the 1850s, as each agency sought to secure new clients and to expand its sphere of operation. However, in order to avoid damaging conflicts, the agencies eventually decided to co-operate by dividing the world up into mutually exclusive territories. By virtue of the Agency Alliance Treaty of 1869, Reuter obtained the territories of the British Empire and the Far East; Havas acquired the French Empire, Italy, Spain and Portugal; and Wolff was granted the exclusive right to operate in German, Austrian, Scandinavian and Russian territories. While the agencies were independent commercial organizations, their domains of operation corresponded to the spheres of economic and political influence of the major European imperial powers. Each agency worked closely with the political and commercial elites of the country which served as its home base, enjoying some degree of political patronage and providing information which was valuable for the conduct of trade and diplomacy.

The triple agency cartel dominated the international collection and dissemination of news until the outbreak of the First World War. Other news agencies were established in the late nineteenth and early twentieth centuries, but most had aligned themselves with one of the three principals. In the wake of the First World War, however, the triple agency cartel was broken by the expansion of two American agencies, Associated Press (AP) and the United Press Association (UPA, subsequently transformed into United Press International or UPI). Associated Press was a cooperative established in 1848 by six New York daily newspapers. AP joined the European cartel in 1893, agreeing to supply the European agencies with news from America in return for the exclusive right to distribute news in the United States. The United Press Association was founded by E. W. Scripps in 1907, partly in order to break the hold of AP in the domestic US news market. In addition to serving the US market, UPA set up offices in South America and sold news to South American and Japanese newspapers. During the First World War and its aftermath, both AP and UPA expanded their activities worldwide, placing increasing pressure on the cartel arrangements. By the early 1930s the triple agency cartel was effectively at an end; in 1934 Reuters signed a new agreement with AP which gave the American agencies a free hand to collect and distribute news throughout the world. While the American agencies expanded rapidly and Reuters maintained a strong position in the global market, the other European agencies underwent major changes. The capitulation of France in 1940 brought about the dissolution of Havas, although it was eventually replaced by a new agency, the Agence France-Presse (AFP), which took over many of the assets and connections of its predecessor. With the rise of Nazism and the subsequent defeat and partition of Germany following the Second World War, the Wolff agency lost its position of influence in the international domain and eventually disappeared.

Since the Second World War, the four major agencies – Reuters, AP, UPI and AFP – have maintained their positions of dominance in the international system for the collection and dissemination of news and other information. Many other agencies have been established and expanded their spheres of operation; and some agencies, such as TASS and the Deutsche Presse Agentur, acquired (at least temporarily) a prominent international role. But the four majors remain the key actors in the global information order. Many newspapers and broadcasting organizations throughout the world depend heavily on them for international news, as well as for news of their own geopolitical region, and many of the smaller agencies are affiliated to them. The major news agencies have also expanded and diversified their activities, taking advantage of new developments in information and communication technology and emerging as central players in the new global market for information and data of various kinds, including information relating to financial and commercial transactions.[6]

The dominance of the major news agencies, combined with other inequalities in the international flow of information and communication, has led to calls from various quarters for a reorganization of the global information order. A series of conferences and commissions sponsored by UNESCO in the 1970s and early 1980s generated a wide-ranging debate on the theme of a 'New World Information and Communication Order' (NWICO). The proponents of NWICO were seeking a more equitable balance in the international flow and content of information, as well as a strengthening of the technological infrastructures and productive capacities of less developed countries in the sphere of communication. But the UNESCO initiatives met with considerable resistance from certain governments and interest groups in the West. In 1984 the United States withdrew from UNESCO, followed by the United Kingdom in 1985; together this deprived UNESCO of around 30 per cent of its budget and greatly limited the effectiveness of any policy recommendations.[7] Nevertheless, the NWICO debate helped to increase awareness of the issues raised by the dominance of the major news agencies and, more generally, by the inequalities associated with the globalization of communication. It also helped to stimulate the development of various forms of cooperation among so-called Third World countries, including the expansion of regional and non-aligned news agencies in Africa and elsewhere.[8]

(3) A third development which played an important role in the globalization of communication also stems from the late nineteenth century: it concerns the development of new means of transmitting information via electromagnetic waves and the succession of attempts to regulate the allocation of the electromagnetic spectrum. In an earlier chapter we briefly considered some of the technical innovations which underpinned this development.[9] The use of electromagnetic waves for the purposes of communication greatly expanded the capacity to transmit information across large distances in a flexible and cost-efficient way, dispensing with the need to lay fixed cables over land or under sea. But the increasing use of electromagnetic waves also created a growing need to regulate the allocation of spectrum space both within and between countries. Each country developed its own legislative framework for spectrum allocation and selective licensing. Initially one of the key concerns of the authorities entrusted with the task of allocating spectrum space was to set aside a segment of the spectrum for military and security purposes, thereby minimizing interference from amateur radio users. But as the commercial potential of the new medium became increasingly clear, political authorities became directly involved in the selective licensing of broadcasting organizations, which were granted exclusive rights to broadcast at designated frequencies in particular regions. The practices of selective licensing were shaped not only by the technical constraints of spectrum scarcity but also by a broader set of political considerations concerning the proper

nature and role of broadcasting organizations, considerations which varied greatly from one country to another.[10]

The international frameworks for the management of spectrum space were less effective. The key organization in this regard was the International Telegraph Union, subsequently transformed into the International Telecommunications Union (ITU). Originally formed in 1865 under a convention signed by 20 European states, the union was concerned primarily with the establishment of international standards and the resolution of technical problems.[11] At its 1906 Berlin conference, it dealt with radio for the first time and agreed to allocate certain sections of the spectrum to specific services, such as the frequencies used by ships at sea. Subsequently the ITU convened a regular conference – the World Administrative Radio Conference or WARC – to address problems of spectrum allocation and related issues. In the early phase of these international activities, frequencies were generally allocated on a first come, first served basis.[12] Users simply notified the ITU of the frequencies they were using or wished to use, and they thereby acquired a 'squatter's right'. But as demands on the radio spectrum increased, the ITU gradually adopted a more active stance. Sections of the spectrum were allocated to particular services, and the world was divided into three broad regions – Europe and Africa, the Americas, and Asia and the South Pacific – which could each be planned in more detail. The systems developed by the ITU have none the less come under increasing pressure in recent years, partly as a result of rising demands by existing users and partly due to new demands by countries hitherto largely excluded from the domain of international telecommunications.

The development of technologies capable of transmitting messages via electromagnetic waves, together with the emergence of national and international organizations concerned with the management of spectrum space, marked a decisive advance in the globalization of communication. It was now possible to transmit increasing quantities of information over large distances in an efficient and virtually instantaneous way. Moreover, the messages transmitted by electromagnetic waves were potentially accessible to anyone who was within range of the signals and who had the equipment to receive them – a fact which was of enormous significance for the commercial exploitation of the medium. However, during the first half of the twentieth century most communication by electromagnetic transmission remained confined to specific geographical locales, such as particular urban areas, nation-states or the regions between land and ships at sea. It was not until the 1960s, with the launching of the first successful geo-stationary communication satellites, that communication by electromagnetic transmission became fully global in scope. I shall return to this development shortly.

Patterns of Global Communication Today: An Overview

While the origins of the globalization of communication can be traced back to the mid-nineteenth century, this process is primarily a phenomenon of the twentieth. For it is during the twentieth century that the flow of information and communication on a global scale has become a regularized and pervasive feature of social life. There are, of course, many dimensions to this process; the twentieth century has witnessed an unparalleled proliferation of the channels of communication and information diffusion. The rapid development of systems of radio and television broadcasting throughout the world has been an important but by no means the only aspect of this process. The globalization of communication has also been a structured and uneven process which has benefited some more than others, and which has drawn some parts of the world into networks of global communication more quickly than other parts. Since the late 1960s, the characteristics of global communication flows have been studied in some detail by researchers in international communication – well before the term 'globalization' gained currency in the social sciences.[13] In this section I shall draw on this literature for the purpose of analysing some of the main patterns of global communication today. I shall not attempt to analyse these patterns in a detailed and comprehensive fashion, but merely to identify some of the main dimensions of globalized communication processes; and I shall be concerned above all to highlight their structured and uneven character. While the range of relevant issues is potentially very wide, I shall restrict my attention to four themes: (1) the emergence of transnational communication conglomerates as key players in the global system of communication and information diffusion; (2) the social impact of new technologies, especially those associated with satellite communication; (3) the asymmetrical flow of information and communication products within the global system; and (4) the variations and inequalities in terms of access to the global networks of communication.

(1) The globalization of communication in the twentieth century is a process that has been driven primarily by the activities of large-scale communication conglomerates. The origins of these conglomerates can be traced back to the transformation of the press in the nineteenth century, as we have seen.[14] The change in the economic basis of newspapers, precipitated and promoted by the introduction of new methods of production, set in motion a long-term process of accumulation and concentration in the media industries. In the course of the twentieth century, this process has increasingly assumed a transnational character. Communication conglomerates have expanded their operations in regions other than their countries of origin; and some of the large industrial and financial concerns have, as part of explicit policies of global expansion and diversification, acquired substantial interests in the information and communication sector. Through mergers, acquisitions and other forms of corporate growth, the large conglomerates have assumed an ever-greater presence in the global arena of the information and communication trade.

The names of some of the largest communication conglomerates are well known: Time Warner, formed by the merger of Time, Inc., and Warner Communications in 1989 and now the largest media enterprise in the world, has subsidiaries in Australia, Asia, Europe and Latin America. The German-based Bertelsmann group, with strong interests in publishing, television, music and high-tech information systems, has operations in Europe, the United States and Latin America. Rupert Murdoch's News Corporation, which has substantial interests in publishing, television and film, probably has the most extensive reach, with subsidiaries in Europe, the United States, Australia and Asia. These and other large communication conglomerates operate increasingly in a worldwide market and organize their activities on the basis of strategies which are effectively global in design. But nearly all of the large conglomerates are based in North America, Western Europe, Australia or Japan; very few are based in Third World countries, although the latter provide important markets for their goods and services.[15] Hence the development of communication conglomerates has led to the formation of large concentrations of economic and symbolic power which are privately controlled and unevenly distributed, and which can deploy massive resources to pursue corporate objectives in a global arena. It has also led to the formation of extensive, privately controlled networks of communication through which information and symbolic content can flow.

The nature and activities of some of the large communication conglomerates have been documented in the literature and I shall not examine them further here.[16] There is a need, however, for more up-to-date comparative research on the activities of these conglomerates, on the ways in which they are adapting to the changing economic and political circumstances of the 1990s, and on their exploitation of new technological developments.

(2) The development of new technologies has played an important role in the globalization of communication in the late twentieth century, both in conjunction with the activities of communication conglomerates and independently of them. Three interrelated developments have been particularly important. One is the deployment of more extensive and sophisticated cable systems which provide much greater capacity for the transmission of electronically encoded information. A second development is the increasing use of satellites for the purposes of long-distance communication, often in conjunction with land-based cable systems. The third development – in many ways the most fundamental – is the increasing use of digital methods of information processing, storage and retrieval. The digitalization of information, combined with the development of related electronic technologies (microprocessors, etc.), has greatly increased the capacity to store and transmit information and has created the basis for a convergence of information and communication technologies, so that information can be converted relatively easily between different communication media.

All three of these technological developments have contributed in fundamental ways to the globalization of communication. Most obviously, the use of telecommunications satellites, positioned in geosynchronous orbits and interlinked, has created a system of global communication which is virtually instantaneous and which dispenses with the need for terrestrial relays and transmission wires. Since their development in the early 1960s, telecommunications satellites have been used for a variety of purposes.[17] The needs of the military and of large commercial organizations have always played an important role, and many multinational corporations make extensive use of satellite communication. Satellites have also been increasingly integrated into the normal telecommunications networks, carrying a growing proportion of the international traffic in telephone, telex, fax, electronic mail and related communication services.

From the outset, telecommunications satellites were also used as relay stations and distribution points for television broadcasting. They formed an integral part of national network systems in the USA, the former USSR and elsewhere, and they were used as distribution points to supply cable systems on a national and international basis. In recent years, however, the development of more sophisticated satellites, capable of transmitting stronger, well-targeted signals, has made possible the introduction of direct broadcasting by satellite (or DBS). The first DBS systems began transmitting programmes in the USA in 1975, and the first European systems began operating in 1986; by the early 1990s, a variety of DBS systems were operating or planned in other parts of the world. Part of the significance of DBS is that it creates new distribution systems outside of the established terrestrially based networks of broadcasting – systems which are often privately owned and controlled and in which the large communication conglomerates may have a substantial stake. Moreover, these new distribution systems are inherently transnational since, from a technical point of view, there is no reason why the reception area (or 'footprint') of a DBS satellite should correspond even roughly to the territorial boundaries of a particular nation-state.

In addition to creating new transnational distribution networks, the development of DBS and other technologies (including cable and video cassette recorders) has expanded the global market for media products. The international flow of films, TV programmes and other materials has increased as producers and distributors seek to exploit the lucrative markets created by satellite and cable channels and by videocassette rentals and sales. This expansion of the global market should be viewed against the blackcloth of earlier trends in the international flow of media products.

(3) A central feature of the globalization of communication is the fact that media products circulate in an international arena. Material produced in one country is distributed not only in the domestic market but also – and increasingly – in a global market. It has long been recognized, however, that the international flow of media products is a structured process in which certain organizations have a dominant role, and in which some regions of the world are heavily dependent on others for the supply of symbolic

goods. Studies carried out in the early 1970s by Nordenstreng and Varis showed a clear asymmetry in the international flow of television programmes: there was, to a large extent, a one-way traffic in news and entertainment programmes from the major exporting countries to the rest of the world.[18] The United States was (and remains) the leading exporter in television programming, selling far more material to other countries (especially to Latin America, Europe, Canada, Australia and Japan) than it imports from abroad. Some European countries, such as Britain and France, were also major exporters (and remain so); but, unlike the United States, they also imported a significant quantity of programming from abroad (mainly from the US). Subsequent studies by Varis and others have tended to confirm the unevenness of flow, although they have also produced a more complex picture and have highlighted the growing importance of intraregional trade (for instance, countries like Mexico and Brazil have emerged as major producers and exporters of programming material to other parts of Latin America).[19]

The structured character of the international flow of symbolic goods is the outcome of various historical and economic factors. In the domain of news, the patterns of dependence reflect the legacy of the international news agencies established in London, Paris and New York (although the precise significance of Western-based news agencies remains a matter of some dispute[20]). In the sphere of entertainment, the economic power of Hollywood continues to exert a major influence on the international flow of films and TV programmes. Many television stations in less developed countries do not have the resources to produce extensive programming of their own. The import of American serials, at prices negotiated on a country-by-country basis, is a relatively inexpensive (and financially very attractive) way to fill broadcasting schedules.

While some of the broad patterns of international flow have been documented over the years, the research remains fragmentary. There are many sectors of the information and communication industries which have yet to be studied in detail from this point of view. And the ways in which existing patterns of international flow will be affected by new technological developments – such as those associated with satellite and cable systems, or those linked more generally to the digitalization of information – is a question which demands a good deal more research. Given the complexity of global networks of transmission and trade and the huge volume of material which passes through them, it is unlikely that our understanding of patterns of international flow will ever be more than partial. But further research could help to shed light on some of the more significant trends.

(4) In addition to analysing the patterns of international flow, it is essential to consider the patterns of access to and uptake of material transmitted through global networks. Much of the research on patterns of international flow has been based on the content analysis of television broadcasting schedules in different countries. But in some parts of the world, access to television broadcasting services was restricted for many years to the relatively small proportion of the population which lived in the major urban areas. For the rural population, which comprises 70–90 per cent of the population in many Third World countries, radio has probably been a more important medium of communication than television.[21] Of course, this situation is changing continuously as more resources are devoted to the development of television services and as more individuals and families are able to gain access to them. But significant inequalities remain in terms of the capacity of individuals in different parts of the world, and in different parts and social strata of the same country, to gain access to the materials which are diffused through global networks.

Quite apart from these inequalities of access, globalized symbolic materials are subjected to different patterns of uptake. Taken on its own, the content analysis of programming schedules tells us relatively little about who watches which programmes, how long they watch them for, etc., and hence tells us relatively little about the extent of uptake of globally distributed material.[22] Moreover, if we wish to explore the impact of the globalization of communication, we must consider not only the patterns of uptake but also the *uses* of globalized symbolic materials – that is, what recipients do with them, how they understand them, and how they incorporate them into the routines and practices of their everyday lives. These are issues to which we shall return.

The Theory of Cultural Imperialism: A Reassessment

So far I have been concerned to retrace the development of the globalization of communication and to examine some of the patterns of global communication in the world today. But what kind of theoretical account can be offered which would help to explain the structured patterns of global communication and which would shed light on their likely consequences? Various theoretical accounts can be found in the literature on international communications.[23] During the last few decades, however, there is one account which has occupied a particularly prominent role: this is the view that the globalization of communication has been driven by the pursuit of the commercial interests of large US-based transnational corporations, often acting in collaboration with Western (predominantly American) political and military interests; and that this process has resulted in a new form of dependency in which traditional cultures are destroyed through the intrusion of Western values. This view was articulated with particular acuity by Herbert Schiller in *Mass Communications and American Empire*, first published in 1969, and the argument has been updated and extended in various publications since then.[24] The argument developed by Schiller and others is generally described as the 'cultural imperialism thesis'.[25] It has been enormously influential: much of the research in international communications in the 1970s and early 1980s (including some of the material drawn on in the previous section) was influenced directly or indirectly by it. But Schiller's work has also been subjected to a great deal of criticism and there are few scholars today who would accept his analysis unreservedly.[26] Nevertheless, it is useful to reconsider briefly Schiller's argument. By identifying some of its main strengths and weaknesses, we can gain a clearer sense of the processes which must be taken into account, and the pitfalls which must be avoided, by a theory of the globalization of communication.

Schiller argues, very broadly, that the period since the Second World War has been characterized by the growing dominance of the United States in the international arena.[27] As the traditional colonial empires of the nineteenth century – the British, French, Dutch, Spanish and Portuguese empires – declined in significance, they were replaced by a new emergent American empire. This new imperial regime is based on two key factors: economic strength, stemming primarily from the activities of US-based transnational corporations; and communications know-how, which has enabled American business and military organizations to take the leading roles in the development and control of new systems of electronically based communication in the modern world. Schiller argues that the American system of broadcasting – essentially a commercial system dominated by the large networks and funded primarily by advertising revenue – exemplifies the way in which some of the most important communication systems have been thoroughly permeated by commercial interests. Moreover, the American system of broadcasting has served as a model for the development of broadcasting systems elsewhere in the world, especially in Third World countries. The dependence on American communications technology and investment, coupled with the new demand for TV programmes and the sheer cost of domestic production, have created enormous pressures for the development of commercial broadcasting systems in many Third World countries and for the large-scale importation of foreign – mainly American – programmes. The result is an 'electronic invasion' which threatens to destroy local traditions and to submerge the cultural heritage of less developed countries beneath a flood of TV programmes and other media products emanating from a few power centres in the West. These programmes are infused with the values of consumerism, since they are geared above all to the needs of the manufacturers who sponsor television through advertising. Hence, when developing countries adopt a commercial system of broadcasting, they are also, argues Schiller, implicated in a process of cultural transformation and dependency in which the values of consumerism override traditional motivations and alternative patterns of value formation, and through which individuals are harnessed increasingly to a global system of communication and commodity production based largely in the US.

Schiller's argument, sketched here only briefly, has the considerable merit of highlighting the global character of electronically based communication systems, of emphasizing their structured character and of underscoring the fact that communication systems are interwoven in fundamental ways with the exercise of economic, military and political power. Moreover, Schiller's argument brings sharply into focus the enormous financial constraints faced by Third World countries seeking to develop their own communication systems, constraints which make the importation of foreign-produced programmes very attractive. However, even if one sympathizes with Schiller's broad theoretical approach and his critical perspective, there are many respects in which his argument is deeply unsatisfactory. I shall not attempt to address all of the difficulties here. Rather, I want to focus on three main problems, all closely linked to the themes I am pursuing in this chapter and elsewhere.

First, let us consider a little further Schiller's portrayal of global structures of power in the post-Second World War period. Schiller's argument was originally developed at a time when American hegemony in the global system seemed – at least to some observers – to be self-evident and secure. The United States, as the major industrial power and the home of many of the largest transnational corporations, appeared to be the military-industrial heartland of the postwar global system; the thesis of cultural imperialism was effectively an argument about the extension and consolidation at the level of communications and information of a power that was fundamentally economic in character. However, this argument provides at best a very partial account of the complex and shifting relations of economic, political, military and symbolic power which characterized the immediate postwar period. It takes relatively little account, for instance, of the fundamental political and symbolic conflicts of the Cold War era, and of the significance of communism and nationalism as mobilizing systems of belief. Moreover, whatever the shortcomings of Schiller's argument with regard to the immediate postwar period, it seems very doubtful indeed whether it could be applied with any degree of conviction to the changing global context of the late twentieth century. In the economic domain alone, the last few decades have witnessed a profound process of global restructuring which has eroded the position of the United States as the preeminent industrial power. The global economy has become increasingly multipolar; Europe (especially Germany), Japan and the newly industrializing countries of South-East Asia have assumed an increasingly important role.[28] Relations of political, coercive and symbolic power have also changed shape in complex ways. The collapse of the communist regimes in Eastern Europe and the dissolution of the Soviet Union have created an altogether new geopolitical situation – not only in Europe but throughout the world. Supranational bodies such as the United Nations and the European Commission are playing an increasing – although as yet relatively limited – role in international affairs. New forms of symbolic power, in some cases linked to the resurgence of nationalism and fundamentalist religious beliefs, have emerged in different parts of the world.

This process of global restructuring has also affected the various industries concerned with information and communication. In terms of the production of electronic components (semiconductors and microprocessors, etc.), the postwar dominance of the United States has been dramatically eroded as production has increasingly shifted to Western Europe, Japan and the Pacific rim. The United States has similarly lost its position of dominance in the manufacture of electronic consumer goods; in television manufacture, for example, Asia is the leading region in the world today and China is the largest single producer, manufacturing 19 per cent of total world output in 1987.[29] The global shift in economic power is also reflected in the growing role of foreign capital in the American market. While Hollywood remains an important producer of films and television entertainment, a growing number of Hollywood studios are owned by foreign-based corporations. In November 1989, Columbia Pictures and Tristar Pictures were bought by the Sony Corporation for $3.4 billion – higher than any price previously paid by a Japanese concern for a US company.[30] Sony had previously acquired CBS Records, so the purchase of Columbia and Tristar represented a further move into the entertainment sector by a company which had established a strong base in the manufacture of audio and video hardware. Shortly after the Sony takeover, another Japanese-based multinational, Matsushita, acquired MCA for $6.9 billion. MCA operates Universal Studios and has a range of other interests in entertainment, retailing, publishing and leisure activities; Matsushita is the largest manufacturer of consumer electronic goods in Japan and one of the largest in the world. Moreover, despite the continued importance of Hollywood, non-North American industries are becoming increasingly important as regional producers and exporters of films and television programmes. This includes industries based in Western Europe and Australia; but it also includes industries based in other parts of the world, such as Mexico, Brazil and India. It would be quite implausible to suggest that this complex and shifting field of global power relations could be analysed in terms of the thesis of cultural imperialism. The thesis is simply too rigid and one-dimensional to do justice to a global situation which is in considerable flux.

Reflecting on his work 25 years later, Schiller recognizes that the cultural imperialism thesis can no longer be sustained in its original form.[31] He acknowledges that since the late 1960s global relations of power have changed in significant ways, and that as a result the thesis would have to be recast today. The global dominance of American culture and media products has not appreciably declined – if anything, argues Schiller, it has become more pronounced, with the collapse of state-socialist regimes in the former Soviet Union and Eastern Europe and with the demise of UNESCO-based attempts to create a new information order. But the economic basis of this dominance has changed. Transnational corporations have assumed an increasingly important role in the global communications industry, and investment capital has been drawn from an increasingly diverse range of sources. So while cultural domination remains American in terms of the form and content of media products, the economic basis of the domination has been internationalized. American cultural imperialism has become, in Schiller's words, 'transnational corporate cultural domination'.[32]

While this revision of the thesis goes some way to address the changes that have taken place in recent decades, it does not go far enough. Schiller still presents too uniform a view of American media culture (albeit a culture which is no longer exclusively at the disposal of American capital) and of its global dominance. He still maintains that American media culture is defined by the overriding objective of promoting consumerism, and that it is this objective which renders it so useful for the global capitalist system. But the composition, the global flow and the uses of media products are far more complex than this characterization would suggest. Schiller's revision of the cultural imperialism thesis is, in effect, a way of acknowledging the globalization of economic activity while still insisting on the continued dominance of American media culture. It would be better to accept that, in the sphere of information and communication as well as in the domain of economic activity, the global patterns and relations of power do not fit neatly into the framework of unrivalled American dominance.

A second problem with Schiller's argument is that it tends to assume that before the electronic invasion led by the United States most Third World countries had indigenous, authentic traditions and cultural heritages which were largely untainted by values imposed from outside. What is at stake in the electronic invasion, explains Schiller, 'is the cultural integrity of weak societies whose national, regional, local or tribal heritages are beginning to be menaced with extinction by the expansion of modern electronic communications'.[33] But this vision of the cultural integrity of Third World countries is a somewhat romantic view which, in many cases, does not stand up to careful scrutiny.[34] The tradi-

tions and cultural heritages of many so-called Third World countries were shaped by a long and often brutal process of cultural
conflict, a process through which many traditional practices were
destroyed and some of the values and beliefs of external powers
were imposed on indigenous populations.[35] But the imposition of
values and beliefs was rarely a straightforward matter. It generally
involved a complex process of adaptation and incorporation
whereby extraneous values and beliefs were adapted to new conditions, selectively appropriated by indigenous populations and
gradually interwoven with pre-existing traditions and practices.
The Spanish conquest of Mexico and the colonization of other
parts of Central and South America offer many vivid examples of
this process.[36]

The issues addressed by Schiller should be placed, therefore, in
a much broader historical perspective. Rather than assuming that
prior to the importation of Western TV programmes etc. many
Third World countries had indigenous traditions and cultural
heritages which were largely unaffected by external pressures, we
should see instead that the globalization of communication
through electronic media is only the most recent of a series of
cultural encounters, in some cases stretching back many centuries, through which the values, beliefs and symbolic forms of
different groups have been superimposed on one another, often in
conjunction with the use of coercive, political and economic
power. Most forms of culture in the world today are, to varying
extents, *hybrid cultures* in which different values, beliefs and practices have become deeply entwined. This does not imply, of
course, that the globalization of communication through the electronic media may not give rise to new forms of cultural domination and dependency. But it does imply that we cannot
understand these new forms, nor can we gain a clear view of
their consequences, if we proceed on the assumption that
previous cultures were largely untainted by values imposed from
outside.

A third problem with Schiller's argument concerns the ways in
which imported media products are thought to affect their recipients in the Third World and elsewhere. Schiller argues, in essence,
that TV programmes which are made for a commercial television
system will unavoidably express consumerist values, both in the
programmes themselves and in the advertising which constitutes
the financial basis of the system; and that these representations
will in turn create wants and foster consumerist motivations in

their recipients, in such a way that these recipients become harnessed to a Western-based system of commodity production and
exchange. No doubt this rather hasty argument, in its concern to
highlight the connection between broadcasting media and a capitalist system of commodity production and exchange, has placed
too much emphasis on the role of consumerist values and has
neglected the enormous diversity of themes, images and representations which characterize the output of the media industries. But
there is another weakness in this argument which is of particular
relevance to the issues that concern us here: the argument presupposes a much too simplified account of what is involved in the
reception and appropriation of media products.[37] Like many arguments influenced by Marxism, Schiller's argument commits a
version of what I have described elsewhere as the 'fallacy of
internalism':[38] Schiller tries to infer, from an analysis of the social
organization of the media industries, what the consequences of
media messages are likely to be for the individuals who receive
them. But inferences of this kind must be treated with scepticism.
Not only are they very speculative but, more importantly, they
disregard the complex, varied and contextually specific ways in
which messages are interpreted by individuals and incorporated
into their day-to-day lives. In short, Schiller's argument ignores
the hermeneutic process of appropriation which is an essential
part of the circulation of symbolic forms (including media
products).

In recent years a number of researchers have shown – through
ethnographic studies in contexts that are particularly suitable for
assessing the plausibility of the cultural imperialism thesis – that
the processes of reception, interpretation and appropriation of
media messages are much more complicated than Schiller's argument assumes. Thus Liebes and Katz, in a well-known study,
examined the reception of *Dallas* among different ethnic groups in
Israel, comparing their responses with groups in the United States
and Japan.[39] They show that different groups found different ways
of making sense of the programme, different ways of 'negotiating'
its symbolic content. The process of reception was not a one-way
transmission of sense but rather a creative encounter between, on
the one hand, a complex and structured symbolic form and, on
the other, individuals who belong to particular groups and who
bring certain resources and assumptions to bear on the activity of
interpretation. So Liebes and Katz found, for instance, that there
were systematic differences in the ways that groups recounted the

programmes they had seen. The groups of Israeli Arabs and Moroccan Jews emphasized kinship relations, interpreting the motivation of characters primarily in terms of the hierarchical order of the family and the continuity of the dynasty. The groups of Russian émigrés, by contrast, paid relatively little attention to kinship relations and were more inclined to take a critical view, seeing the characters as manipulated by the writers and producers of the programme. The groups of kibbutz members and of Americans were also inclined to take a critical view but they interpreted the programme in more psychological terms, as an ongoing saga of interpersonal relations and intrigue.

Studies such as this have shown convincingly that the reception and appropriation of media products are complex social processes in which individuals – interacting with others as well as with the characters portrayed in the programmes they receive – actively make sense of messages, adopt various attitudes towards them and use them in differing ways in the course of their day-to-day lives. It is simply not possible to infer the varied features of reception processes from the characteristics of media messages considered by themselves, or from the commercial constraints operating on the producers of TV programmes. In this respect, Schiller's argument involves a theoretical and methodological short-circuit. The electronic invasion of American films and TV programmes would serve to extend and consolidate a new imperial regime only if it could be reliably assumed that the recipients of these programmes would internalize the consumerist values allegedly expressed in them; but it is precisely this assumption that must be placed in doubt.

This line of criticism presses to the heart of the cultural imperialism thesis. It shows that this thesis is unsatisfactory not only because it is outdated and empirically doubtful, but also because it is based on a conception of cultural phenomena which is fundamentally flawed. It fails to take account of the fact that the reception and appropriation of cultural phenomena are fundamentally hermeneutical processes in which individuals draw on the material and symbolic resources available to them, as well as on the interpretative assistance offered by those with whom they interact in their day-to-day lives, in order to make sense of the messages they receive and to find some way of relating to them. For the cultural imperialism thesis, the process of reception is essentially a 'black box' into which media products infused with consumerist values are poured, and from which individuals oriented towards personal consumption supposedly emerge. But this clearly will not do.

While Schiller's argument is ultimately unsatisfactory, it is nevertheless important as an attempt – indeed, probably the only systematic and moderately plausible theoretical attempt – to think about the globalization of communication and its impact on the modern world. But if Schiller's argument and the cultural imperialism thesis more generally do not provide a satisfactory theoretical framework, what alternatives are there? In the remainder of this chapter I shall try to develop an alternative framework which takes account both of the structured character of global communication and of the contextualized, hermeneutical character of the reception process.

Globalized Diffusion, Localized Appropriation: Towards a Theory of Media Globalization

A satisfactory, theoretically informed account of the globalization of communication and its impact must be based, I shall argue, on two sets of considerations. First, we need to reconstruct historically the ways in which the process of globalization has taken hold, retracing this development with regard to each of the four forms of power and their interrelations. Earlier in this chapter I sketched the beginnings of such an account, focusing on symbolic power and the various institutions and technologies which, since the mid-nineteenth century, have facilitated the process of globalization. But we need a much more elaborate account, one which gives more attention to the multiple, shifting ways in which symbolic power overlapped with economic, political and coercive power in the process of globalization. In this respect, the short-coming of the cultural imperialism thesis is not that it neglects the interplay between these various forms of power: the shortcoming is that it offers an impoverished and ultimately reductionist account of this interplay. Like many arguments influenced by Marxism, the cultural imperialism thesis prioritized economic power and regarded symbolic power as largely a tool of commercial interests (allied with the interests of political and military elites). But the interplay between these forms of power was always more complex and conflict-ridden than such an account would suggest.

The second set of considerations concerns the relation between structured patterns of global communication, on the one hand, and the local conditions under which media products are appropriated, on the other. While communication and information are increasingly diffused on a global scale, these symbolic materials are always received by individuals who are situated in specific spatial-temporal locales. The appropriation of media products is always a localized phenomenon, in the sense that it always involves specific individuals who are situated in particular social-historical contexts, and who draw on the resources available to them in order to make sense of media messages and incorporate them into their lives. And messages are often transformed in the process of appropriation as individuals adapt them to the practical contexts of everyday life. The globalization of communication has not eliminated the localized character of appropriation but rather has created a new kind of symbolic axis in the modern world, what I shall describe as the axis of globalized diffusion and localized appropriation. As the globalization of communication becomes more intensive and extensive, the significance of this axis increases. Its growing importance attests to the dual fact that the circulation of information and communication has become increasingly global while, at the same time, the process of appropriation remains inherently contextual and hermeneutic.

We have already shed some light on the global–local axis by examining some of the patterns of global diffusion. I now want to develop this analysis further by focusing on the process of appropriation and pursuing three interrelated themes. The first theme is this: given the hermeneutical character of appropriation, it follows that the significance which media messages have for individuals and the uses to which mediated symbolic materials are put by recipients depend crucially on the contexts of reception and on the resources that recipients bring to bear on the reception process. This is well illustrated by the Liebes and Katz study of the reception of *Dallas*. It is also vividly demonstrated by the perceptive account by Sreberny-Mohammadi and Mohammadi of the role of communication media in the Iranian Revolution.[40] During the 1970s, traditional religious language and imagery were used in Iran as symbolic weapons in the struggle against the Shah, who was associated with the corrupting importation of Western culture. Although Khomeini was in exile, his speeches and sermons were recorded and smuggled into Iran on audiocassettes, which were easily reproduced and widely diffused. But with the development of an Islamic regime in the post-revolutionary period, Western cultural products began to assume a very different significance for many Iranians. Videos of Western films and tapes of Western pop music circulated as part of a popular cultural underground, taking on a subversive character; they helped to create an alternative cultural space in which individuals could take some distance from a regime experienced by many as oppressive.[41] Examples such as these illustrate well the contextually bounded character of the process of appropriation. As symbolic materials circulate on an ever-greater scale, locales become sites where, to an ever-increasing extent, globalized media products are received, interpreted and incorporated into the daily lives of individuals. Through the localized process of appropriation, media products are embedded in sets of practices which shape and alter their significance.

Let us now consider a second theme: how should we understand the social impact of the localized appropriation of globalized media products? Here I want to emphasize one key feature of this process. I want to suggest that the appropriation of globalized symbolic materials involves what I shall describe as *the accentuation of symbolic distancing from the spatial-temporal contexts of everyday life*. The appropriation of symbolic materials enables individuals to take some distance from the conditions of their day-to-day lives – not literally but symbolically, imaginatively, vicariously. Individuals are able to gain some conception, however partial, of ways of life and life conditions which differ significantly from their own. They are able to gain some conception of regions of the world which are far removed from their own locales.

The phenomenon of symbolic distancing is brought out well by James Lull in his study of the impact of television in China.[42] Television became a widespread medium in China only in the course of the 1980s. In the 1960s and 1970s relatively few television sets were sold in China; they were very expensive relative to normal wages and were generally restricted to the more privileged urban elites. In the 1980s, however, domestic television production increased dramatically; by 1990 most urban families owned at least one TV set, and there was about one set for every eight people nationwide.[43] Broadcasting is dominated by the national network, Central China Television (CCTV), which supplies a large proportion of the programming material to the various regional and local stations operating throughout the country.

What sense do Chinese viewers make of the programmes they

watch? Lull pursues this question through a series of extended interviews with families in Shanghai, Beijing, Guangzhou and Xian. Among other things, he shows that, while many Chinese viewers are critical of the programmes available to them, they value television for the way that it offers new vistas, new lifestyles and new ways of thinking. 'In our daily lives we just go to work and come home, so we want to see something that is different from our own life. TV gives us a model of the rest of the world':[44] this comment by a 58-year-old accountant from Shanghai captures well the effect of symbolic distancing in the age of global communication. Chinese viewers are drawn to programmes imported from Japan, Taiwan, Europe and the United States not only for their information and entertainment value, but also because they give a glimpse – albeit a fleeting and partial one – of what life is like elsewhere. When people watch international news, for instance, they may pay as much attention to street scenes, housing and clothing as to the commentary which accompanies the pictures from foreign lands.

Images of other ways of life constitute a resource for individuals to think critically about their own lives and life conditions. Even if the Chinese broadcasting system is strictly controlled by comparison with Western systems, it nevertheless provides viewers with ample material to engage in symbolic distancing. In so doing, it enables viewers to compare their own life conditions with those that appear to prevail elsewhere; it also enables them to form views both of their own life conditions and of those elsewhere which may diverge from the official government interpretations that are routinely presented to them. As one Beijing viewer remarked, 'Before the Cultural Revolution the government exaggerated the domestic and foreign situations. They said nothing is valuable outside China. But when we look at the TV programs we can see that the West is not so bad.'[45] Individuals distance themselves from their own life conditions and, at the same time, they gain a critical purchase on official interpretations of social and political reality, both in their own country and elsewhere.

In emphasizing the phenomenon of symbolic distancing, I do not want to suggest, of course, that this is the *only* aspect of the process of appropriation which is worthy of consideration. On the contrary, in the actual circumstances of day-to-day life, it is likely that the appropriation of globalized media products will interact with localized practices in complex ways and may, in some respects, serve to consolidate established relations of power or, indeed, to create new forms of dependency. I shall explore some of the more negative aspects of the appropriation of media products in a later chapter. Here I wish only to stress that, given the contextualized character of appropriation, one cannot determine in advance which aspect (or aspects) will be involved in the reception of a particular symbolic form. The relative significance of different aspects can be assessed only by means of careful, ethnographic inquiry.

This brings us to a third theme that I want briefly to consider: the localized appropriation of globalized media products is also a source of tension and potential conflict. It is a source of tension partly because media products can convey images and messages which clash with, or do not entirely support, the values associated with a traditional way of life. In some contexts this discordance may be part of the very appeal of media products: they help individuals to take a distance, to imagine alternatives, and thereby to question traditional practices. So, for instance, it seems that Egyptian soap operas are of interest to young Bedouin women in the Western Desert precisely because they present a set of life-styles – such as the possibility of marrying for love and living separately from the extended family – which diverge from the set of options traditionally available to them.[46]

The tensions and conflicts stemming from the localized appropriation of media products may also be experienced as a form of self-conflict, in so far as the process of self-formation is informed by the symbolic content of media products. Again, we shall return to this theme later when we consider the ways in which, with the development of the media, individuals gain access to new kinds of symbolic materials which can be incorporated reflexively into the project of self-formation. Here it will suffice to highlight the fact that, as these symbolic materials are drawn from more diverse sources, individuals are more likely to experience a clash of values as a personal conflict – that is, as a conflict between competing demands that are made on them or contrasting goals to which they aspire. Individuals are constantly involved in trying to reconcile, or simply hold in an uneasy balance, messages which conflict with one another or with the values and beliefs embedded in the routine practices of their daily lives.

It would be imprudent to claim that the localized appropriation of globalized media products has been a major factor in stimulating broader forms of social conflict and social change in the modern world; most forms of social conflict are extremely complex and involve many diverse factors. But it could be plausibly argued that the increasingly globalized diffusion of media products has played a role in triggering off some of the more dramatic conflicts of recent years. Lull contends that the stream of domestic and international television programmes transmitted throughout China in the 1980s created a cultural reservoir of alternative visions, encouraging people to question traditional values and official interpretations and helping them to imagine alternative ways of living. By itself, this certainly did not bring about the audacious demonstration in Tiananmen Square, nor did it determine the course of the subsequent confrontation. But in the absence of television it seems unlikely that the events of Tiananmen Square would have unfolded in the way they did, nor would they have been witnessed by millions of individuals in China and throughout the world.

In this chapter I have explored some of the contours of the globalization of communication, a phenomenon that has altered the nature of symbolic exchange and transformed in certain respects the life conditions of individuals throughout the world. But does the increasing availability of globalized media products destroy the last residues of tradition? Does the development of the media merely seal the coffin of a traditional way of life whose fate was already decided by the transformative impact of modernity?

6

The Re-mooring of Tradition

One of the most powerful legacies of classical social thought is the idea that, with the development of modern societies, tradition gradually declines in significance and eventually ceases to play a significant role in the daily lives of most individuals. Tradition, it is assumed, is a thing of the past (in more ways than one), and 'modern societies' are contrasted in a general way with the 'traditional societies' that preceded them. 'All that is solid melts into air,' Marx famously remarked; and many other thinkers, whether they shared Marx's perspective or not, have generally concurred in the view that the development of modern societies is accompanied by an irreversible decline in the role of tradition. This view formed an integral part of the various modernization theories which were developed in the 1950s and 1960s. And it is a view which has been revitalized in recent years, albeit in a more qualified fashion, by theorists who contend that the development of modern societies involves a process of 'detraditionalization'.

In this chapter I want to question the received wisdom that tradition is a thing of the past. I want to try to show that, if we pay close attention to the transformative impact of the media, we can gain a rather different view of the changing character of tradition and its role in social life. Prior to the development of the media, most people's sense of the past and of the world beyond their immediate milieu was shaped primarily by the symbolic content exchanged in face-to-face interaction. For most people, the sense of the past, of the world beyond their immediate locales and of the socially delimited communities to which they belonged, was constituted primarily through oral traditions that were produced and reproduced in the social contexts of everyday life. With the development of the media, however, individuals were able to experience events, observe others and, in general, learn about worlds – both real and imaginary – that extended well beyond the sphere of their day-to-day encounters. They were increasingly drawn into networks of communication that were not face-to-face in character. Moreover, as individuals gained access to media products, they were able to take some distance from the symbolic content of face-to-face interaction and from the forms of authority which prevailed in the locales of everyday life. For the purposes of forming a sense of self and of the possibilities open to them, individuals came to rely less and less on symbolic materials transmitted through face-to-face interaction and localized forms of authority. The process of self-formation became more reflexive and open-ended, in the sense that individuals fell back increasingly on their own resources and on symbolic materials transmitted through the media to form coherent identities for themselves.

But did these developments undermine tradition? Not necessarily. For orally transmitted traditions continued to play an important role in the daily lives of many individuals. Moreover, traditions themselves were transformed as the symbolic content of tradition was increasingly inscribed in new media of communication. The mediazation of tradition endowed it with a new life: tradition was increasingly freed from the constraints of face-to-face interaction and took on a range of new traits. Tradition was deritualized; it lost its moorings in the practical contexts of everyday life. But the uprooting of traditions did not starve them of sustenance. On the contrary, it prepared the way for them to be extended and renewed by being re-embedded in new contexts and re-moored to spatial units which exceeded the bounds of face-to-face interaction.

In order to develop this argument, I want to begin by considering the nature of tradition and, in particular, some of the ways in which tradition has been viewed in the literature of social theory. I shall then focus more sharply on the relation between tradition and the media: how have traditions been affected by the development of the media? I shall examine a classic study, conducted broadly within the framework of modernization theory, which answered this question in a way that was to be deeply influential, and which set the terms of the debate for many years. I shall then develop an alternative account which emphasizes that tradition has not been destroyed by the media but rather transformed or 'dislodged' by them. In the final section I shall try to show how this alternative account of the changing character of tradition can shed light on some of the more troubling phenomena of our time.

The Nature of Tradition

What is tradition? How should we understand its nature and role in social life? The notion of tradition has received relatively little direct attention in the literature of social theory.[1] No doubt this neglect is due, in part, to the assumption by most classical social theorists that the development of modern societies would be accompanied by the decline in the role of tradition in social life. This assumption was based on several overlapping sets of considerations. One set was primarily intellectual in character. Classical social theory was in many ways a product of Enlightenment thought; and the Enlightenment was premised on a rejection of tradition, which was regarded by many Enlightenment thinkers as a source of mystification, an enemy of reason and an obstacle to human progress. Another set of considerations was more substantive in character. Many classical social theorists argued that the development of modern societies involved a dynamic that was inherently destructive of tradition. Not only was tradition the enemy of enlightened thought, a legacy of the past to be criticized and dispelled in the name of reason, it was also doomed by the very dynamic set in motion by the emergence of modern societies.

The convergence of these two sets of considerations is evident in the writings of Marx. On the one hand, Marx was deeply influenced by the Enlightenment antipathy towards tradition: for Marx, tradition was primarily a source of mystification, a veil which shrouded social relations and concealed their true nature. On the other hand – and this was one of the central themes of his work – Marx discerned in the capitalist mode of production a dynamic which would tear up the traditional texture of social life. Unlike precapitalist societies, which were basically conservative in their mode of production, modern capitalist society is constantly expanding, changing, transforming itself; the capitalist economy is the scene of feverish activity, since it can continue to exist only by continuously revolutionizing itself. And with this ceaseless activity, the social relations and traditions of precapitalist societies are disrupted and dissolved. Hence, 'All that is solid melts into air, all that is holy is profaned, and man is at last compelled to face with sober senses, his real conditions of life, and his relations with his kind.'[2] The demystification of social relations is thus an inherent aspect of the development of capitalism. By sweeping away the 'train of ancient and venerable prejudices and opinions' which shrouded social relations in the past, capitalism enables individuals to see their social relations for what they are – namely, relations of exploitation – and prepares the way for the kind of enlightened revolutionary transformation envisaged by Marx.

Somewhat similar arguments can be found in the writings of other classical social theorists. While Weber did not share Marx's optimism about the transformation of capitalism, he too thought that the development of industrial capitalism would be accompanied by the demise of traditional world-views. Unlike Marx, Weber argued that certain changes in religious ideas and practices were preconditions for the emergence of capitalism in the West. But once capitalism had established itself as the predominant form of economic activity, it acquired a momentum of its own and dispensed with the religious ideas and practices that had been necessary for its emergence. The development of capitalism, together with the associated rise of the bureaucratic state, progressively rationalized action and adapted it to criteria of technical efficiency. The purely personal, spontaneous and emotional elements of traditional action were squeezed out by the demands of purposive-rational calculation. This 'disenchantment' of the modern world was part of the price to be paid for the rationalization of the West; Weber regarded it, with some regret, as the 'fate of modern times'.[3]

The views of Marx and Weber, among others, had a formative impact on subsequent ways of thinking about the fate of tradition. The modernization theories of the 1950s and 1960s generally took for granted a broad opposition between 'traditional' and 'modern' societies, and generally assumed that given the right conditions the passage from the former to the latter would be a one-way process of social change. In more recent years, social theorists such as Ulrich Beck and Anthony Giddens have put forward a more qualified view.[4] They argue that in the early phases of modernization many institutions depended crucially on traditions that were characteristic of premodern societies – in the way, for example, that many early modern productive organizations depended on the continuation of traditional forms of family life. But as the process of modernization enters a more advanced phase (what Beck calls 'reflexive modernization' and what Giddens calls 'late modernity'), pre-existing traditions are increasingly undermined: modern societies are 'detraditionalized'. Traditional practices do not altogether disappear from the modern world but their status changes in certain ways. They become less taken for granted and less secure as they are increasingly exposed to the corrosive impact of public scrutiny and debate. As traditions are called on to defend themselves, they lose their status as unquestioned truths. But they may survive in various forms – for example, by being transformed into a kind of fundamentalism which rejects the call for discursive justification and seeks, against a background of generalized doubt, to reassert the inviolable character of tradition.

I shall not examine the views of particular theorists in further detail here. I want instead to focus on the general question raised by their work: has the development of modern societies been accompanied by the decline of the role of tradition in social life? While it is common among classical and contemporary social theorists to answer this question in the affirmative, there are, in my view, two major problems with this response. The first problem is that it makes it difficult to understand why certain traditions and traditional belief systems continue to have a significant presence in the late twentieth century. If traditions were bound to be swept aside by the development of modern societies, then why do traditions – including religious beliefs and practices – remain such pervasive features of social life today? For those who adhere to the general thesis of the decline of tradition, it is difficult to understand the persistence or resurgence of traditional beliefs and practices in any terms other than those of regression or reaction. For the proponents of the general thesis of decline, the persistence of tradition can only be understood as a return to the past, a refuge for backward souls, a refusal to give up something which is doomed to disappear. We may wonder, however, whether this perspective is somewhat presumptuous; it can see tradition only as a legacy of the past, a remnant of an earlier age, thereby precluding the possibility that, in certain respects, tradition may be an integral part of the present.

The second problem with the general thesis of decline is that, in most versions of the thesis, little or no attention is given to the role

of the media. It is generally assumed that the dynamic characteristic of modern societies – whether this is understood as capitalist
economic activity or, more generally, as the rationalization of
action – has had a direct and deleterious impact on traditional
forms of life. But what role do the media play in the transformation of traditional life-forms? Can we understand this transformation without considering the ways in which the development of the
media has affected the social organization of everyday life? These
are questions which are, for the most part, neglected by the
proponents of the general thesis of decline. But these questions
are central and they will provide the starting point for the more
detailed analyses that follow.

Before embarking on these analyses, I want to examine further
the notion of tradition. What is tradition? How should we understand its traits? In its most general sense, 'tradition' means a
traditum – that is, anything which is transmitted or handed down
from the past.[5] Tradition may involve elements of a normative
kind (for instance, that past practices should serve as a guide to
future action), but this is not necessarily an aspect of all traditions.
In order to clarify this point, it is helpful to distinguish between
four different aspects of tradition. I shall describe these as the
'hermeneutic aspect', the 'normative aspect', the 'legitimation
aspect' and the 'identity aspect'. In practice these four elements
often overlap or merge together. But by distinguishing between
them we can get a clearer sense of what is involved in the existence
of tradition.

Consider first the hermeneutic aspect. One way of understanding tradition is to view it as a set of background assumptions that
are taken for granted by individuals in the conduct of their daily
lives, and transmitted by them from one generation to the next. In
this respect, tradition is not a normative guide for action but
rather an interpretative scheme, a framework for understanding
the world. For as hermeneutic philosophers such as Heidegger
and Gadamer have emphasized, all understanding is based on
presuppositions, on some set of assumptions which we take for
granted and which form part of a tradition to which we belong.[6]
No understanding can be entirely presuppositionless. Hence the
Enlightenment critique of tradition must, in Gadamer's view, be
qualified. In juxtaposing the notions of reason, scientific knowledge and emancipation to those of tradition, authority and myth,
the Enlightenment thinkers were not dispensing with tradition as
such but rather were articulating a set of assumptions and meth-

ods which formed the core of another tradition, that of the Enlightenment itself. In the hermeneutic sense of tradition, the Enlightenment is not the antithesis of tradition but is, on the contrary, one tradition (or cluster of traditions) among others – that is, a set of taken-for-granted assumptions which provide a framework for understanding the world.

Many traditions also have what we may describe as a normative aspect. What I mean by this is that sets of assumptions, forms of belief and patterns of action handed down from the past can serve as a normative guide for actions and beliefs in the present. We can distinguish two ways in which this may occur. On the one hand, material handed down from the past can serve as a normative guide in the sense that certain practices are *routinized* – that is, they are done as a matter of routine, with relatively little reflection on why they are being done in that way. Large parts of most people's everyday lives are routinized in this sense. On the other hand, material handed down from the past can serve as a normative guide in the sense that certain practices can be *traditionally grounded*, that is, grounded or justified by reference to tradition. This is a stronger sense of normativity precisely because the grounds for action are made explicit and raised to the level of self-reflective justification. The question of grounds can be raised by asking why one believes something or behaves in a certain way; and these beliefs or practices are traditionally grounded if one replies by saying 'That's what we've always believed' or 'That's what we've always done', or some variant thereof.

The third aspect of tradition is what one could call the legitimation aspect. What I mean by this is that tradition can, in certain circumstances, serve as a source of support for the exercise of power and authority. This aspect is brought out well by Max Weber.[7] According to Weber, there are three principal ways in which the legitimacy of a system of domination can be established. Claims to legitimacy can be based on rational grounds, involving a belief in the legality of enacted rules (what Weber calls 'legal authority'); they can be based on charismatic grounds, involving devotion to the sanctity or exceptional character of an individual ('charismatic authority'); or they can be based on traditional grounds, involving a belief in the sanctity of immemorial traditions ('traditional authority'). In the case of legal authority, individuals are obedient to an impersonal system of rules. In the case of traditional authority, by contrast, obedience is owed to the person who occupies the traditionally sanctioned position of authority and whose actions are bound by tradition. Weber's account of traditional authority is helpful because it highlights the fact that, in certain contexts, tradition may have an overtly political character: it may serve not only as a normative guide for action but also as a basis for exercising power over others and for securing obedience to commands. It is in this respect that traditions may become 'ideological': that is, they may be used to establish or sustain relations of power which are structured in systematically asymmetrical ways.

Finally, let us consider the nature of tradition in relation to the formation of identity – what I called the identity aspect of tradition. There are two types of identity formation which are relevant here – what we may call 'self-identity' and 'collective identity'. Self-identity refers to the sense of oneself as an individual endowed with certain characteristics and potentialities, as an individual situated on a certain life trajectory. Collective identity refers to the sense of oneself as the member of a social group or collectivity; it is a sense of belonging, a sense of being part of a social group which has a history of its own and a collective fate. What is the relevance of tradition to these two types of identity formation? As sets of assumptions, beliefs and patterns of behaviour handed down from the past, traditions provide some of the symbolic materials for the formation of identity both at the individual and at the collective level. The sense of oneself and the sense of belonging are both shaped – to varying degrees depending on social context – by the values, beliefs and forms of behaviour which are transmitted from the past. The process of identity formation can never start from scratch; it always builds on a pre-existing set of symbolic materials which form the bedrock of identity. But it may well be that, with the development of communication media, the nature of this pre-existing set of symbolic materials has changed in significant ways, and this may in turn have implications for the process of identity formation. These are issues to which we shall return.

Having distinguished these various aspects of tradition, we are now in a position to consider the ways in which the role of tradition has changed with the development of modern societies. Let me summarize the salient points of the argument I shall develop.

– With the development of modern societies, there is a gradual decline in the traditional grounding of action and in the role of traditional authority – that is, in the normative and the legitimation aspects of tradition.

– In other respects, however, tradition retains its significance in the modern world, particularly as a means of making sense of the world (the hermeneutic aspect) and as a way of creating a sense of belonging (the identity aspect).

– While tradition retains its significance, it has been transformed in a crucial way: the transmission of the symbolic materials which comprise traditions has become increasingly detached from social interaction in a shared locale. Traditions do not disappear but they lose their moorings in the shared locales of day-to-day life.

– The uprooting of traditions from the shared locales of everyday life does not imply that traditions float freely; on the contrary, traditions will be sustained over time only if they are continuously re-embedded in new contexts and re-moored to new kinds of territorial unit. The significance of nationalism can be partly understood in these terms: nationalism generally involves the re-mooring of tradition to the contiguous territory of an actual or potential nation-state, a territory that encompasses but exceeds the limits of shared locales.

But if tradition remains an important feature of the modern world, is it plausible to speak of the passing of traditional society? Is not the broad contrast between 'traditional' and 'modern' societies somewhat misleading in this regard? No doubt it is, and I shall be concerned to show that the relation between tradition and modernity is more puzzling and paradoxical than a sharp opposition of this kind would suggest. We can understand the paradox of tradition and modernity by focusing on this consideration: the decline of traditional authority and the traditional grounding of action does not spell the demise of tradition but rather signals a shift in its nature and role, as individuals come to rely more and more on mediated and delocalized traditions as a means of making sense of the world and of creating a sense of belonging.

So far I have distinguished certain aspects of tradition and outlined an argument about the changing role of tradition in the modern world, but I have not yet considered in detail the relation between tradition and the media. This I shall do in the following sections. I shall argue that the transformation of tradition is linked in a fundamental way to the development of communication media. The link is twofold: on the one hand, the development of

communication media facilitates the decline of traditional authority and the traditional grounding of action; on the other hand, new
communication media also provide the means of separating the
transmission of tradition from the sharing of a common locale,
thus creating the conditions for the renewal of tradition on a scale
that greatly exceeds anything that existed in the past.

Tradition and the Media (1): Tradition Destroyed?

In order to explore the impact of the media on the nature and role
of tradition, I want to begin by re-examining the arguments of a
classic work – Daniel Lerner's *The Passing of Traditional Society.*[8]
This work is a detailed study of the process of modernization in
the Middle East. The work is well known in the field of development studies and, in particular, among those who are concerned
with communication and development; together with the work of
Wilbur Schramm,[9] it established the main framework within
which problems of communication and development were debated for several decades. Lerner is regarded by many as the
proponent of a rather old-fashioned and ethnocentric theory of
modernization, a theory that was based on Western prototypes
and was largely endogenous in character. These reservations are
not without substance; no doubt Lerner's theory of modernization
was to some extent a product of its time, and it hardly did justice
to the complexity and interconnectedness of the modern world.
Nevertheless, Lerner's work remains of interest for the light that it
sheds on the question of the relation between tradition and the
media. *The Passing of Traditional Society* is one of the few studies
that pursues this question in a detailed, empirically oriented way;
and some of Lerner's analyses are valuable and insightful, despite
the evident shortcomings of his approach. It is in this spirit that I
want to re-examine some aspects of his work.

Lerner assumes a broad distinction between traditional societies and modern societies, where the latter are modelled on contemporary Western societies, and he seeks to determine the
conditions which underlie the transition from the former to the
latter. What are the characteristics of traditional society, in
Lerner's view? Traditional societies are fragmented into communities which are isolated from one another and in which kinship

relations play a predominant role. People's horizons are limited by locale, and their interactions with others are largely restricted to known persons who share their immediate milieu. Everyday life in traditional societies is routinized according to traditional patterns; there is no need to defend or justify these traditional patterns simply because, for most individuals, there are no other ways on the agenda. The individual in traditional societies is not concerned with matters that do not bear directly on his or her daily life. There is an absence of curiosity and an absence of knowledge about events that take place in distant locales. There is relatively little self-experimentation, as individuals carry out their daily lives in accordance with routines that are largely unquestioned. The self in traditional society is a 'constrictive self': it is rooted in the familiar and the routine, and the trajectory of the self is organized with minimum awareness of alternatives to existing practices.

By contrast, the individual in modern societies is characterized by a degree of flexibility and mobility which is quite alien to the closed world of the constrictive self. The growth of travel and the physical movement of individuals – including large-scale migration – has certainly increased the flexibility of individuals and their capacity to imagine themselves in new situations, confronted with new possibilities. But this opening up of the self has also been stimulated by the diffusion of mediated experience through mass communication. In this respect, the media are a 'mobility multiplier': they make available to individuals a vast array of experiences that otherwise would have been unavailable to them, and they do so while obviating the need for physical travel. Moreover, precisely because mediated experience is vicarious experience, it cultivates the individual's faculty of imagination. The individual becomes increasingly capable of seeing himself or herself in the place of the other – in a new situation that may be radically different from his or her own. The rigidity of traditional ways of life begins to break down as individuals are confronted with alternatives that were previously unimaginable. Social life begins to seem more uncertain as individuals start to wonder what will happen next rather than assuming that the future will resemble the past as it has always done.

Lerner uses the term 'empathy' to describe the capacity – stimulated by exposure to the media – to imagine oneself in the place of the other, and he regards this capacity as a key feature of modern social life. Empathy enables individuals to distance themselves imaginatively from their immediate circumstances and inclines them to take an interest in matters that do not bear directly on their day-to-day lives. With the development of empathy, the self becomes more expansive, desirous, open-ended; rather than seeing oneself as located at a fixed point in an unchanging order of things, one sees one's life as a moving point along a trajectory of things imagined. Like the grocer of Balgat, the empathic self can imagine a world beyond the immediate locale, a world of risks and opportunities in which a new life can be forged through the continuous assimilation of actual and vicarious experience.

Exposure to the media also affects the ways in which individuals relate to power and authority. This is brought out well by Lerner's account of the impact of communication media in rural Lebanon. In the traditional communication network, human sources were more important than the media: villagers got their news and spread it largely through encounters with known others in face-to-face interaction. Village chiefs, landed patriarchs, priests and elders were the traditional moulders of opinion; so long as the village remained relatively isolated from the outside world, they commanded respect. But as isolation gave way to growing traffic with towns and cities, the respect traditionally accorded to village elders began to wane. A new group of intermediaries – young men who travelled to the towns and cities and had contact with the media – played an increasingly important role in transmitting information, shaping opinion and interpreting the news. Lacking mobility and literacy, the village elders gradually forfeited influence to younger men who were tied into new networks of communication and capable of relaying news and information to others.

While Lerner's study is in many ways very dated now (the original research was carried out in the early 1950s, prior to the development of television in the Middle East and to the upheavals which have characterized the region in recent decades), nevertheless the study highlights a number of points which retain their significance today. Perhaps most important in this respect is Lerner's emphasis on the fact that the media play a crucial role in the cultural transformations associated with the rise of modern societies. It may well be that Lerner interprets this role in a way that is too unambiguous, too overdetermined by a theory of modernization oriented towards a particular goal (what he calls 'the participant society'); but Lerner's emphasis on the centrality of the media is a salutary antidote to the legacy of classical social theory. A second aspect of Lerner's work which remains of interest is his characterization of the media as a 'mobility multiplier':

the media enable individuals to experience vicariously events which take place in distant places, thereby stimulating their capacity to imagine alternatives to the ways of life characteristic of their immediate locales. Again one may not be entirely persuaded by Lerner's interpretation of this phenomenon as a kind of 'empathy' which enables individuals to take the standpoint of the other, thus preparing the psychological ground for the emergence of a participant society. But the key idea that the media enable individuals to acquire experience across space and time, through forms of interaction that are not face-to-face in character, is surely correct and is only accentuated by the advent of television.

A third theme of Lerner's work which merits further consideration is his suggestion that, through exposure to the media, the self becomes more expansive and open-ended, less constrained by the precedents of tradition and more open to experimentation, to the search for new opportunities and new styles of life. There is, in my view, a good deal of substance to this suggestion – though it may be that the point is overstated somewhat, and that it neglects the mobilizing potential of traditions that have been transformed in certain respects. Finally, Lerner calls attention to some of the ways in which, with the development of new networks of communication, traditional forms of power and authority may be challenged, called into question or simply bypassed, as they were in the villages of Lebanon and Anatolia.

What emerges much less clearly from Lerner's study is a plausible answer to the question of why Islam should remain such a potent force in the Middle East, despite the modernizing tendencies which he was so concerned to document. Of course, Lerner did not suggest that the transition from a 'traditional' to a 'modern' society would be a smooth and unproblematic process; he allowed for the possibility that social change could become 'out of phase', as he put it, creating an unstable situation that could erupt in violence. But this qualification hardly provides a satisfactory way of accounting for the enduring significance of Islam in the countries of the Middle East (and, indeed, elsewhere in the world today).

Why this failure? How can we account for what seems, in retrospect, to be a fatal flaw in Lerner's analysis? Part of the explanation lies, no doubt, in the rather simplistic theory of modernization employed by Lerner, a theory which envisaged modernization as a largely one-way track from a traditional to a modern, 'participant' society. Part of the explanation also lies in

the fact that this theory of modernization was based on an endogenous model of social change and hence, like most endogenous
models, accorded relatively little significance to the relations between states and to the role of military conflict. Yet there can be
little doubt that in the Middle East military conflict has played an
enormously important role in the second half of the twentieth
century and has, in some respects, accentuated the significance of
Islam as a rallying cry, as a means of unifying and mobilizing
people in pursuit of political and military goals.

But there is another reason why Lerner failed to anticipate the
enduring significance of Islam, a reason which is more closely
linked to our current concerns. In Lerner's view, the persistence
of traditional ways and the adoption of modern lifestyles were
mutually exclusive options, and the shift from the former to the
latter was more or less inevitable: 'The symbols of race and ritual
fade into irrelevance when they impede living desires for bread
and enlightenment.'[10] But it seems clear that this way of presenting the issues is unsatisfactory. For many people, the option of
maintaining traditional ways or adopting modern lifestyles does
not present itself as an either/or choice. On the contrary, they are
able to organize their day-to-day lives in such a manner as to
integrate elements of tradition with new styles of living. Tradition
is not necessarily abandoned in the quest for 'bread and enlightenment' but is, on the contrary, reshaped, transformed, perhaps
even strengthened and reinvigorated through the encounter with
other ways of life.

The development of Islam in the 1970s and 1980s provides an
instructive example of this process. The Iranian Revolution of
1979 is a particularly vivid testimony to the resurgent power of
Islam: here the mobilization of traditional religious beliefs, facilitated by the diffusion of audiocassettes and printed materials
circulating through informal communication networks and outside the sphere of the state-controlled media, helped to discredit
the Western-oriented policies of the Shah and to undermine the
monarchical regime.[11] But the dramatic developments in Iran,
culminating in the abdication of the Shah and the establishment
of a Shiite Islamic Republic, were somewhat exceptional and were
not necessarily indicative of developments taking place in the
Sunni countries of the Middle East. In the latter, the conquest of
state power by revolutionary Islamic movements had been largely
unsuccessful; there was, however, a gradual process of what Gilles
Kepel calls 're-Islamization from below'.[12] The beliefs and prac-

tices of Islam were renewed and deepened within local communities and networks, often by means of organizations which also provided social services and forms of support for individuals and families which had yet to see the fruits of economic development. For these individuals, Islam was a way of rebuilding an identity and a sense of belonging in a world that had promised much but delivered relatively little. By the end of the 1980s, the movements of re-Islamization from below had established powerful networks which, in some cases, controlled large areas and served as intermediaries between state authorities and marginalized social groups. As their power bases strengthened, those at the head of these movements and networks began to intervene more actively in political life. The outcome of this development can be seen not only in the Islamic countries of the Middle East, but also in the countries of Western Europe, like Britain and France, where there are significant Muslim populations.

It is no doubt the case that the resurgence of Islam in recent decades has characteristics that make it unique; there are doctrinal aspects of Islam, together with some of the social and political conditions of its resurgence, which cannot be directly compared to developments elsewhere. It is nevertheless striking that the revival of religious beliefs and practices is by no means unique to the Islamic world. In Europe and the United States, in the countries of the former communist world, in Latin America and elsewhere, religious movements of varying creeds have gained strength and begun to assert their power in the political sphere. How should we understand this remarkable development, which seems to fly in the face of classical theories of modernization? Should this be interpreted merely as a kind of cultural retrenchment, a return to the certainties of scriptural truth as a way of coping with the radical indeterminacy of life in the modern age?

Perhaps. There may be some substance in the view that, in the modern age, religion survives as a refuge for individuals who are unable or unwilling to live in a world from which the certainties of tradition have been stripped away. But it is difficult to believe that there is nothing more to it than that. To view the renewal of religious belief as merely a defensive reaction to the process of modernization is to fail to see that there are certain aspects of tradition which are neither eliminated nor made redundant by this process – aspects which provide a foothold for the continued cultivation of religious and other forms of belief in the modern world.

Contrary to what some commentators may have thought, the development of modern societies does not eliminate the need to formulate a set of concepts, values and beliefs to make sense of the world and one's place within it. If the development of modern societies seemed to destroy this hermeneutic aspect of tradition, it was only because the rise of modern societies was accompanied by the emergence of a new set of concepts, values and beliefs – involving a combination of progress, scientific knowledge and secular humanism – which appeared to some as self-evident.[13] But what seemed self-evident to some was to others nothing more than a choice; it was a privileging of certain concepts, values and beliefs at the expense of others, a privileging which had some indisputable gains but also, in the eyes of critics, some losses. Among the losses is what one could describe as a 'moral deficit' – that is, an incapacity to deal with certain questions of a fundamental kind concerning life and death, right and wrong, etc. This moral deficit has helped to keep alive, for many people, a belief in the continuing relevance of religious tradition. Religious beliefs retain their relevance precisely because, for many people, the values of secular humanism have proven to be inadequate as a means of dealing with the basic ethical problems of human life. Secular humanism is morally insufficient – or even, in the eyes of some, morally bankrupt.

There is another reason why religious beliefs and practices persist in the modern world. Like other forms of tradition, religious beliefs and practices are often interwoven with the activities of everyday life in a way which provides individuals with a sense of belonging to a community, a sense of identity as an integral part of a broader collectivity of individuals who share similar beliefs and who have, to some extent, a common history and a collective fate. This identity-forming aspect of tradition has not been eliminated by the development of modern societies; it has, at most, been reshaped (in part by the media) and relativized to the growing autonomy of the individual as a reflexive agent capable of refashioning his or her self-identity. These are issues to which we shall return. Here I wish only to emphasize the enduring significance of tradition (including religious tradition) as a means of nourishing a sense of identity and providing individuals with a sense of belonging, a sense of being part of a community.

I have been concerned to argue that, if we wish to understand the cultural impact of communication media in the modern world, we should put aside the view that exposure to the media will lead invariably to the abandonment of 'traditional' ways of life and to the adoption of 'modern' lifestyles. Exposure to the media does not entail, in and by itself, any particular stance *vis-à-vis* tradition. Communication media can be used not only to challenge and undermine traditional values and beliefs, but also to extend and consolidate traditions. It is not difficult to provide examples of the way in which media have been used effectively in the service of tradition, from the diffusion of printed bibles and prayer books in early modern Europe to the tele-evangelism of today.

But if the development of the media has not led to the demise of tradition, it has nevertheless transformed tradition in certain fundamental respects. With the development of communication media, the formation and transmission of tradition have become increasingly dependent on forms of communication which are not face-to-face in character, and this in turn has several consequences. Let me emphasize three.

(1) Since many forms of mediated communication involve some degree of fixation of symbolic content in a material substratum, they endow this content with a temporal permanence which is generally lacking in the communicative exchanges of face-to-face interaction. In the absence of material fixation, the maintenance of tradition over time requires the continual re-enactment of its symbolic content in the activities of day-to-day life. Practical repetition is the only way of securing temporal continuity. But with the fixation of symbolic content in a material substratum of some kind, the maintenance of tradition over time can be separated to some extent from the need for practical and continual re-enactment. The cultivation of traditional values and beliefs becomes increasingly dependent on forms of interaction which involve media products; the fixing of symbolic content in media products (books, films, etc.) provides a form of temporal continuity which diminishes the need for re-enactment. Hence the decline of some of the ritualized aspects of tradition (church attendance, etc.) should not necessarily be interpreted as the decline of tradition as such; it may simply express the fact that the maintenance of tradition over time has become less dependent on ritualized re-enactment. Tradition has, in effect, become increasingly *deritualized*.

The deritualization of tradition does not imply that *all* elements of ritual will be eliminated from tradition, nor does it imply that

tradition will become entirely divorced from the face-to-face interaction which takes place in shared locales. While the symbolic
content of tradition may become increasingly fixed in media products, many traditions remain closely tied to the practical encounters of daily life within the family, the school and other
institutional settings. Moreover, media products are commonly
appropriated within contexts of face-to-face interaction, and
hence the renewal of tradition may involve a constantly changing
mixture of face-to-face and mediated quasi-interaction. This is
evident to parents and teachers who come to rely more and more
on books, films and television programmes to convey to children
the main themes of a religious or other tradition, and who see their
own role more in terms of elaboration and explication than in
terms of the cultivation of tradition from scratch.

(2) To the extent that the transmission of tradition becomes
dependent on mediated forms of communication, it also becomes
detached from the individuals with whom one interacts in day-to-
day life – that is, it becomes *depersonalized*. Once again, this
process of depersonalization is never total, since the transmission
of tradition remains interwoven with face-to-face interaction. But
as mediated forms of communication acquire an increasing role,
so the authority of tradition is gradually detached from the individuals with whom one interacts in the practical contexts of daily
life. Tradition acquires a certain autonomy and an authority of its
own, as a set of values, beliefs and assumptions which exist and
persist independently of the individuals who may be involved in
transmitting them from one generation to the next.

The depersonalization of tradition is not, however, a uniform
and unambiguous process, and we can see that, with the development of electronic media and especially television, the conditions
are created for a renewal of the link between the authority of
tradition and the individuals who transmit it. But the nature of
this link is new and unprecedented: it is a link which is established
and sustained largely within the framework of mediated quasi-
interaction. For most people, evangelists such as Billy Graham
and Jerry Falwell are known only as TV personalities. They are
individuals one can witness and observe, watch and listen to
(credulously or not, as the case may be), but they are not individuals with whom one is ever likely to interact in day-to-day life.
Hence, while such individuals may succeed in 'repersonalizing'
tradition, it is a quite distinctive kind of personalization: for most
people, it lacks the reciprocity of face-to-face interaction and it is

dissociated from the individuals encountered in the shared locales of everyday life. It is a form of what I shall describe in the following chapter as 'non-reciprocal intimacy at a distance'.

(3) As the transmission of tradition becomes increasingly linked to communication media, traditions are also increasingly detached from their moorings in particular locales. Prior to the development of the media, traditions had a certain rootedness: that is, they were rooted in the spatial locales within which individuals lived out their daily lives. Traditions were integral parts of communities of individuals who interacted – actually or potentially – with one another. But with the development of the media, traditions were gradually uprooted; the bond that tied traditions to specific locales of face-to-face interaction was gradually weakened. In other words, traditions were gradually and partially *delocalized* as they became increasingly dependent on mediated forms of communication for their maintenance and transmission from one generation to the next.

The uprooting or 'delocalization' of tradition had far-reaching consequences that I want to pursue in the remaining sections of this chapter. It enabled traditions to be detached from particular locales and freed from the constraints imposed by oral transmission in circumstances of face-to-face interaction. The reach of tradition – both in space and in time – was no longer restricted by the conditions of localized transmission. But the uprooting of traditions from particular locales did not lead them to wither away, nor did it destroy altogether the connection between traditions and spatial units. On the contrary, the uprooting of traditions was the condition for the re-embedding of traditions in new contexts and for the re-mooring of traditions to new kinds of territorial unit that exceeded the limits of shared locales. Traditions were delocalized but they were not deterritorialized: they were refashioned in ways that enabled them to be re-embedded in a multiplicity of locales and reconnected to territorial units that exceed the limits of face-to-face interaction.

Tradition and the Media (2): Tradition Dislodged

I have argued that, as traditions become increasingly interwoven with communication media, they are gradually uprooted from

particular locales and rendered increasingly dependent on a form
of interaction which is not face-to-face in character. Traditions
that are uprooted in this way are more readily adapted, transformed or codified by individuals who have access to the means of
production and distribution of mediated symbolic forms. But
traditions that have become mediated to some extent are not, for
all that, free-floating. If these traditions are to be sustained over
time, they have to be re-embedded in the practical contexts of
everyday life. Traditions that are not re-embedded in this fashion
will gradually decline in significance.

What is involved in the uprooting and re-mooring of tradition?
How should we analyse the process by which traditions are dislodged from particular locales and re-embedded in the practical
contexts of daily life, though now in ways that reconnect traditions
to new kinds of spatial unit?

We can gain some insight into this process by considering what
is sometimes referred to as 'the invention of tradition'. As Eric
Hobsbawm and others have shown,[14] some of the traditions that
are commonly regarded today as stretching back for centuries are,
in fact, relatively recent inventions, often dating from the late
eighteenth century. So, for example, the Highland tradition of
Scotland, expressed by the bagpipe and the tartan kilt woven in
colours and patterns which signify different clans, is often presented as having existed from time immemorial; but it seems that
it was largely an invention of the late eighteenth and early nineteenth centuries.[15] The kilt, far from being a traditional Highland
costume, was invented by an English Quaker from Lancashire,
who designed it for use in a smelting factory that he had established near Inverness in 1727. Following the great rebellion of
1745, the Highlanders were disarmed by the British government
and the kilt, among other things, was outlawed. By 1780 it had
largely disappeared. The renewal of the kilt, and the establishment
of the connection between patterns and clans, were largely the
work of a few zealous individuals. Societies were established in
London and Edinburgh dedicated to the preservation and cultivation of Highland traditions. Books were published – including the
Vestiarium Scoticum and *The Custome of the Clans* by the brothers
Allen – which claimed to establish a connection, stretching back
to the Middle Ages, between tartan patterns and Highland clans.
Gradually a tradition was fashioned in which the tartan kilt – its
differentiated colours and patterns allegedly referring to ancient
clans – became a symbol of the national integrity of Scotland, to

be paraded on those occasions when Scots gather together to celebrate their national identity.

Much of the literature on the invention of tradition has been concerned to emphasize the degree of fabrication involved in the retrospective cultivation of traditional practices and beliefs. Not only are many traditions less ancient than they seem, but they are also replete with myths and half-truths whose origins are so obscure that they are no longer recognized as such. But this literature also highlights another theme which is of particular interest to the issues we are considering here: it attests to the role played by the media in the reinvention of tradition and in the re-mooring of tradition to territorial units of various kinds. The books of the brothers Allen, which forged the links (almost certainly spurious) between tartan patterns and Highland clans and which helped to establish the kilt as a national symbol of Scotland, exemplify the capacity of media products to take up the symbolic content of traditions and adapt it in various ways, enabling it to be re-moored in particular regions and locales. Let us consider another example which effectively illustrates this point.

Many of the traditions associated with the British monarchy are a good deal less ancient than they seem. Of course, royal rituals were a common feature of Tudor and Stuart courts, as they were of courtly life in other parts of Europe. But, as David Cannadine has shown, many of the ceremonial practices associated with the British monarchy today are in fact a creation of the late nineteenth and early twentieth centuries.[16] Prior to the late nineteenth century, royal ceremonies were performed largely for the benefit of other members of the court and aristocracy; they were, by and large, group rites in which London-based elites reaffirmed their corporate solidarity. During the first three-quarters of the nineteenth century, the major ceremonies of the British monarchy were extensively reported in the metropolitan and the provincial press. But the attitude of the press was largely hostile, and the monarchy was a popular object of criticism and caricature. The ceremonies themselves were generally conducted in a dreadfully incompetent fashion. 'In 1817, at the funeral of Princess Charlotte, the daughter of the Prince Regent, the undertakers were drunk. When the duke of York died, ten years later, the Chapel at Windsor was so damp that most of the mourners caught cold, Canning contracted rheumatic fever and the bishop of London died.'[17] The coronations of George IV, William IV and Victoria were poorly managed and unrehearsed, and were subjected to scathing criticisms by royal commentators at the time.

From the late 1870s on, however, the royal rituals and public image of the British monarchy began to change. A great deal more effort was invested in the planning and organization of the major occasions of state, beginning with Queen Victoria's Golden Jubilee in 1887. Ceremonies that had previously been rather ungainly affairs were gradually transformed into pageants of unprecedented splendour, meticulously planned and carefully rehearsed. Moreover, with the emergence in the late nineteenth century of the mass-circulation popular press, there was a significant shift in the public portrayal of the monarchy. The mocking caricatures and critical editorials of earlier decades were replaced by an increasingly respectful representation of the monarchy in the popular press, and the great royal ceremonies were described in a sentimental and reverential way. At a time when the real political power of the monarchy was declining significantly, the position of the monarch as head of state and symbol of national unity was enhanced through the renewal and elaboration of royal rituals and their celebration in the popular press. Traditions that previously had been restricted primarily to London-based elites were now reshaped and made available, via the printed media, to a much larger constituency. These traditions were not only transformed, indeed invented, in certain fundamental respects: they were also disconnected from their historical embeddedness in courtly life and increasingly made available to the population as a whole. The traditions of royal ritual were re-embedded in the daily lives of ordinary individuals through the appropriation of media products; and they were reconnected to the territorial boundaries of the nation-state, the unity and integrity of which these rituals were designed increasingly to represent.

In the period after the First World War, the role of the monarchy as the politically impartial embodiment of national unity was extended further by the advent of broadcasting. John Reith, the first Director General of the BBC, was a devotee of the monarchy and quickly recognized the potential of radio as a means of conveying a sense of participation in the great ceremonial occasions of state.[18] The major royal ceremonies were broadcast live on radio, beginning with the Duke of York's wedding in 1923. Great care was taken to position microphones in a way which would enable listeners to hear the sounds of bells, horses, carriages and cheering crowds. In an age of rapid social change, the anachronism of the ceremonies merely enhanced their grandeur. They took on a fairytale quality. With the development of television in the 1950s, the anachronistic grandeur of royal ceremonies was made available in all its splendour. Now it was possible for a substantial proportion of the population not only to hear but also to see the ceremonies as they occurred. The coronation of Queen Elizabeth in 1953 was the first occasion on which the crowning of a British sovereign could be seen by the public at large.[19]

By considering the ways in which royal ceremonies have changed over time, we can get a sense not only of the invented character of many traditions but also of the extent to which their significance and scope have changed. While royal rituals were once performed largely for the benefit of members of the elite who were physically present on the occasions of their performance, increasingly they have been detached from the face-to-face contexts of courtly life and made available, via the media, to an extended range of recipients. And in so doing, the meaning and purpose of these rituals have changed. Today they are no longer concerned with the reaffirmation of the corporate solidarity of metropolitan elites; rather, the great ceremonial occasions of the monarchy have become mediated celebrations of national identity which all citizens, wherever they may be, are able to witness and in which they are invited vicariously to take part.

It is not surprising that traditions which have become so dependent on the media should also be vulnerable to them. In an age of mediated visibility, the monarchy is in a precarious position. On the one hand, the appeal of the monarchy, and of the royal rituals associated with it, stems from its capacity to stand above the mundane world of party politics and to present itself as a body whose integrity and probity is beyond reproach, a body clothed in ancient costumes and governed by time-honoured customs which, when re-enacted before us all in the carefully managed ceremonies appearing on our television screens, endow the monarchy and its temporal representatives with an other-worldly glow. On the other hand, in an increasingly mediated world, it is difficult for the temporal representatives of the monarchy to avoid appearing as ordinary individuals, as men and women who are little different from other individuals apart from the accident of their birth, and who are prone to the same temptations, driven by the same desires and subject to the same weaknesses as ordinary mortals. It is this tension between the other-worldly and the mundane, between the aloofness of the monarchy and the all-too-ordinary lives of its representatives, which lies at the heart of the scandals that have shaken the monarchy in recent years and renewed the speculation about its future.

In this section I have explored some of the ways in which traditions have been taken up, reshaped and, to some extent, reinvented in the course of their enactment and elaboration over time. Now it might be argued that the examples we have considered, precisely because of their 'invented' character, are instances of 'artificial traditions' that are imposed on people from above, in contrast to the 'authentic traditions' of the past which, it might be claimed, arose spontaneously from below. Unlike the latter, it might be argued, these 'pseudo-traditions' are not rooted in the day-to-day lives of individuals; they are not created and sustained by them through their practical activities but, instead, are imposed on them by political elites, entrepreneurs, promoters of the tourist industry and an odd assortment of self-proclaimed guardians of the past.[20]

While this line of argument is not without interest, it does not, in my view, press to the heart of the matter. By insisting on the distinction between authentic and artificial traditions (and relegating the former largely to the past), this line of argument fails to grasp the significance of the fact that traditions have become increasingly interwoven with mediated symbolic forms. When the symbolic content of tradition is articulated in media products, it is necessarily and to some extent distanced from the practical contexts of daily life; the establishment and maintenance of traditions over time become increasingly dependent on forms of interaction which are not face-to-face in character. But traditions which rely heavily on mediated symbolic forms are not *ipso facto* less authentic than those which are transmitted exclusively through face-to-face interaction. In a world increasingly permeated by communication media, traditions have become increasingly dependent on mediated symbolic forms; they have become dislodged from particular locales and re-embedded in social life in new ways. But the uprooting and re-mooring of traditions does not necessarily render them inauthentic, nor does it necessarily spell their demise.

Migrant Populations, Nomadic Traditions: Some Sources of Cultural Conflict

We have considered some of the ways in which traditions have been uprooted, reworked and re-moored to new kinds of territorial unit. But the uprooting and re-mooring of traditions are also interwoven in complex ways with other trends and developmental characteristics of modern societies. One characteristic which is particularly important in this regard is the migration, dislocation and resettling of populations. As people move (or are forcibly moved) from one region or part of the world to another, they often carry with them the sets of values and beliefs that form part of traditions. These mobile, nomadic traditions may be sustained partly through ritualized re-enactment and the retelling of stories in contexts of face-to-face interaction. With the passage of time, nomadic traditions may gradually alter in character, as they become increasingly remote from their contexts of origin and increasingly interwoven with symbolic contents derived from the new circumstances in which they are re-enacted.

While nomadic traditions may be sustained partly through ritualized re-enactment, they may also become closely interwoven with mediated symbolic materials, precisely because communication media tend to uproot traditions from particular locales and endow their symbolic content with some degree of temporal permanence and spatial mobility. Communication media provide a way of sustaining cultural continuity despite spatial dislocation, a way of renewing tradition in new and diverse contexts through the appropriation of mediated symbolic forms. Hence communication media can play an important role in the maintenance and renewal of tradition among migrant or dislocated groups. This role is likely to be particularly significant when the groups are settled in countries where different languages are spoken, and where traditions and customs diverge from their own. This is well illustrated, for example, by the popularity of Hindi films among families of South Asian origin who are settled in Britain and other parts of the world.[21]

The dispersion of traditions through the media and through the movements of migrant populations has created a cultural landscape in the modern world of enormous complexity and diversity. It has also given rise to forms of tension and conflict which are, in some respects, new. We can discern these tensions in different contexts and at different levels. Within the context of the family, for instance, parents and children of migrant populations may have divergent views of the merits of traditions which are linked to a distant place of origin. Parents may place greater value on these traditions and on the maintenance of some degree of cultural continuity with a distant past; children, who may be more assimilated to the communities in which they have settled, may be more likely to view these traditions with scepticism or even contempt. Hence the appropriation of media products – such as the family viewing of a film on video – may be a somewhat discordant occasion, as parents may see the activity of appropriation as a valuable opportunity to renew traditional ties while children may regard it as little more than a disagreeable obligation.

This kind of intergenerational tension and conflict can also be experienced subjectively, by a particular individual, as sets of values and beliefs which pull in different directions. A person may feel some attraction to and some sympathy with the traditions linked to a distant place of origin, and yet may also feel that these traditions have little bearing on the actual circumstances of his or her life. Despite the ritualized re-enactment of traditions and the continual appropriation of media products, it may be difficult to re-embed these traditions in the practical contexts of daily life. The individual may feel torn between a set of values and beliefs which provides a link to a past which is distant both in space and in time, on the one hand, and a cluster of values and beliefs which seem to point towards the future, on the other.

From this point of view, we can gain some appreciation of the complexity and ambiguity of what might be described as 'the quest for roots'. As a kind of cultural project that may be expressed in particular media products and linked to their appropriation, the quest for roots bears a strong but ambivalent relation to migrant populations. The appeal of the quest is that it offers a way of recovering and, indeed, inventing traditions which reconnect individuals to (real or imaginary) places of origin. The greater the distance of these origins in time and space, the more appealing the quest for roots may be, for it may help one to refashion an aspect of self which has been suppressed, ignored or stigmatized in some way. And yet individuals may also feel deep ambivalence towards the project of recovering the traditions associated with an alleged place of origin. For they may feel that, whatever the facts of migration and dislocation may be, these traditions have little to do with the kind of life they want to build for themselves. 'Parents use . . . films to represent their culture to their children,' remarked one young Londoner of South Asian descent, 'but that will not work because those are not my roots, that place [India] has nothing to do with me anymore.'[22]

There are other ways in which the maintenance and renewal of tradition among migrant or dislocated groups may be a source of tension and conflict. The traditions of different groups are increasingly brought into contact with one another, partly as a result of cultural migrations and partly due to the globalization of media products. But the increasing contact between traditions is not necessarily accompanied by an increase of mutual comprehension on the part of the individuals who belong to different groups. On the contrary, the encounter of traditions may give rise to intense forms of conflict which are based on varying degrees of incomprehension and intolerance – conflicts which are all the more intense when they are linked to broader relations of power and inequality. The Salman Rushdie affair is a particularly vivid example of this kind of cultural conflict. As a media product circulating in a global domain, *The Satanic Verses* precipitated a violent clash of values that are rooted in different traditions; and while the spatial barriers between these traditions have been eroded by cultural migrations and communication flows, the gulf of understanding remains.

Contact between traditions can also give rise to intensified forms of boundary-defining activity. Attempts may be made to protect the integrity of traditions, and to reassert forms of collective identity which are linked to traditions, by excluding others in one's midst. These boundary-defining activities can be both symbolic and territorial – symbolic in the sense that the primary concern may be to protect traditions from the incursion of extraneous symbolic content, territorial in the sense that the protection of traditions may be combined with the attempt to re-moor these traditions to particular regions or locales in a way that forcibly excludes others. A region becomes a 'homeland' which is seen by some as bearing a privileged relation to a group of people whose collective identity is shaped in part by an enduring set of traditions. And we know only too well how this kind of boundary-defining activity – especially when combined with the accumulated means of political and coercive power – can manifest itself in the most brutal forms of violence.

I have dwelt on some of the ways in which the intermingling of populations and traditions can be a source of tension and conflict. But it should be stressed that this process of intermingling is also a source of enormous cultural creativity and dynamism. In the sphere of literature or popular music, of art or cinema, the weaving together of themes drawn from different traditions – this continuous hybridization of culture – is the basis of some of the most original and exciting work. It creates a kind of cultural restlessness which is constantly shifting directions, assuming new forms and departing from established conventions in unexpected ways.[23] And it attests to the fact that, in a world increasingly traversed by cultural migrations and communication flows, traditions are less sheltered than ever before from the potentially invigorating consequences of encounters with the other.

Self and Experience in a Mediated World

In this chapter I want to focus on the nature of the self, experience and everyday life in a mediated world. My starting point is the view that, with the development of modern societies, the process of self-formation becomes more reflexive and open-ended, in the sense that individuals fall back increasingly on their own resources to construct a coherent identity for themselves. At the same time, the process of self-formation is increasingly nourished by mediated symbolic materials, greatly expanding the range of options available to individuals and loosening – without destroying – the connection between self-formation and shared locale. This connection is loosened in so far as individuals increasingly have access to forms of information and communication which stem from distant sources and which are made available to individuals via the expanding networks of mediated communication; in other words, individuals increasingly have access to what we may describe in a general way as 'non-local knowledge'. But the connection between self-formation and shared locale is not destroyed, since non-local knowledge is always appropriated by individuals in specific locales and the practical significance of this knowledge – what it means to individuals and how it is used by them – is always dependent on the interests of recipients and on the resources they bring to bear on the process of appropriation.

The development of the media not only enriches and transforms the process of self-formation, it also produces a new kind of intimacy which did not exist before and which differs in certain fundamental respects from the forms of intimacy characteristic of face-to-face interaction. In contexts of face-to-face interaction, individuals are able to achieve forms of intimacy which are essentially reciprocal in character; that is, their intimate relations with others involve a two-way flow of actions and utterances, of gains and losses, of rights and obligations. Of course, reciprocity is not the same as equality. Intimate relations may be reciprocal and yet may be – and often are – structured in asymmetrical ways. With the development of mediated forms of communication, however, new kinds of intimate relationship become possible. In the case of mediated interaction, such as that sustained through the exchange of letters or through telephone conversation, individuals can establish a form of intimacy which is reciprocal in character but which lacks some of the features typically associated with the sharing of a common locale. By contrast, in the case of mediated quasi-interaction, individuals can create and establish a form of intimacy which is essentially non-reciprocal. It is this new form of mediated, non-reciprocal intimacy, stretched across time and space, which underlies, for example, the relationship between fan and star. It can be exhilarating, precisely because it is freed from the reciprocal obligations characteristic of face-to-face interaction. But it can also become a form of dependence in which individuals come to rely on others whose very absence and inaccessibility turn them into an object of veneration.

Just as the development of the media produces a new form of non-reciprocal intimacy, so too it creates a new and distinctive intermingling of experience which runs counter to other trends characteristic of modern societies. In the spatial-temporal contexts of day-to-day life, modern societies involve a relatively high degree of institutional and experiential segregation: certain social phenomena (illness, madness, death, etc.) are separated off from everyday social contexts and handled by specialized institutions and professional personnel. For many individuals today, the experience of someone dying, or suffering from chronic physical or mental illness, is a rare occurrence rather than an ordinary, routine feature of day-to-day life. But alongside this segregation or 'sequestration' of experience, a parallel development has occurred: the development of the media has increased the capacity of individuals to experience, through mediated quasi-interaction, phenomena which they are unlikely ever to encounter in the locales of their daily lives. Few people in the West today are likely to encounter someone suffering from extreme dehydration or starvation, someone shot by sniper fire or maimed by mortar shells; but most will have witnessed suffering of this kind on their television screens. Today we live in a world in which the capacity to experience is disconnected from the activity of encountering. The sequestration of experience in the spatial-temporal locales of our daily lives goes hand-in-hand with the profusion of mediated experience and with the routine intermingling of experiences which most individuals would rarely encounter face-to-face.

How do individuals cope with the influx of mediated experience in their day-to-day lives? They deal with it selectively, of course, focusing on those aspects which are of particular interest to them and ignoring or filtering out others. But they also struggle to make sense of phenomena that defy easy comprehension, and struggle to relate them to the contexts and conditions of their own lives. It is not so much that individuals are lost in an information blizzard, unable to find their way and numbed into inactivity by the profusion of mediated images and points of view. Rather, the problem that confronts most people today is a problem of symbolic dislocation: in a world where the capacity to experience is no longer linked to the activity of encountering, how can we relate mediated experiences to the practical contexts of our day-to-day lives? How can we relate to events which take place in locales that are remote from the contexts in which we live out our daily lives, and how can we assimilate the experience of distant events into a coherent life trajectory that we must construct for ourselves?

I shall return to these questions later in the chapter. I want to begin by examining in more detail the ways in which self-formation has become increasingly interwoven with mediated symbolic forms. I shall then explore the new kind of intimacy created by the media, using the relation between fan and star as a limit-case of non-reciprocal intimacy. In the third section I shall examine the nature of mediated experience and its relation to lived experience, before returning to the question of how individuals cope with the influx of mediated experience in their day-to-day lives.

The Self as a Symbolic Project

One of the less fortunate legacies of much critical social theory in recent decades – especially those forms of social theory which have had most impact in critical media studies – has been an impoverished conception of the self. For authors working within a broadly 'structuralist' tradition, or whose approach has been influenced in some significant way by the assumptions of structuralist linguistics, the self is viewed largely as a product or construct of the symbolic systems which precede it. A variety of terms have been introduced, from Althusser's 'interpellation' to Foucault's 'techniques' or 'technologies' of the self, to try to specify the ways in which individuals are turned into subjects who think and act in accordance with the possibilities that are laid out in advance. Of course, the dominant symbolic systems (what some used to call 'ideologies', but what many now prefer to call 'discourses') will not define an individual's every move. Like a game of chess, the dominant system will define which moves are open to individuals and which are not – with the non-trivial difference that, unlike chess, social life is a game that one cannot choose not to play.

In this chapter I shall develop an account of the self which differs fundamentally from the kind of approach outlined above. The account I shall develop here is indebted primarily to the tradition of hermeneutics,[1] but it also bears an affinity to the work of symbolic interactionists and others. According to this account, the self is viewed neither as the product of an external symbolic system, nor as a fixed entity which the individual can immediately and directly grasp; rather, the self is a symbolic project that the individual actively constructs. It is a project that the individual constructs out of the symbolic materials which are available to him or her, materials which the individual weaves into a coherent account of who he or she is, a narrative of self-identity. This is a narrative which for most people will change over time as they draw on new symbolic materials, encounter new experiences and gradually redefine their identity in the course of a life trajectory. To recount to ourselves or others who we are is to retell the narratives – which are continuously modified in the process of retelling – of how we got to where we are and of where we are going from here. We are all the unofficial biographers of ourselves, for it is only by constructing a story, however loosely strung together, that we are able to form a sense of who we are and of what our future may be.

To emphasize the active, creative character of the self is not to suggest that the self is socially unconditioned. On the contrary, the symbolic materials which form the elements of the identities we construct are themselves distributed unevenly.[2] These symbolic resources are not available to everyone in a similar way, and access to them may require skills that some individuals possess and others do not. Moreover, the ways in which individuals draw on symbolic resources to construct their sense of self will depend to some extent on the material conditions of their lives, as individuals typically adjust their expectations and evaluations to their continuously revisable assessments of what, given the circumstances of their lives, they could realistically hope to achieve.

If we adopt this general approach to the nature of the self, then we can see that the development of communication media has had a profound impact on the process of self-formation. Prior to the development of the media, the symbolic materials employed by most individuals for the purposes of self-formation were acquired in contexts of face-to-face interaction. For most individuals, the formation of the self was bounded by the locales in which they lived and interacted with others. Their knowledge was 'local knowledge',[3] handed down from generation to generation through oral exchange and adapted to the practical necessities of life. The horizons of understanding of most individuals were limited by the patterns of face-to-face interaction through which information flowed. In some cases these patterns extended well beyond the immediate locales of day-to-day life, thanks to the activities of travellers, itinerant pedlars and so on. But even in such cases, it seems likely that the interpretation of information stemming from distant sources, and relayed via extended networks of face-to-face interaction, was strongly shaped by authoritative individuals within the local community.

These various conditions are altered fundamentally by the development of communication media. The process of self-formation becomes increasingly dependent on access to mediated forms of communication – both printed and, subsequently, electronically mediated forms. Local knowledge is supplemented by, and increasingly displaced by, new forms of non-local knowledge which are fixed in a material substratum, reproduced technically and transmitted via the media. Expertise is gradually detached from the relations of power established through face-to-face interaction, as individuals are able to gain access to new forms of knowledge which are no longer transmitted face-to-face. Individuals' horizons of understanding are broadened; they are no longer limited by patterns of face-to-face interaction but are shaped increasingly by the expanding networks of mediated communication. The media become, in Lerner's terms, a 'mobility multiplier', a form of vicarious travel which enables individuals to distance themselves from the immediate locales of their day-to-day lives.

By opening up the self to new forms of non-local knowledge and other kinds of mediated symbolic material, the development of the media both enriches and accentuates the reflexive organization of the self. It enriches this organization in the sense that, as individuals gain access to mediated forms of communication, they are able to draw on an expanding range of symbolic resources for the purposes of constructing the self. Like symbolic materials exchanged through face-to-face interaction, mediated materials can be incorporated into the process of self-formation; increasingly the self becomes organized as a reflexive project through which the individual incorporates mediated materials (among others) into a coherent and continuously revised biographical narrative.[4] The development of the media also deepens and accentuates the reflexive organization of the self in the sense that, with the expansion of symbolic resources available for the process of self-formation, individuals are continuously confronted with new possibilities, their horizons are continuously shifting, their symbolic points of reference are continuously changing. It becomes more and more difficult to fall back on the relatively stable frameworks of understanding which are embodied in oral traditions and tied to particular locales. The reflexive organization of the self becomes increasingly important as a feature of social life – not because it did not exist previously (no doubt it did in some way and to some extent), but because the tremendous expansion of mediated symbolic materials has opened up new possibilities for self-formation and placed new demands on the self in a way and on a scale that did not exist before.

The mediated accentuation of the reflexive organization of the self can have unsettling consequences, both for individuals and for the communities of which they are part. The profusion of mediated materials can provide individuals with the means of exploring alternative forms of life in a symbolic or imaginary mode; it can provide individuals with a glimpse of alternatives, thereby enabling them to reflect critically on themselves and on the actual circumstances of their lives. Through a process of symbolic distancing, individuals can use mediated materials to see their own lives in a new light – like the Chinese viewers in Lull's study, for whom the attraction of watching international news on television lay not so much in the explicit content of the news but rather in the opportunity to see street scenes from foreign cities, domestic scenes from foreign households and, in general, to get a sense of how people live in other parts of the world, a sense which would give them a point of comparison to reflect critically on their own conditions of life.[5]

So far I have been concerned to highlight some of the ways in which the development of the media has enriched and accentuated the reflexive organization of the self, but I have not yet dwelt on the more negative aspects of this relation. I now want to consider several respects in which the growing role of media products can have negative consequences for self-formation. I shall describe these as (1) the mediated intrusion of ideological messages; (2) the double-bind of mediated dependency; (3) the disorienting effect of symbolic overload; and (4) the absorption of self in mediated quasi-interaction. Let me briefly consider each in turn.

(1) The notion of ideology has been much debated and much criticized in recent years, so much so that some analysts would prefer to leave the notion aside altogether. That is not my view. I have tried to show elsewhere that the notion of ideology still has a useful and important role to play in the analysis of symbolic forms, provided that this notion is stripped of some of the assumptions that have overburdened it in the past.[6] I have proposed a dynamic, pragmatic conception of ideology which focuses our attention on the ways in which symbolic forms serve, in particular circumstances, to establish and sustain relations of domination. According to this conception, specific symbolic forms are not ideological *as such*: they are ideological only in so far as they serve, in particular circumstances, to establish and sustain systematically asymmetrical relations of power.

If we conceptualize ideology in this way, we can see that the development of the media greatly increases the capacity to transmit potentially ideological messages across extended stretches of space and time, and to re-embed these messages in a multiplicity of particular locales; in other words, it creates the conditions for the mediated intrusion of ideological messages into the practical contexts of everyday life. However, it is crucial to emphasize the contextual character of ideology: whether mediated messages are ideological will depend on the ways in which they are taken up by the individuals who receive them and incorporated reflexively into their lives. Texts and media programmes which are replete with stereotypical images, reassuring messages, etc., may in fact be taken up by recipients and used in quite unexpected ways. To understand the ideological character of media messages, one must consider the ways in which these messages are incorporated into the lives of recipients, how they become part of their projects of self-formation and how they are used by them in the practical contexts of their day-to-day lives.

This is not the place to discuss the methodological issues raised by this conception of ideology and its usefulness for the analysis of mediated symbolic forms – I have examined these issues in some detail elsewhere.[7] Here I want to concentrate on the broader and more substantive aspects of this account. While the development of the media has enriched and accentuated the reflexive organization of the self, and while the reflexive appropriation of media messages may have unsettling consequences both for the individual and for established relations of power, it would be misleading and inaccurate to suggest that these consequences are *always* unsettling. Clearly they are not; it seems clear that in some contexts the appropriation of media messages serves to stabilize and reinforce relations of power rather than to disrupt or undermine them. Moreover, when mediated symbolic forms are incorporated reflexively into projects of self-formation – as they are, for example, with conceptions of masculinity and femininity, conceptions of ethnic identity and so on – then media messages can assume a quite powerful ideological role. They become deeply ingrained in the self and are expressed not so much in explicit beliefs and opinions, but rather in the ways that individuals carry themselves in the world, relate to themselves and others and, in general, come to understand the contours and the limits of their selves.

(2) Let us now consider a second respect in which the development of the media can have negative consequences for the process of self-formation. While the availability of media products serves to enrich and accentuate the reflexive organization of the self, at the same time it renders this reflexive organization increasingly dependent on systems over which the individual has relatively little control. This is what I refer to as the double-bind of mediated dependency: the more the process of self-formation is enriched by mediated symbolic forms, the more the self becomes dependent on media systems which lie beyond its control. In this respect, reflexivity and dependency are not necessarily opposed to one another. A deepening of the reflexive organization of the self

can go hand in hand with a growing dependence on the systems which provide the symbolic materials for self-formation.

The double-bind of mediated dependency is part of a more general trend characteristic of modern societies. I have described how, with the development of modern societies, individuals are obliged increasingly to fall back on themselves and to construct, with the symbolic and material resources at their disposal, a coherent life-project. The self becomes increasingly organized as a reflexive project through which the individual constructs, in the form of an autobiographical narrative, a sense of self-identity. At the same time, however, individuals are increasingly dependent on a range of social institutions and systems which provide them with the means – both material and symbolic – for the construction of their life-projects.[8] Entry into the educational system, the labour market, the welfare system and so on are possible moves in a life-project to which an individual may aspire, but the opportunities to make these moves are differentially distributed and dependent on the decisions of others. Access to these and other systems is governed by agencies and processes which most individuals may be unable significantly to influence, and yet these agencies and processes may have a very significant impact on individuals' life chances and self-perception. This is the paradox with which individuals are increasingly confronted in the late twentieth century: the accentuation of the reflexive organization of the self takes place under conditions which render the individual increasingly dependent on social systems over which he or she has relatively little control.

This paradox of reflexivity and dependency – or, in Beck's terms, of individualization and institutionalization – is a pervasive feature of modern social life; it is by no means restricted to the domain of the media. But if we focus our attention on the relation between the development of the media and the process of self-formation, we can appreciate the significance of this paradox. Just as the increasing availability of media products provides individuals with the symbolic means to distance themselves from the spatial-temporal contexts of their daily lives and to construct life-projects which incorporate reflexively the mediated images and ideas they receive, so too individuals become increasingly dependent – in respect of their self-formation and what one might loosely call the life of the imagination – on complex systems for the production and transmission of mediated symbolic forms, systems over which most individuals have relatively little control.

(3) The growing availability of mediated symbolic materials may not only enrich the process of self-formation: it can also have a disorienting effect. The enormous variety and multiplicity of messages made available by the media can give rise to a kind of 'symbolic overload'. Individuals are confronted not just with another narrative of self-formation which enables them to reflect critically on their own lives, not just with another vision of the world which contrasts with their taken-for-granted view: they are confronted with countless narratives of self-formation, countless visions of the world, countless forms of information and communication which could not all be effectively and coherently assimilated. How do individuals cope with this ever-increasing flow of mediated symbolic materials?

Partly they cope by being very selective in terms of the material they assimilate. Only a small portion of the mediated symbolic materials available to individuals are assimilated by them. But individuals also develop, or avail themselves of, systems of expertise which enable them to steer a path through the increasingly dense forest of mediated symbolic forms. These systems of expertise may themselves be part of media networks – as, for example, when individuals come to rely on the opinions of film or TV critics to guide their viewing choices. But individuals also commonly rely on significant others with whom they interact in their day-to-day lives, and whose opinions they have come to respect as a source of expert advice about which symbolic materials are worth assimilating and which are not, and about how such materials are to be interpreted.

The reliance on significant others as a source of expert advice concerning media messages has been well documented in various studies, from the early work of Katz and Lazarsfeld to a variety of more recent studies.[9] Consider, for example, Janice Radway's study of readers of romantic fiction.[10] Avid followers of romantic fiction are confronted with a bewildering array of books. Dozens of new titles are published or reissued every month. How do individuals cope with this avalanche of new material? Partly they develop their own systems of expertise which enable them to exercise selectivity – for instance, they learn which authors and imprints are most likely to please them, and they learn how to interpret the publishers' blurbs and to decode the iconography of the cover. But individuals also seek advice from others whose opinions they have come to value. In the case of Radway's readers, the role played by a local bookstore attendant, Dorothy ('Dot')

Evans, was crucial. Dot was extremely knowledgeable about the world of romantic fiction, and many women in the local community came to rely on her as a source of advice about which novels were worth reading and which were not. They had come to trust her judgement; since Dot offered expert advice which was independent of any particular publisher, she helped readers to experiment with new authors and new 'lines' in a way that minimized the risk of disappointment and wasted expense. Moreover, Dot had started a newsletter, 'Dorothy's Diary of Romance Reading', which made her advice available to readers who did not know her through the bookstore. As her reputation grew, publishers began to send her the proofs of forthcoming books in the hope of getting a review in the newsletter. Dot increasingly took on the role of a cultural intermediary who helped readers to sift through the outpourings of the publishing houses and enabled them to find – with the aid of Dot's expert advice – the particular novels that would satisfy their needs.

This example illustrates well the way in which individuals build up and avail themselves of systems of practical expertise in order to cope with the ever-increasing flow of mediated symbolic forms. Of course, the development of systems of practical expertise is not confined to the sphere of individuals' appropriation of media products. In other spheres of life – in learning how to deal with welfare systems, for example, or how to cope with personal relationships, or how to adjust to serious illness or injury – individuals commonly build up systems of practical expertise which enable them to sift through the options and weigh up the opinions of professionals and others.[11] And, in building up these systems, individuals often draw on media products as a resource. Books, manuals, radio and TV programmes, etc., provide a constant source of advice about how to cope with the difficulties and complexities of life. Again, Radway's romantic fiction readers illustrate this point well: having drawn on the expertise of Dot to select their novels from among the countless titles available to them, they then incorporate the messages they draw from the texts into a system of practical expertise for dealing with personal relationships and coping with the demands of daily life. Reading romantic fiction is a practical lesson in how to manage a relationship which promises much but delivers a good deal less, and in which the path to happiness is strewn with painful obstacles that have to be confronted, endured and eventually overcome. It is, as Geertz would say, a form of sentimental education.[12]

The development of the media is thus an integral part of a broader dynamic characteristic of modern societies, a dynamic that we may describe as the interplay of complexity and expertise. As the social environment of individuals grows more and more complex (in part through the massive growth in mediated symbolic forms), individuals build up systems of practical expertise (drawing in part on mediated materials as a resource) which enable them to cope with this complexity and to deal with the demands of living in the modern world. The media thus both contribute to the growth of social complexity and provide individuals with a constant source of advice about how to cope with it.

(4) Let us consider a fourth respect in which the development of the media can have negative consequences for the process of self-formation. I have tried to show that the development of the media creates a new kind of interactive situation – what I have called mediated quasi-interaction. For most individuals, the participation in mediated quasi-interaction is one among many aspects of everyday social activity; mediated symbolic materials are a rich and varied resource for the process of self-formation, but they are not the only or even the principal resource. Individuals also draw extensively on the symbolic materials exchanged through face-to-face interaction with members of the family, friends and others they encounter in the course of their day-to-day lives. However, it is clear that in some cases individuals can come to rely very heavily on mediated symbolic materials; these materials become not so much a resource that individuals draw on and incorporate reflexively into their projects of self-formation, but rather an object of identification to which individuals become strongly and emotionally attached. The reflexive character of the self, whereby individuals are able reflexively to incorporate symbolic materials (mediated and otherwise) into a relatively autonomous process of self-formation, fades almost imperceptibly into something else: the self becomes absorbed in a form of mediated quasi-interaction.

The absorption of the self does not necessarily involve a suspension of reflexivity; rather, it could be seen as a kind of extension and accentuation of the reflexive character of the self. It is precisely because the individual is able reflexively to incorporate mediated symbolic materials into the process of self-formation that these materials can become ends in themselves, symbolic constructs around which the individual begins to organize his or her life and sense of self. Hence the absorption of the self in mediated quasi-interaction is not a phenomenon which is qualitatively different from the reflexive organization of the self: it is a version of it, extended to the point where mediated symbolic materials are not merely a resource for the self but its central preoccupation.

Why should mediated symbolic materials have this drawing power for individuals? What is it about the nature of mediated quasi-interaction which might enable it to become not merely one form of social involvement among others, but rather a primary form of involvement around which other aspects of an individual's social life and sense of self are organized? In order to answer these questions, we need to examine further the distinctive character of mediated quasi-interaction and the forms of involvement, at the level of personal intimacy, that it makes possible.

Non-reciprocal Intimacy at a Distance

There are two aspects of mediated quasi-interaction which are of particular importance for the nature of the personal relationships that can be formed through the media. First, since mediated quasi-interaction is stretched across space and time, it makes possible a form of intimacy with others who do not share one's own spatial-temporal locale; in other words, it makes possible what has been aptly described as 'intimacy at a distance'.[13] Second, since mediated quasi-interaction is non-dialogical, the form of intimacy established through it is non-reciprocal in character. That is, it is a form of intimacy which does not involve the kind of reciprocity and mutuality characteristic of face-to-face interaction.

This distinctive kind of non-reciprocal intimacy at a distance has some attractions for individuals as well as some costs. It enables individuals to enjoy some of the benefits of companionship without the demands typically incurred in contexts of face-to-face interaction. It provides individuals with an opportunity to explore interpersonal relations in a vicarious way, without entering into a web of reciprocal commitments. The distant others whom one comes to know through mediated quasi-interaction are others who can be slotted into the time-space niches of one's life more or less at will. They are regular and dependable companions who can provide entertainment, offer advice, recount events in distant locales, serve as a topic of conversation and so on – all in a way that avoids the reciprocal demands and complexities that are characteristic of relationships sustained through face-to-face interaction.

The non-reciprocal character of mediated relationships does not imply that recipients are at the mercy of distant others and are unable to exercise any control; on the contrary, the very fact that others are not situated in the same spatial-temporal locales as recipients, and are not normally participants in face-to-face interactions with recipients, means that recipients have a great deal of leeway in shaping the kind of relationship they wish to establish and sustain with distant others. Part of the attraction of the kind of intimacy created through mediated quasi-interaction consists precisely in that: it is a kind of intimacy which allows individuals a great deal of scope in defining the terms of engagement and in fashioning the character of intimate others. Individuals can conceive of the others they come to know through the media in a way that is relatively unconstrained by the reality-defining features of face-to-face interaction.

In one form or another, most individuals in modern societies establish and sustain non-reciprocal relations of intimacy with distant others. Actors and actresses, news readers and talk show hosts, pop stars and others become familiar and recognizable figures who are often discussed by individuals in the course of their day-to-day lives, who may be referred to routinely on a first-name basis and so on. But it is also clear that in some cases these non-reciprocal relations of intimacy may assume a much greater significance in the lives of particular individuals. They can become such an important aspect of an individual's life that they begin to overshadow other aspects, in such a way that forms of everyday interaction are redefined in their terms, sometimes with painful and confusing results. Consider the account of Joanne, a 42-year-old married woman with three children:

> When I make love with my husband I imagine it's Barry Manilow. All the time.
> And after, when my husband and I have made love and I realize it's not him, I cry to myself.
> It's usually dark when the tears flow and somehow I manage to conceal them.

It happens to an awful lot of people, too. I didn't realize how many until I got involved with Barry fans. A lot of them are married and around my age and they feel the same way and do the same thing. It's comforting to know I'm not the only one.

But it's still not easy sometimes. It can be very, very upsetting. 'Cos sometimes, besides everything else, I've got this terrible guilty feeling . . .

I suppose it's the same kind of thing people get out of religion. I can't really explain it more than that. But they obviously get something from God to help them through their lives. And Barry is – maybe I shouldn't say it, but it's the way I feel – he's the same sort of thing. He helps me through my life.

But also it isn't just that, because I'm attracted to him as well. I am definitely attracted to him. It's what I describe as a one-sided love affair. He's my lover in my fantasies. He's my friend when I'm depressed. He's there and he seems to serve as something I need to get through my life.[14]

This frank and disconcerting account is no doubt somewhat exceptional, but it is interesting for the light that it sheds on the nature of non-reciprocal relations of intimacy with distant others. Joanne's one-sided love affair with Barry Manilow has become an integral aspect of her life, so much so that she cannot exclude it from the intimate relationships she sustains through face-to-face interaction. As a distant other encountered primarily through the media, Barry Manilow is a malleable object of affection, a companion who can be summoned up more or less at will and who can be shaped according to Joanne's own wishes, feelings and desires. He is a companion whose very distance from the practical contexts of daily life is one of the sources of his enduring appeal, since it is this distance which elevates, which keeps him apart while rendering him permanently available in a mediated or imaginary form, and which enables Joanne to imagine him as she would like him to be. And yet the intrusion of this non-reciprocal relationship into the contexts of daily life can be a source of confusion and even pain. It can be difficult to bear the guilt of knowing that you are leading a double life, enacting an intimate relationship through face-to-face interaction while imagining that you are with someone else – someone, indeed, with whom you could never sustain anything other than a non-reciprocal relation of intimacy at a distance.

Joanne had developed a non-reciprocal relation of intimacy with Barry Manilow before she became involved with Barry fans, but getting involved with Barry fans was an important new step. It enabled her to feel part of a collectivity of individuals who shared similar concerns, and this sense of belonging was itself a source of reassurance – 'It's comforting to know that I'm not the only one.' What is a fan? The term is not a particularly helpful one, since it conjures up too many stereotypical images (the horde of screaming teenagers struggling to catch a glimpse of their favourite star, the obsessed loner who stalks and threatens to kill the person he or she adores, etc.). The term itself is an abbreviation of 'fanatic' and was probably first used in the late nineteenth century to describe enthusiastic spectators of sport. While the term 'fan' is often used today in a broadly descriptive fashion, it has not entirely lost the connotation of religious fervour, frenzy and demonic possession conveyed by its etymological derivation.

In the account I shall develop here, being a fan is an altogether ordinary and routine aspect of everyday life. To be a fan is to organize one's daily life in such a way that following a certain activity (like a spectator sport), or cultivating a relation to particular media products or genres, becomes a central preoccupation of the self and serves to govern a significant part of one's activity and interaction with others. Being a fan is one way of reflexively organizing the self and its day-to-day conduct. Viewed in this way, there is not a clear-cut dividing line between a fan and a non-fan. It is only a matter of degree – of the degree to which an individual orients himself or herself towards certain activities, products or genres and begins to refashion his or her life accordingly.

In many cases, an important part of being a fan is the cultivation of non-reciprocal relations of intimacy with distant others. There are many individuals, such as Joanne, for whom the activity of being a fan is rooted in a non-reciprocal relation of intimacy, and it is this relation which gives meaning and purpose to the associated fan activities. But there are forms of fandom which do not necessarily involve the intensive cultivation of non-reciprocal relations of intimacy; many sports fans, for example, may develop bonds of loyalty to particular teams rather than relations of intimacy with particular players. Moreover, being a fan typically involves a good deal more than an affective orientation towards a distant other. Fans typically engage in a multitude of practical social activities, such as collecting records, tapes, videos and other media products; building up collections of memorabilia or scrapbooks of photos and newspaper clippings; going to concerts, films, matches, etc.; writing letters to other fans; subscribing to newsletters and 'fanzines'; joining fan clubs; attending fan conventions; and, perhaps most importantly, engaging in regular conversation – face-to-face, over the telephone and even, for the more dedicated fans, through computer networks – with other individuals with whom one may have little in common apart from the shared fact of being a fan.

Those who have studied fans have highlighted the fact that the world of the fan is often a complex and highly structured social world with its own conventions, its own rules of interaction and forms of expertise, its own hierarchies of power and prestige, its own practices of canonization, its own divisions between the *cognoscente* and the amateur, the fan and the non-fan, and so on.[15] The world of the fan may be dependent on products of the media industries which are generally available, but these products are taken up, transformed and incorporated into a structured symbolic universe inhabited only by fans. Among the most dedicated fans, this transformative process can become extremely elaborate, resulting in the creation of whole new genres of books, videos, artwork, etc., which, while parasitic on the original media products, often move well beyond them.[16] But participation in the world of the fan often assumes less elaborate forms. Letters exchanged between fans are full of code-words and esoteric knowledge which help to turn the world of the fan into something special: a world which is set apart from the mundane world of non-fans who, while they may watch the same programmes or listen to the same music or read the same books, have not reorganized their lives around these activities and made them an integral aspect of their sense of self.

What is the appeal of being a fan? Why should anyone want to become a fan? The process of becoming a fan can be understood as a strategy of self – that is, as a way of developing the project of the self through the reflexive incorporation of the symbolic forms associated with fandom. For individuals who have established a non-reciprocal relation of intimacy with a distant other, becoming a fan is a way of extending and consolidating this relationship; it is a way of enacting a relationship which cannot normally be enacted in reciprocal contexts of face-to-face interaction. (Even on occasions when the distance which normally separates the fan and the star is temporally breached – as it is, for example, at a concert – the non-reciprocity of the relationship is generally sustained; a concert is an occasion for fans to enact a non-reciprocal relation of intimacy with distant others whose distance has been temporarily suspended.) By providing individuals with the means of enacting a relationship or forming a bond, becoming a fan has a great deal to offer. It enables individuals to tap into a rich source of symbolic materials which can be used to develop a non-reciprocal relation of intimacy or to cultivate a bond, and which can thereby be incorporated reflexively into a project of self-formation.

Fandom has other attractions too. Most importantly, it offers the possibility of becoming part of a group or community, of developing a network of social relations with others who share a similar orientation. The community of fans is a quite distinctive kind of community. It is a community which is, for the most part, not restricted to a particular place. Fans may come together from time to time, as when they meet at concerts or conventions, but their association is not based on the sharing of a common locale. Hence forms of mediated communication – letters, newsletters, telephone, computers, etc. – are crucial to the development of the fan community. This is a community with which individuals can nevertheless feel deeply involved at a personal and emotional level. Partly this involvement stems from the fact that being a fan is viewed by many people as a somewhat unworthy pursuit. It is a stigmatized activity which, in some contexts, may give rise to feelings of guilt and self-doubt. Finding oneself in the company of fellow-travellers can be a source of enormous relief from the guilt and doubt which weighs down on the stigmatized self.

But the deep personal and emotional involvement of individuals in the fan community is also a testimony to the fact that being a fan is an integral part of a project of self-formation. It is precisely because individuals have wrapped up a significant part of their identity in the experience of being a fan that the act of associating with other fans can be immensely gratifying. To associate with other fans is to discover that the choices one has made in constructing one's life-project are not entirely idiosyncratic. It is to discover that one's chosen life trajectory overlaps significantly with the life trajectories of others, in such a way that certain aspects of the self – including, in some cases, one's innermost feelings and desires – can be shared unashamedly with others.

If we understand fandom in this way, we can also understand why for some individuals the experience of being a fan can take on an ever-greater significance. For many individuals, being a fan is merely one among other aspects of the life-projects which they build for themselves. They move between the world of the fan and the practical contexts of their everyday lives with relative ease. They have not lost sight of the symbolic boundary which separates these worlds; indeed, it is the very existence of this boundary, and the ability to move across it more or less at will, which is part of the pleasure of being a fan. But for some individuals, the attractions of fandom can become overwhelming. The experience of being a fan can become a kind of addiction – that is, a form of activity which becomes compulsive and from which the individual cannot extricate himself or herself at will. The individual becomes increasingly preoccupied with the cultivation of a relation of intimacy with a distant other (or with the development of a similar bond); the self becomes increasingly absorbed in the world of the fan. When this occurs, the individual may find it difficult to sustain the distinction between the world of the fan and the practical contexts of daily life. These worlds become inextricably entangled, and the project of the self becomes inseparable from, and increasingly shaped by, the experience of being a fan.

With this merging of the self and the other, of the world of the fan and the world of everyday life, the individual may begin to feel that his or her life is slipping out of control. Being a fan may gradually cease to be an activity that is chosen, one activity among the many that comprise the practical engagements of the self; it may become an activity that one cannot do without. The narrative of the self becomes interwoven with a narrative of the other in such a way that one can no longer prise them apart. 'The star expresses something up there that's very real to you and so you mistake that thing for yourself. And you get caught up in his life':[17] this view, expressed by a former David Bowie fan, captures the way in which the reflexive appropriation of mediated symbolic materials can become a compulsive preoccupation with the other, a preoccupation in which the self gradually loses control. 'But you're another person' – she goes on to say, reflecting on her experiences as a fan – 'with another story to tell.'[18]

Desequestration and the Mediation of Experience

The formation of non-reciprocal relations of intimacy with distant others is not the only mode of experience that individuals sustain through the media. More generally, the media make available a range of experience that individuals would not normally acquire in the practical contexts of their day-to-day lives. We can appreciate the significance of this phenomenon if we view it in a broad historical perspective. The development of modern societies has involved a complex reordering of spheres of experience. With the emergence of specialized systems of knowledge such as medicine and psychiatry, and specialized institutions like hospitals, hospices and asylums of various kinds, certain forms of experience have been gradually removed from the locales of everyday life and increasingly concentrated in particular institutional settings. The experience, for instance, of chronic illness (physical and mental) or of the death of a loved one are experiences which for most people are increasingly shaped by a range of institutions which specialize in the care of the sick and the dying. These and other forms of experience are separated out from the practical contexts of day-to-day life and reconstituted in specialized institutions, access to which may be restricted or controlled in certain ways.

Perhaps the most dramatic examples of this 'sequestration' of experience can be found in the development of prisons and insane asylums from the early nineteenth century on. These institutions forcibly isolated certain categories of individuals from the rest of the population and enclosed them within high walls and secure gates.[19] In previous centuries individuals convicted of criminal offences were often subjected to forms of public humiliation and punishment, such as flogging, branding, the pillory and the gallows; offenders were physically marked and displayed for all to see. But from the early nineteenth century on, convicted criminals were increasingly locked away in institutions where they would be largely excluded from public view. Today the punishment of convicted criminals, like the treatment of the mentally ill, is no longer a phenomenon which people routinely encounter in the course of their day-to-day lives. It is a phenomenon which has become the province of specialists and which most individuals encounter, if they encounter it at all, as something extraordinary.

But the institutional sequestration of experience has gone hand in hand with another development which in some ways runs counter to it: the massive expansion of forms of experience which are mediated in character. Just when many forms of experience are being separated out from the practical contexts of day-to-day life and reconstituted within specialized institutional settings, individuals are confronted with an explosion of mediated forms of experience. And some of the forms of experience which have been

separated out from the normal flow of everyday life are reintro-
duced – perhaps even amplified and accentuated – through the
media. While we may rarely encounter certain kinds of illness and
death in the practical contexts of our daily lives, we may well
acquire some experience of them, and some knowledge about
them, through the media.

The desequestration of experience through the media is a significant development, but it tells only part of the story. For the
media make available forms of experience which are altogether
new, irrespective of whether they were gradually separated out
from the normal flow of everyday life. Anyone who watches television today on a moderately regular basis will have witnessed
countless instances of death and murder (both simulated and
real), will have seen children dying of disease and starvation, will
have seen wars, conflicts and the violent suppression of demonstrations as they occurred in different parts of the world, will have
seen assassinations and attempted assassinations, coups and
aborted coups, revolutions and counter-revolutions – they will
have seen these and many other events unfolding before them on
their TV screens, events which, prior to the advent of television,
may never have been seen by most people. The media produce a
continuous intermingling of different forms of experience, an
intermingling that makes the day-to-day lives of most individuals
today quite different from the lives of previous generations.

How should we make sense of this distinctive intermingling of
different forms of experience? How should we analyse its constitutive features and its consequences? I shall begin to answer these
questions by drawing a broad distinction between two types of
experience. Following Dilthey and other authors within the
hermeneutic and phenomenological traditions, I shall use the
term 'lived experience' (*Erlebnis* in Dilthey's terms) to refer to
experience as we live through it in the course of our day-to-day
lives.[20] It is the experience we acquire in the temporal flow of our
daily lives; it is immediate, continuous and, to some extent, pre-
reflexive, in the sense that it generally precedes any explicit act of
reflection. Lived experience, as I shall construe it here, is also
situated experience, in the sense that it is the experience we
acquire in the practical contexts of our everyday lives. It is the
practical activities of our daily lives and our encounters with
others in contexts of face-to-face interaction which provide the
content of our lived experience.

We can distinguish lived experience in this sense from what I shall call 'mediated experience'. Mediated experience is the kind of experience we acquire through mediated interaction or quasi-interaction, and it differs from lived experience in several ways. Here I shall concentrate on the experience acquired through mediated quasi-interaction and examine four respects in which it differs from lived experience.

In the first place, to experience events through the media is to experience events which, for the most part, are distant spatially (and perhaps also temporally) from the practical contexts of daily life. They are events which one is unlikely to encounter directly in the course of one's day-to-day activity. Hence they are events which, for the individuals who experience them through the media, have a certain refractory character: that is, they are events which are unlikely to be affected by the actions of these individuals. They are not 'at hand' or 'within reach', and are therefore not readily amenable to the actions of recipients. They are also events which, by virtue of their spatial (and perhaps also temporal) distance, are unlikely to impinge directly and perceptibly on the lives of the individuals who experience them through the media. There may be causal connections between the events experienced through the media and the practical contexts of one's daily life, but these connections are likely to involve many intermediaries and to be so extended as to be imperceptible.

A second aspect of mediated experience is that the experience takes place in a context which is different from the context in which the event actually occurs. Mediated experience is always recontextualized experience; it is the experience of events which transpire in distant locales and which are re-embedded, via the reception and appropriation of media products, in the practical contexts of daily life. The recontextualized character of mediated experience is a source both of its charm and of its ability to shock and disconcert. Its charm: the media enable individuals to move with relative ease, and without altering the spatial-temporal contexts of their lives, into new and quite different realms of experience. Realms of experience are not delimited by spatial-temporal contexts but are, as it were, superimposed upon them, in such a way that one can move between them without altering the practical context of daily life. But the recontextualized character of mediated experience is also the source of its capacity to shock and disconcert, precisely because this experience takes place in a context which may be far removed – in space, possibly in time, but also in terms of the social and material conditions of life – from the

context in which the event itself occurs. The shocking, disconcerting character of television images from the Sudan, Bosnia, Soma-
lia, Rwanda and elsewhere stems not only from the desperate life
conditions of the people portrayed in these images, but also from
the fact that their life conditions diverge so dramatically from the
contexts within which these images are re-embedded. It is the
clash of contexts, of divergent worlds suddenly brought together
in the mediated experience, that shocks and disconcerts. Who has
not felt the need, from time to time, to turn away from the images
that appear on the TV screen, to close off temporarily the realm of
experience opened up by this medium and return to the familiar,
reassuring realities of one's day-to-day life?

A third aspect of mediated experience has to do with what we
may describe as its 'relevance structure'.[21] If we understand the
self as a symbolic project which the individual shapes and reshapes
in the course of his or her life, then we must also see that this
project involves a continuously modifiable set of priorities which
determine the relevance or otherwise of experiences or potential
experiences. This set of priorities is an integral part of the life-
project that we construct for ourselves. We do not relate to all
experiences or potential experiences equally, but rather orient
ourselves towards these experiences in terms of the priorities that
are part of the project of the self. From the viewpoint of
the individual, therefore, experiences and potential experiences
are structured in terms of their relevance to the self.

Both lived experience and mediated experience are structured
in this way, but the characteristics of mediated experience endow
it with a somewhat different relevance structure. Let us first
consider lived experience. As one moves along the time-space
paths of daily life, one is constantly immersed in lived experience;
this experience is continuous, immediate and, at least to some
extent, unavoidable. Lived experience forms an environment for
the self; it is the experience of events which occur (or of others
who are situated) in the same spatial-temporal locale as the self,
and which the self can potentially influence through its actions (or
with whom the self can potentially interact). The relevance of
lived experience to the self is direct and largely unquestioned, for
it is primarily through this experience that the project of the self is
formed and reformed over time.

In the case of mediated experience, the relevance structure is
somewhat different. Since mediated experience generally involves
events which are distant in space (perhaps also in time) and which

are refractory to the individuals who experience them, it is more likely to bear a rather tenuous, intermittent and selective relation to the self. Mediated experience is not a continuous flow but rather a discontinuous sequence of experiences which have varying degrees of relevance to the self. For many individuals whose life-projects are rooted in the practical contexts of their day-to-day lives, many forms of mediated experience may bear a tenuous connection to their lives: they may be intermittently interesting, occasionally entertaining, but they are not the issues that concern them most. But individuals also draw selectively on mediated experience, interlacing it with the lived experience that forms the connective tissue of their daily lives; and in so far as mediated experience has been incorporated reflexively into the project of the self, it may acquire a deep and enduring relevance.

For any particular individual, we could in principle construct a map of the relevance structure of different forms of experience as he or she moves through the time-space paths of daily life. At one end of the spectrum, there is the individual who values only lived experience and who has relatively little contact with mediated forms. For this person, the project of the self is shaped overwhelmingly by lived experience and, while mediated experiences may occur at various points along the time-space path, these experiences have little bearing on the self: they may be noticed, perhaps remembered for the purposes of accomplishing some task at hand, but they remain peripheral to the core concerns of the self. At the other end of the spectrum, there is the individual for whom mediated experience has become central to the project of the self. Like the dedicated fan, this person organizes his or her life in such a way that mediated experience is a regular and integral feature of it. Taken to an extreme, mediated experience may even supplant or become confused with lived experience in such a way that individuals may find it difficult to distinguish between them, as we have seen.

For most individuals, the relevance structure of different forms of experience lies somewhere between these two poles. As they move through the time-space paths of their day-to-day lives they acquire both lived experience and mediated experience, incorporating them into a continuously evolving life-project. They organize their time-space paths in such a way that certain mediated experiences are planned features of them – the evening news bulletin, for instance, or the episodes of a televised serial or soap opera, or the live broadcast of a sports event. The planning of mediated experiences is an index of their relevance to the self: the more relevant they are felt to be, the more likely it is that an individual will integrate them into his or her daily schedules. Through routinization they become settled features of everyday life. But even when mediated experiences become routinized in this way, they often have a somewhat tenuous relation to the self, precisely because the events experienced through the media take place in locales which are remote from the practical contexts of day-to-day life.

Let us now consider a fourth and final aspect of mediated experience, what I shall describe as its 'despatialized commonality'. In the case of lived experience, the commonality of experience is linked to the sharing of a common locale and to the overlapping of life trajectories in the shared circumstances of day-to-day life. In so far as different individuals have experiences in common, in the sense of lived experience, this commonality is often rooted in the fact that the practical life contexts of these individuals are the same or very similar: the commonality of lived experience is rooted in spatial proximity. It is this commonality of lived experience which formed the basis of many traditional kinds of political organization, such as trade unions and class-based political parties. Of course, these traditional kinds of political organization often made extensive use of mediated communication, in the form of partisan newspapers, pamphlets, etc. But ultimately they were rooted in a certain commonality of lived experience, of shared experiences based on shared life conditions, and mediated communication was used to call attention to this common basis.

However, the development of mediated communication creates a new kind of experience which to some extent undercuts these traditional kinds of political organization, for it is a kind of experience in which commonality is no longer linked to the sharing of a common locale. Individuals can acquire similar experiences through the media without sharing similar life contexts. This is not to say that the life contexts of individuals are irrelevant to the nature and significance of mediated experience: on the contrary, as I have repeatedly stressed, the life contexts of individuals play a crucial role in shaping the ways that individuals appropriate media products and incorporate them into their lives. But, unlike lived experience, the commonality of mediated experience is not rooted in spatial proximity. Whether individuals share the same or similar experiences, in the sense of mediated experience, has less to do with spatial proximity and the overlapping of life trajectories than with their common access to mediated forms of communication. I shall pursue the political implications of this point in the following chapter. But first I want to consider in a more general way some of the consequences of living in a world in which mediated experience has become more and more pervasive.

New Options, New Burdens: Living in a Mediated World

What is it like to live in a world increasingly permeated by mediated forms of information and communication? What happens to the self in a world where mediated experience has come to play a substantial and expanding role in the daily lives of individuals? Some of the recent literature in social and cultural theory suggests a certain way of answering these questions: the profusion of mediated messages and images has, it is sometimes argued, effectively dissolved the self as a coherent entity. The self has, in effect, been absorbed into a disjointed array of mediated signs. As the individual becomes more and more open to mediated messages, the self becomes more and more dispersed and decentred, losing whatever unity and coherence it may have had. Like the images refracted through a hall of mirrors, the self becomes an endless play of signs that shift with every movement. Nothing is stable, nothing is fixed, and there is no separate entity of which these images are a reflection: in this age of media saturation, the multiple, shifting images *are* the self.[22]

How convincing is this as an account of the self and of the impact of mediated communication? Certainly it is an account which has been influential: it lurks in much of the literature associated with postmodernism,[23] even if it is seldom stated in an explicit form. But as a characterization of the self in the contemporary media age, this account is, in my view, misguided. The self has not been dissolved by the profusion of mediated messages, and the metaphor of the hall of mirrors does not capture well the predicament of the self in the contemporary world. The self has been transformed, the conditions of self-formation have been altered; but we need to think about this transformation in a different way.

With the increasing availability of mediated materials, the self,

understood as a reflexively organized symbolic project, has become increasingly unconstrained by its location in the practical
contexts of day-to-day life. While still situated in these contexts
and organizing much of their lives in terms of the demands arising
from them, individuals can also experience distant events, interact
with distant others and move temporarily into mediated
microworlds which, depending on one's interests and priorities,
exercise varying degrees of holding power. As these mediated
experiences are incorporated reflexively into the project of self-
formation, the nature of the self is transformed. It is not dissolved
or dispersed by media messages, but rather is opened up by them,
in varying degrees, to influences which stem from distant locales.

Living in a mediated world involves a continuous interweaving
of different forms of experience. For most individuals, as they
move along the time-space paths of their daily lives, lived experience continues to exert a powerful influence on the project of self-
formation: we think of ourselves and our life trajectories primarily
in relation to the others whom, and the events which, we encounter (or are likely to encounter) in the practical contexts of our daily
lives. However, if we compare our lives today with the lives of
individuals who lived two or three centuries ago, it seems clear
that the structure of experience has changed in significant ways.
While lived experience remains fundamental, it is increasingly
supplemented by, and in some respects displaced by, mediated
experience, which assumes a greater and greater role in the process of self-formation. Individuals increasingly draw on mediated
experience to inform and refashion the project of the self.

The growing availability of mediated experience thus creates
new opportunities, new options, new arenas for self-experimentation. An individual who reads a novel or watches a soap opera is
not simply consuming a fantasy; he or she is exploring possibilities, imagining alternatives, experimenting with the project of the
self. But as our biographies are opened up by mediated experience, we also find ourselves drawn into issues and social relations
which extend well beyond the locales of our day-to-day lives. We
find ourselves not only to be observers of distant others and
events, but also to be involved with them in some way. We are
released from the locales of our daily lives only to find ourselves
thrown into a world of baffling complexity. We are called on to
form a view about, to take a stand on, even to assume some
responsibility for, issues and events which take place in distant
parts of an increasingly interconnected world.

Living in a mediated world thus carries with it a new burden of responsibility which weighs heavily on the shoulders of some. It gives rise to a new dynamic in which the immediacy of lived experience and the moral claims associated with face-to-face interaction are constantly played off against the claims and responsibilities stemming from mediated experience. Some individuals turn away from the latter claims and seek to maintain their distance from events which are, in any case, distant from the pressing demands of their day-to-day lives. Others, stirred by media images and reports, throw themselves into campaigns on behalf of distant groups or causes. The case of Graham Bamford, who doused himself in petrol and set himself alight in Parliament Square to protest against the British government's failure to intervene in the Bosnian tragedy, is certainly an extreme example; but it illustrates vividly the extent to which a sense of responsibility for distant others, acquired through mediated experience, can bear down on the project of the self.[24] Most individuals try, as best they can, to steer a path between the claims and responsibilities arising from the practical contexts of their day-to-day lives, on the one hand, and those stemming from mediated experience, on the other. They try to find a balance they can live with and justify to themselves.

This moral circumstance, in which mediated experience can give rise to claims on the self and to a sense of responsibility for distant others or events, is relatively new as a widespread phenomenon. It has highlighted a set of issues – concerning, among other things, the long-range impact of human action and the high-risk stakes of an increasingly interconnected world – which cannot be readily accommodated within the traditional frameworks of moral and political thought. In the final chapter I shall explore some of these issues and pursue the task of rethinking some of the notions that traditional frameworks have bequeathed to us.

8

The Reinvention of Publicness

In previous chapters I have raised but not pursued questions of a more normative character concerning the media and their role in modern societies. How should the media be organized at an institutional level? What contribution should they make to social and political life? What kinds of opportunities do the media open up, and what limitations do they impose on the forms of communication that are possible in the modern world? These are some of the questions I want to pursue in this final chapter. In so doing I shall be concerned to develop a particular argument: today, I shall argue, we must look for new ways to reinvent publicness. But what does it mean to reinvent publicness? How should we conceptualize this task and how can we translate it into practical terms? We can begin to answer these questions by recalling the distinction, drawn in chapter 4, between two senses of the public–private dichotomy. According to the first sense, the public–private dichotomy has to do with the relation between the state, on the one hand, and those activities or spheres of life that were excluded or separated from it, on the other. The second sense of the dichotomy has to do with the relation between visibility and invisibility. If we bear in mind this distinction, then we can see that the argument concerning the reinvention of publicness has to be pursued at two separate levels.

At one level, the reinvention of publicness involves the creation of new forms of public life which lie beyond the state. This was, of course, the theme that Habermas wished to highlight in his arguments concerning the emergence of the bourgeois public sphere: this sphere was important, he argued, because it was separate from the state and stood in a relation of potential criticism *vis-à-vis* the exercise of state power. This theme retains its significance today, although it needs to be rethought in relation to the developmental trends which have transformed the conditions under which media organizations operate. Today the reinvention of publicness must take place in a symbolic environment which is already shaped by substantial concentrations of resources and which extends well beyond the boundaries of particular nation-states.

There is, however, a second level at which the argument about the reinvention of publicness must be pursued. Our ways of thinking about politics have been profoundly shaped by a certain model of what public life should be. It is a model derived from the assemblies of the classical Greek city-states, a model in which individuals come together in the same spatial-temporal setting to discuss issues of common concern. But we must seriously question whether this traditional model of publicness as co-presence is adequate to the social and political conditions of the late twentieth century. The problem is not simply that modern societies have developed on a scale that renders the traditional model quite impractical as a means of conceptualizing the involvement of most individuals in many of the political decisions that affect their lives. There is a further problem: namely, that the development of communication media has created a new kind of publicness which is very different from the traditional conception of public life. This new kind of mediated publicness does not involve individuals coming together in a shared locale to discuss issues of common concern. Rather, it is a publicness of openness and visibility, of making available and making visible, and this visibility no longer involves the sharing of a common locale.

What are the consequences of this new kind of mediated publicness for the way we think about the conduct and content of politics? What opportunities does it open up in the modern world, and what risks does it introduce? What limitations does it impose on the forms of political activity that are possible in the late twentieth century? These are some of the questions I shall try to address. I shall begin by situating the task of reinventing publicness within a broader set of debates concerning the nature of politics and the state; here the reinvention of publicness involves the creation of new forms of public life which lie beyond the institutions of the state. In the second section I shall develop the argument that the reinvention of publicness requires us to move beyond the traditional notion of publicness as co-presence. In the third section I shall explore the notion of mediated publicness in more detail and examine some of the consequences of mediated visibility. Drawing together these lines of argument, I shall conclude by considering some of the opportunities for, and the limitations on, the renewal of politics and moral-practical thinking in an age of global communication.

Publicness Beyond the State

In an earlier chapter we considered how, with the formation of the modern state, the term 'public' came increasingly to refer to state-related activity, while 'private' referred to the areas of economic activity and personal relations which fell outside of direct state control. This sense of the public–private dichotomy has had a profound impact on the ways in which public life and politics have been understood. It has become customary to think of public life and politics as co-extensive with the activities of the state and – in Western democratic regimes, at any rate – with the regularized competition for control of the state by political parties operating within the established rules of the game.

But the tendency to identify public life with state-related activity has not gone unchallenged. If we go back to the beginnings of modern societies, we can retrace the development of social and political activities which contributed to the formation of a vibrant political culture beyond the sphere of the state. These ranged from the salons, coffee houses and 'table societies' of bourgeois social life to a variety of popular and working-class organizations. Moreover, as Habermas among others has shown, the development of communication media based on print played an important role in the emergence of these forms of public life and in the articulation of a kind of 'public opinion' which was distinct from, and potentially critical of, the official doctrines of the state.

It is in this context that we can appreciate the significance of the classical liberal defence of the freedom of the press. Writing in the early nineteenth century, at a time when the newspaper industry in Britain was campaigning against the stamp duties, the early liberal thinkers such as Jeremy Bentham, James Mill and John Stuart Mill gave an eloquent defence of the freedom of the press and an insightful account of its role in the cultivation of public life beyond the state.[1] They saw the free expression of opinion through the organs of an independent press as a principal means by which a diversity of viewpoints could be expressed, an enlightened public opinion could be formed, and the abuses of state power by corrupt or tyrannical governments could be checked. A free and independent press would play the role of a critical watchdog; not only would it articulate a diversity of opinions and thereby enrich the sphere of knowledge and debate, but it would also expose and criticize the activities of those who rule and the principles on which their decisions are based.

As a set of arguments concerned with the cultivation of public life independent of state power, there is still much to commend in the classical liberal defence of the freedom of the press. The liberty to express thoughts and opinions in public, however uncomfortable they may be for established authorities, is a vital feature of a modern democratic order – a feature which is by no means characteristic of all political regimes in the world today. But, having said that, the world of the late twentieth century is very different from early nineteenth-century England, and it would be misleading to suggest that the traditional liberal theory of the free press could be transposed to the conditions of the late twentieth century without substantial modification. Two developments, which distance our world today from that of the early nineteenth century, are particularly significant in this regard.

One development is the growing concentration of resources in the media industries, leading to the formation of large-scale communication conglomerates with interests in a diversified array of media activities. As we have seen, the origins of this development can be traced back to the early nineteenth century, when new methods of production and distribution greatly increased the productive capacity of the newspaper industry and prepared the way for the transformation of news and other media organizations into large-scale commercial concerns. The second development is the intensification of processes of globalization. Today the world is much more interconnected than it was two hundred years ago. In the sphere of communication, the origins of the process of globalization can be traced back to the mid-nineteenth century, as we saw in a previous chapter. With the development of submarine cable networks and, more recently, the deployment of integrated satellite and cable systems capable of transmitting large quantities of information around the world, with the growth of transnational communication conglomerates which conduct their commercial activities in a global arena, and with an expanding global trade in information and communication products, the globalization of communication has continued unabated.

As a consequence of these two developments, the configuration of issues that confront us in the late twentieth century is quite different from that which faced liberal thinkers two centuries ago. For the early liberal thinkers, the main threat to individual liberty and freedom of expression was a threat that stemmed from the state: the rights of the individual had to be protected against the excessive use of state power. The early liberal thinkers took it for granted that free enterprise was the foundation of freedom of expression. The free expression of thoughts and opinions could be practically achieved, in their view, only in so far as the institutions of the press were independent of the state and situated in the private domain where they could carry out their activities with a minimum of constraint: in traditional liberal theory, a laissez-faire approach to economic activity was the natural counterpart to individual liberty of thought and expression.[2] The early liberal thinkers also took it for granted that the natural framework of sovereignty and accountability for a modern democratic society was the territorially bounded nation-state.[3] The political leaders of a state were accountable to its citizens, and the state was the supreme and sovereign authority within the territory of its jurisdiction.

But today these assumptions can no longer be taken for granted. With the transformation of media organizations into large-scale commercial organizations, the freedom of expression was increasingly confronted by a new threat, a threat stemming not from the excessive use of state power, but rather from the unhindered growth of media organizations *qua* commercial concerns. A laissez-faire approach to economic activity is not necessarily the best guarantor of freedom of expression, since an unregulated market may develop in a way that effectively reduces diversity and limits the capacity of most individuals to make their views heard. The history of the newspaper industry in Western countries provides ample evidence of this law of diminishing diversity. In Britain, for instance, the growth in overall circulation during the first half of the twentieth century was accompanied by a decline in the number of newspapers published and an increasing concentration of resources in the hands of large media conglomerates. As overall circulation began to decline from the mid-1950s on, the competition between the remaining newspapers intensified, leading to the demise of titles that were unable to command a sufficiently large circulation, or a sufficient proportion of the advertising revenue, to cover their costs.[4] Left to itself, the market does not necessarily cultivate diversity and pluralism in the sphere of communication. Like other domains of industry, the media industries are driven primarily by the logic of profitability and capital accumulation, and there is no necessary correlation between the logic of profitability and the cultivation of diversity.

Just as traditional liberal theory underestimated the dangers that would stem from the dependence of media institutions on a highly competitive process of capital accumulation, so too the early liberal thinkers did not anticipate the extent to which the autonomy and sovereignty of particular nation-states would be limited by the development of transnational networks of power and by the activities and policies of institutions which operate increasingly on a global scale. Particular nation-states were never isolated entities; they were always part of an interconnected system of nation-states, linked together in shifting alliances and dependent on accumulation processes that extended well beyond their territorial boundaries. But in the course of the nineteenth and twentieth centuries, the degree of interconnectedness has increased significantly. This is true in the sphere of information and communication just as it is in other sectors of commodity production. In an age when global communication conglomerates are key actors in the production and distribution of symbolic goods, a reflection on the conditions of the freedom of expression cannot be restricted to the territorial framework of the nation-state.

So how, in the late twentieth century, can we create the conditions for a renewal of public life? How can we stimulate a kind of publicness which is neither part of the state nor wholly dependent on the autonomous processes of the market? We can best pursue this goal, in my view, by seeking to implement what I have described elsewhere as *the principle of regulated pluralism*.[5] What is regulated pluralism? It is the establishment of an institutional framework which would both accommodate and secure the existence of a plurality of independent media organizations. It is a principle which takes seriously the traditional liberal emphasis on the freedom of expression and on the importance of sustaining media institutions which are independent of state power. But it is a principle which also recognizes that the market left to itself will not necessarily secure the conditions of freedom of expression and promote diversity and pluralism in the sphere of communication. To secure these conditions and promote these goals, it may be necessary to intervene in the market and to regulate market processes in such a way that diversity and pluralism are not undermined by the concentration of economic and symbolic power.[6]

The principle of regulated pluralism establishes certain broad parameters for the development of media institutions. On the one hand, the principle calls for a deconcentration of resources in the media industries: the trend towards the growing concentration of resources should be curtailed and the conditions should be created, so far as possible, for a flourishing of independent media organizations. This requires not only restrictive legislation – that is, legislation which limits mergers, takeovers and cross-ownership in the media industries – but also enabling legislation which is concerned to create favourable conditions for the development of media organizations that are not part of the large conglomerates. Legislative intervention in the media industries should therefore be seen not simply as a means of curtailing the excessive power of large conglomerates: it is also a means of facilitating the development of new centres of symbolic power which lie outside the spheres of the conglomerates and their ramified networks of production and exchange. On the other hand, while the principle of regulated pluralism calls for legislative intervention in the media industries, it also requires, so far as the routine operation of media institutions is concerned, a clear separation of media institutions from the exercise of state power. As the early liberal thinkers argued, media institutions should be free to articulate views which are critical of the policies and officials of the state, and any attempt to restrict this freedom – either through overt forms of censorship or indirectly, through financial pressure, threats, incentives or disincentives of various kinds[7] – should be firmly resisted.

These twin aspects of regulated pluralism – the deconcentration of resources in the media industries, the separation of media institutions from the state – define a broad institutional space for the development of media organizations, but they do not specify in detail the forms of ownership and control which should prevail in the media industries. This agnosticism with regard to forms of ownership and control is intentional, for it seems to me both

impractical and undesirable to try to prescribe the most appropriate forms of organization. It is impractical because, in the actual
circumstances of the late twentieth century, a substantial proportion of media products are produced and distributed by large
communication conglomerates. It is possible to regulate the activities of these conglomerates, to limit their acquisitions and to
seek to create a symbolic environment in which the large conglomerates are not the only players. But to suppose that scholarly
debates about ideal forms of ownership and control in the media
industries will have a significant impact on the activities of the
large conglomerates is, in all likelihood, a will-o'-the-wisp.

There are also good grounds for doubting the desirability of
trying to prescribe in detail the most appropriate forms of organization for the media industries. The main problem with any such
attempt is that the form of ownership and control in the media
industries is not necessarily a reliable indicator of the content and
orientation of the material produced. In Britain, for example,
some of the most critical and innovative television programmes
have been produced by the private sector (both by the ITV
companies and by independent production companies commissioned by Channel Four), while the BBC has remained relatively
cautious in its programming. Similarly, in the sphere of publishing, some of the most innovative steps in recent years, such as
publishing new work by women, have been taken by small, independent publishing houses. The organization of media institutions on a commercial basis does not necessarily lead to a dulling
of criticism, a downgrading of quality and a hijacking of public
discourse for commercial ends.[8]

Hence, for the purposes of cultivating diversity and pluralism in
the media, it seems sensible and desirable to allow for a variety of
organizational forms. The principle of regulated pluralism defines
a broad institutional space which allows for this kind of variety.
But this space is not without limits. It is a space between market
and state; or, more precisely, it is a space beyond the state which
is regulated with a view to cultivating diversity and pluralism.

There is another sense in which the institutional space of the
media lies beyond the state: today the major actors in the media
industries are transnational corporations, and media products
circulate well beyond the boundaries of particular nation-states.
The institutional space of the media is increasingly transnational
in character, and any attempt to rethink problems of regulation
and diversity must therefore be situated at a level which extends

beyond the domestic policies of individual states. The traditional way of posing problems of media regulation – in terms of the relation between state and society, where 'society' is understood, explicitly or implicitly, as the society defined by the territorial boundaries of a given nation-state – is no longer satisfactory in a world where national boundaries are increasingly porous with regard to the flow of symbolic goods. Today it is no longer possible (if it ever was) to think of the international dimension of communication as supplementary to a national policy for media regulation; on the contrary, the international dimension must be placed at the centre of any reflection on what a coherent and viable national policy should be.

There is, of course, a history of attempts to regulate communication media at an international level, a history which we briefly considered in an earlier chapter. But most earlier attempts were concerned with a relatively narrow set of issues involving the allocation of scarce resources, such as spectrum space for radio transmission and orbital slots for satellites, or with the problems of regulating transborder communication flows. While these issues are important, there is a growing need to broaden the range of issues addressed by international bodies and to consider the question of how, at the international level, the activities of trans-national communication conglomerates can be regulated in a way that would cultivate diversity and pluralism. Today the creation of a pluralistic public sphere in any particular society is increasingly dependent on the cultivation of diversity and pluralism at the international level, for all societies are increasingly affected by flows of information and communication over which any particular nation-state has only limited control.

Visibility Beyond the Locale

So far I have been concerned with the question of reinventing publicness at the institutional level, that is, at the level of creating media institutions which lie beyond the state and which contribute to a diverse and pluralistic media culture. But there is another sense of publicness that we need to consider at this stage: not the sense of publicness that has to do with the relation between the state and those aspects of social life that are separate from it, but

244   *The Reinvention of Publicness*

rather the sense that has to do with visibility versus invisibility. What might it mean, in the late twentieth century, to reinvent publicness in this sense?

Our ways of thinking about social and political life have been shaped in a quite profound manner by a certain model of publicness that stems from the ancient world, from the assemblies and market squares of the classical Greek city-states. This is the traditional model of publicness as co-presence, the idea that public life consists in the coming together of individuals in a common space, a shared locale, to engage in debate about matters of general concern. It is a model which defines publicness in spatial and dialogical terms. The very essence of public life, on this account, is the to-and-fro of argument between individuals who confront one another face-to-face.

Today we must recognize that this traditional model of publicness no longer provides an adequate way of thinking about the nature of public life. The development of communication media – beginning with print, but including the more recent forms of electronic communication – has created new forms of publicness which do not share the features of the traditional model. These new forms of mediated publicness are not localized in space and time: they detach the visibility of actions and events from the sharing of a common locale. The new forms of mediated publicness are also, for the most part, non-dialogical in character. The roles of producer and recipient are differentiated and the process of symbolic exchange through the media acquires characteristics which distinguish it, in many cases, from dialogical interaction.

How should we respond to this discrepancy between the traditional way of thinking about public life, on the one hand, and the new forms of publicness created by the media, on the other? There are two kinds of response which should, in my view, be avoided. One response is to hold on to the traditional model and to champion it as the only legitimate account of what public life should be. Now it may be that the traditional model remains relevant in some respects to the social and political conditions of the late twentieth century. It may be that there are some contexts of social and political life today – such as meetings and public gatherings of various kinds – which still bear some resemblance to the assemblies of the classical Greek city-states. But, for the most part, this model of publicness is far removed from the practical life contexts of most individuals today. If we champion this model as our ideal, then we shall be inclined to take a rather dim view of the quality of public life in the late twentieth century. And we shall be obliged to interpret the ever-growing role of mediated communication as a slope of steady decline.

A second possible response – equally unsatisfactory, in my view – is to suppose that mediated communication could be understood simply as an extension of the traditional model. Thus it might be supposed that the kind of mediated communication which takes place on radio and television, in books and newspapers, etc., is merely a conversation writ large, and that it differs from ordinary conversation in face-to-face situations only in terms of its scale: mediated communication is a conversation that embraces thousands and potentially millions of people, not just two or three. But this image of mediated communication as a conversation writ large is, for the most part, an illusion. Of course, there are forms of mediated communication, such as telephone communication, which are conversational in character. But the forms of communication involving radio, television, etc., are not conversational in this sense, because most listeners and viewers are not participants in a dialogue but rather recipients of messages which are produced and transmitted independently of their actual or potential response.[9]

There is a third – and, in my view, a more promising – way of responding to the discrepancy highlighted above: we can put aside the traditional model, with its emphasis on dialogical communication in a shared locale, and try to free our way of thinking about public life from the grip of the traditional approach. We can focus our attention on the kind of publicness created by the media and seek to analyse its characteristics – its strengths and its limitations, the opportunities opened up by it and risks associated with it. We can try to refashion our way of thinking about public life at the same time as we reflect on the new kind of publicness created by the media.

So how should we think about the nature of mediated publicness? Let us focus our attention on the kind of publicness created by printed materials like books and newspapers, and by electronic media like radio and television. These media create a new kind of publicness which consists of what we may describe as *the space of the visible*: it is the non-localized, non-dialogical, open-ended space of the visible in which mediated symbolic forms can be expressed and received by a plurality of non-present others. Some aspects of this space deserve further comment.

Mediated publicness is a *non-localized* space in the sense that it is not tied down to particular spatial-temporal locales. It is a 'space' in the sense that it is an opening, a sphere of possibilities in which mediated symbolic forms can appear; but it is not a 'place', that is, a particular locale in which individuals act and interact. Just as the development of communication media enables symbolic forms to be circulated beyond the contexts of their production, so too it detaches the phenomenon of publicness from the sharing of a common locale: the sphere of mediated publicness is extended in time and space, and is potentially global in scope.

Mediated publicness is *non-dialogical* in the sense that the producers and the recipients of mediated symbolic forms are generally not engaged in a dialogue with one another. Producers generally produce media messages for an indefinite range of potential recipients, and recipients generally receive these messages under conditions which do not enable them to respond, in any direct and discursive manner, to the producers. The roles of producer and recipient are differentiated, and the relation between them is asymmetrical. 'But,' it might be said, 'what of the talk shows on radio and TV, the phone-in programmes where listeners and viewers are invited to put questions to members of a panel, and so on: don't these examples show that mediated publicness can be dialogical in character?' No, they don't. A talk show is a hybrid form of interaction where the individuals involved in producing the show are engaged in face-to-face interaction in a studio (or, in some cases, mediated interaction with a small number of individuals who have written or phoned in), while the vast majority of individuals who watch or listen to the talk show are engaged only in a form of mediated quasi-interaction. The individuals who watch or listen to a talk show are, of course, watching or listening to a dialogue, but they are not participating in a dialogue as an interlocutor. And, apart from a small number of self-selected individuals who avail themselves of another communication medium (the letter or the telephone) in order to put a question to a panel or to offer their opinions on some matter, most individuals are unlikely to participate in any role other than that of recipient.

Mediated publicness is an *open-ended* space in the sense that it is a creative and uncontrollable space, a space where new symbolic forms can be expressed, where new words and images can suddenly appear, where information previously hidden from view can be made available, and where the consequences of becoming visible cannot be fully anticipated and controlled. Mediated publicness is open-ended in the sense that the contents of mediated materials cannot be entirely delimited in advance – although the degree to which these contents are delimited will depend on the organization of media institutions and their relation to forms of economic and political power. And when symbolic materials become available in the media, their consequences are indeterminate. A few sentences that initially appear on the back page of a local newspaper can be picked up by the national press and turned into a major story; an image captured by an amateur photographer can be picked up by television networks and relayed around the world; and the consequences of these and similar processes cannot be determined in advance.

If we bear in mind these features of mediated publicness, we can appreciate the significance that *struggles for visibility* have come to assume in the social and political life of late twentieth-century societies. In earlier forms of society, where visibility depended on the sharing of a common locale, there was no public arena that extended beyond the localized spheres of face-to-face interaction: if individuals wanted to express their grievances or concerns, they had to do so (either in person or through intermediaries) face-to-face. There was no way of gaining recognition of their concerns, no way of making themselves heard, other than by expressing their concerns, in words or in actions, to others with whom they interacted in contexts of co-presence. Struggles were, for the most part, localized struggles, and issues became known to outsiders only if they were relayed to them by messengers or by word of mouth.

Today the situation is quite different. Since the development of print and especially the electronic media, struggles for recognition have increasingly become constituted as struggles for visibility within the non-localized space of mediated publicness. The struggle to make oneself heard or seen (and to prevent others from doing so) is not a peripheral aspect of the social and political upheavals of the modern world; on the contrary, it is central to them. The development of social movements, such as the women's movement and the civil rights movement, provide ample testimony to the fact that the claims of hitherto subordinate or marginalized groups are advanced through struggles for visibility in the media. The development of such movements also attests to the fact that, by achieving some degree of visibility in the media, the claims and concerns of particular individuals can gain some recognition from others, and hence can serve as a rallying cry for individuals who do not share the same spatial-temporal context.

This account of mediated publicness also enables us to understand why the achievement of visibility can set in motion a chain of events which unfold in unpredictable and uncontrollable ways. Media images and messages can tap into deep divisions and feelings of injustice that are experienced by individuals in the course of their day-to-day lives. The media can *politicize the everyday* by making it visible and observable in ways that previously were not possible, thereby turning everyday events into a catalyst for action that spills well beyond the immediate locales in which these events occurred. This is vividly illustrated by the events surrounding the trial of the police officers accused of assaulting Rodney King, the black motorist who, while driving at night in Los Angeles in 1991, was stopped by police, dragged from his car, and kicked, beaten with batons and shot with a stun gun as he lay on the ground. The events were captured on video by an amateur photographer who happened to be nearby. The videotape was used as evidence in the subsequent trial of the officers, but it was also repeatedly shown on television (and frames were reprinted in newspapers and magazines) throughout the United States and, indeed, throughout the world. When the police officers were eventually acquitted by the jury in spring 1992, the announcement of the verdict was followed by violent rioting in Los Angeles and in other American cities. The amateur videotape had touched a raw nerve. It had captured a distressing but nevertheless altogether ordinary event, lifted it out of its spatial-temporal setting and turned it into a visible, repeatable and seemingly incontrovertible testimony to a kind of brutality that was felt by many individuals in the black community to be a routine part of their day-to-day lives. The anger felt by many on hearing the verdict was rooted not simply in the feeling that justice had not been done in this case: the announcement of the verdict would not have unleashed such dramatic events if it had not tapped into a much broader sense of injustice concerning the position of blacks in American society and the differential treatment of ethnic groups by the police and judicial systems. The videotape of the beating of Rodney King did not by itself give rise to the riots in LA and elsewhere. But it turned the everyday experience of one individual into a visible testimony to the experience of many; and this, when juxtaposed to a verdict that seemed palpably unfair, served to spark off an uncontrollable sequence of events which spread well beyond the inner-city region of LA.

This example also illustrates that, in an era of mediated publicness, questions of justice – and, more generally, questions of politics – cannot be easily contained within particular institutions and locales. However hard the Los Angeles authorities may have tried to keep the Rodney King affair within the boundaries of the judicial system, the videotape endowed the affair with a degree of visibility which propelled events out of their control. The affair raised questions of justice and injustice which were of interest not only to residents of the local community: they became issues of national and even international concern. And the way in which these questions were dealt with by the established judicial system was subjected to extensive criticism by individuals who were neither participants in the judicial process nor witnesses of the original events, but who formed their own opinion on the basis of an amateur videotape. In this respect, the development of mediated publicness has contributed to a more general transformation in the nature of power and politics in modern societies. Let us consider this transformation in more detail.

Towards a Renewal of Democratic Politics

Democracy has become the one idea, and seemingly the only idea, which is capable of underwriting the legitimate exercise of political power in the late twentieth century. The story of the remarkable triumph of this idea – from its parochial origins in sixth-century Athens to its well-nigh universal appeal today – has been retold many times.[10] It is a story that is all the more remarkable for the fact that, for most of its 2,500-year history, the idea of democracy was regarded by most commentators as a pretty distasteful recipe for the administration of human affairs. It is only since roughly the late eighteenth century that the democratic ideal has been taken up once again and seriously advanced as a principle for the organization of political power. But in this context – that is, in the context of the emergence of modern societies – the idea of democracy was adapted in ways that distanced it quite significantly from the practices of the ancient Athenians. For many early modern political thinkers, democracy was conceived of primarily as a way of organizing political power within the framework of the emerging nation-state. It was not a system aimed at ensuring the maximum degree of citizen self-rule, but rather a mechanism intended to secure some degree of accountability of rulers to those over whom they ruled. Given the sheer scale of modern nation-states and the vastness of the populations circumscribed by them, it was in any case difficult to see how democracy could be practically implemented in the modern world in anything other than a representative form. Moreover, the development of institutions of representative democracy in the emerging nation-states went hand in hand with the development of a market economy and of autonomous economic institutions organized on a capitalist basis. While the connection between representative democracy and the capitalist economy may have been a historical contingency, today it has become increasingly difficult to envisage how a democratic regime could operate effectively and durably without some degree of autonomous and market-oriented development in the economy.

The apparent triumph of democracy in the modern world is thus a victory in which, since the struggle began some two and a half millennia ago, both the battlefield and the adversaries have changed almost beyond recognition. While the classical Greek ideal of autonomous citizens ruling themselves continues to provide a source of inspiration for the political imagination today, the actual form in which democracy has triumphed in the modern world is a faint reflection of that ideal: it is, by and large, the form of representative democracy, institutionalized primarily at the level of the nation-state and coupled with a relatively autonomous market economy over which it has assumed some degree of regulatory control.[11] While certainly not a Pyrrhic victory, the triumph of democracy in this sense has been achieved only at a certain cost. The development of representative democracy has, to some extent, created new problems which threaten to undermine the very legitimacy that the idea of democracy seemed to bestow. Let us briefly consider four of these problems.

First, the development of representative democracy has been accompanied by significant and growing levels of cynicism and disillusionment on the part of ordinary individuals towards the established political institutions. This is reflected in opinion polls, in fluctuating (and, in some cases, very low) rates of voter turnout, and in declining support for the major political parties. This trend is neither new nor particularly surprising. Its social and political conditions were analysed many decades ago by Max Weber among others.[12] With the professionalization of politics and the bureaucratization of political parties, active participation in the political process has become increasingly restricted to full-time officials who have turned politics into a career. For the vast majority of individuals, participation in this process amounts to little more than a choice exercised every four or five years between candidates who appear increasingly indistinguishable in terms of their overall policies and increasingly ineffective in terms of their capacity to alter the course of events. Since political parties depend on electoral support to win power, they constantly seek to distinguish themselves from other parties through the reiteration of distinctive slogans, the denunciation of their rivals, etc. But for many individuals, these activities appear like the all-too-predictable moves in a game with which they have little sympathy or empathy, and towards which they express their lack of sympathy by declining the occasional invitation to play.

A second problem stems from the coexistence of representative democracy with a complex array of market-generated inequalities. Historically the institutions of representative democracy have developed in a close and reciprocal relation with the wealth-generating organizations of a privatized market economy. As Marx and others emphasized, these economic organizations generated not only wealth but also massive inequalities in terms of the distribution of resources and life chances. But the various experiments which have been undertaken in the course of the twentieth century to eliminate these inequalities through the partial or total abolition of the privatized market economy – whether in the form of the large-scale programmes of nationalization undertaken in some Western countries, or in the form of the centralized command economy attempted in the former Soviet Union and elsewhere – have proven to be equivocal successes at best, dismal failures at worst. Less radical attempts to intervene in the economy through fiscal policy, regulatory bodies and welfare institutions have succeeded to some extent in reducing the inequalities generated by the market, but they have by no means eliminated them. Given the sheer scale and complexity of the problems involved in managing a modern economy, and the uncertainty about the extent to which the reduction of inequalities can be reconciled with the maintenance of dynamic economic activity, it seems doubtful whether representative democratic regimes could succeed in eliminating market-generated inequalities. These regimes are dependent on market economies which they can regulate but never completely control; and hence they are always vulnerable to the criticism that, while formally enfranchising all citizens by providing them with the right to vote, they have nevertheless acquiesced in the process by which individuals are unequally empowered, in terms of their economic resources and life chances, through the relatively autonomous operations of the market.

The third problem is that, by translating democratic practices into a set of rules which define the conditions under which political parties can compete for and exercise power, representative democracy effectively limits the scope of these practices. As parties are engaged first and foremost in struggles with one another, competing for electoral support within a political field defined by the rules of the democratic game, they can easily lose touch with the concerns of ordinary individuals and they may be slow to respond to the changes that are affecting their lives. Moreover, if democratic practices are restricted to the sphere of institutionalized politics, then there are many spheres of social life – from the workplace to the home, from the relations of authority between employers and employees to the relations of intimacy between friends – which are effectively excluded from the operation of democratic decision-making procedures.

It is significant that some of the most serious challenges to representative democracy in recent years have been directed against this historically effective restriction of democratic practices to the sphere of institutionalized politics. These challenges are directed against, not the idea of democracy as such, but rather the near-exclusive embodiment of democratic principles in the parliamentary institutions of the modern state. The rise of extraparliamentary social movements and pressure groups – including the civil rights movement, the women's movement and environmental groups – is an indication of the fact that many individuals feel that the established political institutions have not addressed with a sufficient degree of urgency some of the issues which concern them most. By organizing themselves in extraparliamentary movements and groups, these individuals have placed new issues on the political agenda and opened up areas of social life – hitherto largely neglected by the established parties – to critical scrutiny. They have also set in motion processes of democratization beyond the sphere of institutionalized politics –

for example, at the level of relations between the sexes[13] – whose consequences have yet to be fully played out.

A fourth problem stems from the fact that representative democracy has been institutionalized primarily at the level of the nation-state, and the theorists of representative democracy have generally taken it for granted that the territorially bounded nation-state was the most appropriate framework for the operation of democratic rule. But the globalizing tendencies of modern social life have rendered this territorial delimitation increasingly problematic.[14] Particular nation-states are increasingly embedded in networks of power (economic, political, coercive and symbolic) which extend well beyond their boundaries and which limit, to an extent which varies greatly from one country to another, the room to manoeuvre of democratically elected national governments. Moreover, there are a range of issues – concerning, for instance, the activities of transnational corporations, problems of pollution and environmental degradation, the resolution of armed conflict and the proliferation of weapons of mass destruction – which cannot be satisfactorily addressed within the political framework of the nation-state.

It seems clear that the problems confronting the institutions of representative democracy today are enormous; once the self-congratulatory rhetoric of democracy's most vociferous champions has faded away, the grounds for celebration appear to be rather thin. What is much less clear is what, if anything, can be done to rectify the situation. Is there a feasible way to bridge the gulf between electors and their representatives? To stem the tide of cynicism and disillusionment? To create a more active and participatory form of democratic government?

It is undoubtedly tempting to respond to such questions by turning back to the classical model of the polis for inspiration and by trying to imagine a new world in which the issues that affected people's lives would be actively discussed by them, in which anyone concerned about an issue would have the right to express their opinion on it, and in which decisions would be based on the consent (perhaps even the consensus) of those involved. From a moral point of view, there is much to be said in favour of this model of direct, participatory democracy. It recognizes all individuals as equal and autonomous agents who bear responsibility for their own fate. It emphasizes the importance of dialogue and argument, rather than violence and force, as the means of resolving differences. It reduces the risks of particular individuals or

groups pursuing their interests at the expense of others and without taking the views of others into account. And it endows individuals with the status of agents who actively shape their lives and
history, rather than regarding them merely as bodies that are
swept along by the tide.

While the model of direct, participatory democracy has considerable moral appeal, it is hardly compelling as a practical response
to the dilemmas of democratic politics in the modern age. For the
model presupposes certain social and symbolic conditions which
are rarely met by the circumstances under which most decision-
making processes take place today.[15] It presupposes, first, a shared
spatial-temporal locale in which individuals can come together to
discuss issues of common concern. Second, it presupposes a
certain equality of status among the participants. Third, it presupposes a process of dialogue through which individuals are able to
express their views, question the views of others, engage in argument and debate, and thereby arrive at a discursively formed
judgement. In short, the model presupposes a process of
dialogical communication among individuals of more or less equal
status who come together to form, through argument and debate,
a collective will.

Now there may well be circumstances where this model of
direct, participatory democracy could be applied with some degree of effectiveness today – in relatively small-scale local communities and associations, for example. But at the levels at which
many of the most important decisions are taken today (and the
levels at which, given the growing interconnectedness of the modern world, more decisions will have to be taken in the future), the
model of direct, participatory democracy is a forlorn hope. It has
no practical purchase on the problems raised by the need to make
decisions which will affect the lives of countless individuals who
are widely dispersed in time and space. The difficulty is not simply
one of implementation, as if the model itself were fine but the
process of putting it into practice had encountered certain obstacles. The difficulty is more fundamental: the model is based on
certain conditions which, given the scale and complexity of modern societies and the growing interconnectedness of the modern
world, are increasingly remote from the actual circumstances in
which many decisions have to be taken today.

If the model of direct, participatory democracy is of limited
value, what alternatives are there? Are there practical and effective
ways of reinvigorating the democratic ideal today, without either

resigning oneself to the existing institutions of representative democracy, which seem to deliver too little, or succumbing to the allure of the classical model, which seems to promise too much? Here it is helpful, in my view, to consider the idea of 'deliberative democracy' – not so much as an alternative to representative institutions but as a way of developing and enriching them.[16] By 'deliberative democracy' I mean a conception of democracy which treats all individuals as autonomous agents capable of forming reasoned judgements through the assimilation of information and different points of view, and which institutionalizes a variety of mechanisms to incorporate individual judgements into collective decision-making processes. The deliberative conception of democracy focuses attention on the *processes* by which judgements are formed and decisions are taken. Individuals are called on to consider alternatives, to weigh up the reasons and arguments offered in support of particular proposals and, on the basis of their consideration of different points of view, to form reasoned judgements. In a deliberative conception of democracy, the legitimacy of a decision stems from the fact that the decision is the outcome of a process of generalized deliberation. A deliberative conception does not assume that each individual already possesses a predetermined will or set of preferences, nor does it define legitimacy as merely the arithmetic summation of individual preferences. Rather, the process of deliberation itself is crucial, for it is through this process, through the weighing up of arguments and different points of view, that individuals come to form their wills.[17]

The process of deliberation is necessarily open-ended. As more information is made available and as individuals consider the arguments and claims advanced by others, they may question and gradually modify their original views. The horizons of their understanding may be broadened as they strive to take account of the points raised by others. This open-ended process of argument and counterargument, claim and counterclaim, may be brought to a temporary close by a vote, which provides an index at a particular point in time of the views of individuals who have engaged – with varying degrees of involvement, no doubt – in a process of generalized deliberation. It follows that, within the framework of deliberative democracy, the majority principle provides a justifiable basis for decision-making. For if, given the opportunity to consider various alternatives, a majority is persuaded of the merits of a particular proposal, then that proposal carries legitimacy for the time being, until a point is reached (if ever it is) when a majority is persuaded otherwise.[18]

If the idea of deliberative democracy enables us to preserve and elaborate some of the key ideas handed down by the tradition of democratic thought, it also enables us to avoid some potential pitfalls. In the first place, it is important to stress that a *deliberative* conception of democracy is not necessarily a *dialogical* conception. The formation of reasoned judgements does not require individuals to participate in dialogue with others.[19] There are no good grounds for assuming that the process of reading a book or watching a television programme is, by itself, less conducive to deliberation than engaging in a face-to-face conversation with others. On the contrary, by providing individuals with forms of knowledge and information to which they would not otherwise have access, mediated quasi-interaction can stimulate deliberation just as much as, if not more than, face-to-face interaction in a shared locale. This is not to say that all forms of mediated communication will, in practice, stimulate deliberation – doubtless that would be untrue. But it is to say that we should free ourselves from the idea that the process of deliberation, and of the formation of reasoned judgement, bears a privileged relation to the dialogical form of symbolic exchange.

By separating the idea of deliberative democracy from dialogical communication and from face-to-face interaction in a shared locale, we can also see why the idea of deliberative democracy is distinct from – and, indeed, bears no necessary connection to – the model of direct, participatory democracy. To engage in a process of deliberation does not require individuals to gather together in a shared locale to express their views and to listen to the opinions of others; it does not presuppose that citizen assemblies, or some other type of gathering, is the only legitimate (or the most appropriate) forum for deliberation. On the contrary, it may well be that in some contexts and in some respects citizen assemblies obstruct rather than facilitate the process of reasoned, level-headed deliberation. Rather than encouraging the careful weighing-up of alternatives, assemblies may arouse the passions and induce individuals to take decisions on the basis of considerations which have little to do with reasoned judgement.[20] So the idea of deliberative democracy is not vulnerable to the criticisms that can be levelled at the model of direct, participatory democracy. Advocating the process of deliberation does not commit oneself to the view that forms of direct, participatory democracy are the most appropriate mechanisms for institutionalizing the deliberative process.

What, then, are the practical implications of the idea of deliberative democracy? Can anything more concrete be said about the institutional conditions that would favour its development? In practical terms, the challenge posed by the idea of deliberative democracy is to find new ways of expanding and institutionalizing deliberative processes, and new mechanisms for feeding the results of deliberation into decision-making procedures. The more that individuals are able to participate in deliberation concerning the issues that affect them, and the more that the results of such deliberation are fed into decision-making procedures, the greater their democratic stake will be in the social and political organizations that shape their lives. The challenge is to find ways of deepening the democratic stake by enlarging the scope of deliberative processes, enhancing their quality and ensuring that they have perceptible consequences for the decisions taken at various levels of social and political life.

Viewed from this perspective, we can see that media institutions have a particularly important role to play in the development of a deliberative democracy. For they are the principal means by which individuals acquire information and encounter different points of view on matters about which they may be expected to form reasoned judgements. They also provide individuals with a potential mechanism for articulating views which have been marginalized or excluded from the sphere of mediated visibility. The cultivation of diversity and pluralism in the media is therefore an essential condition of the development of deliberative democracy, not an optional and dispensable extra. Deliberation thrives on the clash of competing views; nothing is more destructive of the process of deliberation than an orchestrated chorus of opinion which allows for no dissent. By securing the conditions under which power can be challenged and a diversity of views can be expressed, the principle of regulated pluralism provides part of the institutional framework within which the idea of deliberative democracy could be practically developed.

In the actual conditions of modern societies, a deliberative democracy would therefore be, to a significant extent, a mediated democracy, in the sense that processes of deliberation would depend on media institutions both as a means of information and as a means of expression. There is no need to assume that the relation between deliberative democracy and the media would find its most appropriate expression in some kind of electronic town hall, or in other somewhat fanciful forms of 'tele-democracy' which have become staple features in the writings of futurologists.[21] Rather, the vigorous application of the principle of regulated pluralism, coupled with the development of new mechanisms which would enable the reasoned judgements of ordinary individuals to be incorporated reflexively into decision-making processes at various levels of social and political life, would go some way towards a renewal of democratic politics. It would help to disperse power outwards and downwards, creating multiple centres of power and diversified networks of communication and information flow. It would help to draw ordinary individuals into processes of deliberation and thereby deepen their democratic stake in social and political life, while at the same time recognizing that, in the complex and interconnected world of the late twentieth century, different levels of decision-making involving representative bodies are indispensable.

It would be ingenuous to suppose that these proposals for a deliberative democracy would succeed in overcoming, or even ameliorating to a significant degree, the problems confronted by democratic politics in the modern age. These problems are rooted in fundamental features of social organization and long-term processes of social change, and they do not admit of easy resolution. But they may help to steer us away from the lure of immediacy which the model of direct, participatory democracy continues to exercise on the modern political imagination. And they may help us to envisage a form of democratic life which recognizes all individuals to be autonomous and responsible agents capable of forming reasoned judgements, without expecting them to be, or supposing that they realistically could be, partners in a dialogue.

Towards an Ethics of Global Responsibility

Is there a normative or ethical dimension to the new kind of publicness created by the media? This question may seem strangely old-fashioned to some. For it has become customary in some circles of social and cultural theory to regard ethical reflection as a preoccupation of the past, as a residual expression of a legislating reason that sought – fruitlessly and, in some cases, with disastrous consequences – to derive universally binding principles of human conduct. The collapse of the universalist project has left the nature and scope of ethical inquiry surrounded in a haze of uncertainty. Some have argued that moral-practical questions can be properly raised and answered only *in situ*, as part of a process through which the members of a community renew the bonds that tie them together. Others have suggested that, rather than trying to pare down the aims of ethical inquiry by acknowledging its situated, historical character, it would be better to put it aside altogether: ethical precepts, however encompassing in scope, could only serve to encumber the self and restrict its creative self-formation. Ethics should give way to an aesthetics of the self, to a conception of the self as a work of art that is freely and continuously re-created over time.

While the question of whether mediated publicness has a normative or ethical dimension may seem old-fashioned to some, to others it may seem oddly out of place. For the media are one domain, it may seem, from which serious ethical concerns were banished long ago. With the growing commercialization of media institutions, the moral and political ideals held by some of the early media entrepreneurs were increasingly displaced by criteria of efficiency and profitability. Media products themselves – or so the argument goes – became increasingly standardized and stereotypical; they trivialized and sensationalized, they concerned themselves with fleeting events, and they relinquished any capacity they once may have had to transcend the banalities of daily life. And the reception of media products has become just another form of consumption, a source of excitement, entertainment and pleasure. Of course, the reception of media products may have certain distinctive characteristics (require certain skills to decode, give rise to certain kinds of gratification, etc.); but in terms of its ethical significance, it may seem little different from the consumption of refrigerators or potatoes or any other commodity. The rise of the media, or so it seems, was not good news for ethics.

Part of the enduring appeal of Habermas's original account of the transformation of the public sphere is that it offers a sharp critical perspective on what one might describe as the ethical hollowing-out of public life. The emergence of the bourgeois public sphere in eighteenth-century Europe was not just an institutional development: it also had a moral-practical dimension. The bourgeois public sphere was a realization – albeit very partial

– of what Habermas sometimes refers to as 'the critical principle of publicity' (or of 'publicness' – *Öffentlichkeit*). This is an idea which Habermas traced back to Kant's writings on enlightenment;[22] it is the idea that the personal opinions of private individuals could evolve into a public opinion through a process of rational-critical debate which was open to all and free from domination. Habermas maintained that despite the decline of the bourgeois public sphere, which provided a partial and imperfect realization of this idea, the critical principle of publicity retains its value as a normative ideal, a kind of critical yardstick by means of which the shortcomings of existing institutions can be assessed and the outlines of alternative forms of social organization can be sketched.

The normative issues that Habermas was addressing in *Structural Transformation* have continued to preoccupy him over the years, but the way in which he addresses these issues has changed in certain respects. Habermas became increasingly convinced that his earlier approach – in which normative issues were addressed largely through an immanent critique of a historically emerging set of ideas – was unsatisfactory. It did not provide a sufficiently compelling account of why the principles once expressed in the bourgeois public sphere should continue to have any hold on us today. Habermas therefore moved away from the kind of immanent critique developed in *Structural Transformation* and tried to show – eventually by means of his theory of communicative action and his notion of discourse ethics – that the normative problems confronting a critical theory of society could be handled in terms of a conception of rationality which has a certain binding and unavoidable character.[23]

Habermas's reworking of the normative dimension of the public sphere in terms of his theory of communicative action has not gone unchallenged. There is an extensive critical literature dealing with Habermas's conception of discourse ethics and his analysis of moral-practical issues.[24] Many commentators have cast doubt on what they see as an attempt to resurrect, in a somewhat modified form, the Kantian principle of universalizability – an attempt which is unlikely, in their view, to be any more successful than the many attempts which have gone before. Other commentators, while more sympathetic to Habermas's overall project, have doubted whether, in view of the plurality of evaluative and interpretative standpoints characteristic of modern societies, it makes sense to try to construct a moral and political theory on the basis of a notion of rational consensus. For Habermas's proposal is that a norm would be valid or just (*richtig*), or an institution would be legitimate, only if, were the norm or institution to be openly discussed by everyone affected by it under conditions free from constraint, it would elicit their consent; but this requirement seems much too strong, and it is difficult to see how it could be applied with any hope of success to the controversial moral and political issues of our time.

Apart from these objections, which have been well aired in the critical literature, there is a further problem with Habermas's approach which has hardly been considered by his critics, but which bears directly on our concerns. As I argued in an earlier chapter, Habermas's conception of the public sphere – whether in the form of the bourgeois public sphere which emerged in the eighteenth century, or in the form of his own, philosophically more elaborate model of practical discourse – is a spatial and dialogical conception. It is based on the idea that individuals come together in a shared locale to engage in dialogue with one another, as equal participants in a face-to-face conversation. The problem, however, is that this conception bears little relation to the kinds of action and communication which have become increasingly common in the modern world. Today actions can affect individuals who are widely dispersed in space and time; and the media have created forms of communication which do not involve dialogical conversation in a shared locale. Habermas's model of practical discourse is essentially an extension (albeit a highly elaborate one) of the traditional conception of publicness as co-presence. Hence it is difficult to relate this model to the kinds of action and communication – and to the distinctive type of publicness created by the media – with which we are so familiar today.

Viewed from this perspective, we can see through some of the hazy unreality that surrounds Habermas's work. In principle it may seem plausible to suggest that an action would be correct or a norm would be just if and only if everyone affected by it, having had the opportunity to discuss it together under conditions free from domination, were willingly to assent to it. But what could this possibly mean in practice in a world where many actions and norms affect thousands or even millions of individuals who are widely dispersed in space (and perhaps also in time)? Actions leading to the destruction of the rain forests or the depletion of the ozone layer, for example, are likely to affect populations across the globe and could seriously impair the life conditions of future generations. What could it mean in practice to suggest that the correctness or otherwise of such actions would be determined by the outcome of a debate in which everyone affected by them would have the opportunity to participate as free and equal conversational partners? Such a debate is simply not feasible, and any attempt to stage a debate on this scale would be little more than pretence. Millions would be reduced to silence while others spoke in their name, and the concerns of future generations would find no place on the agenda of the living.

Examples of this kind highlight the fact that ways of thinking about moral-practical issues have not kept pace with the developments that have transformed (and continue to transform) our world. As Hans Jonas has shown, our ways of thinking are rooted in a traditional conception of ethics which was fundamentally anthropocentric in orientation and which was narrowly circumscribed in spatial and temporal terms.[25] Matters of ethical significance, according to this traditional conception, were essentially interhuman in character: they had to do with the relations between human beings (or with an individual's relation to himself or herself). The ways in which human beings dealt with the nonhuman world of nature was, to all intents and purposes, ethically neutral. Moreover, the spatial and temporal scope of ethical reflection was relatively limited. Ethics was geared to forms of action whose effective range was small, and to forms of interaction which were essentially face-to-face. The ethical universe was composed of contemporaries, of individuals situated in the here and now, and ethical reflection was a morality of proximity.

Today we can no longer think about moral-practical issues in this way. Today, thanks to the development of technologies and the massive concentration of resources, actions can have consequences that stretch far beyond the immediate locale. The ethical universe can no longer be thought of as a world of co-present contemporaries. The conditions of nearness and contemporaneity no longer hold, and the ethical universe must be enlarged to comprise distant others who, while remote in space and time, may nevertheless be part of an interconnected sequence of actions and their consequences. Moreover, as we have become increasingly aware of the devastating impact of human action on the environment, it has become increasingly doubtful whether the non-human world of nature can be treated simply as the ethically neutral backdrop to human action and interaction. We seem to bear some responsibility for the world of the non-human, even though the inhabitants of this world (as well as the succeeding generations of human beings who will inherit the world) are in no position to press their claims upon us.

We must seek to develop a way of thinking about moral-practical issues which does justice to the new and historically unprecedented circumstances under which these issues arise today. It is a way of thinking that must be based on a recognition of the interconnectedness of the modern world and the fact that spatial and temporal proximity has ceased to be relevant as a measure of ethical significance. It is a way of thinking that must be based, at least in part, on a sense of responsibility for others – not just the formal sense of responsibility, according to which a responsible individual is one who is accountable for his or her own actions, but a stronger and more substantive sense, according to which individuals bear some responsibility for the well-being of others and share a mutual obligation to treat others with dignity and respect.[26] It is a way of thinking which must recognize that our substantive responsibility extends well beyond the proximate sphere of others with whom we interact in our day-to-day lives; in an increasingly interconnected world, the horizons of responsibility extend increasingly to others who are distant in space and time, as well as to a non-human world of nature whose destiny is increasingly interwoven with our own. And, finally, it is a way of thinking that must take full account of the enormity of the stakes, as the growth of power at the disposal of human beings has reached the point at which the survival of the species and of the planet can no longer be assured.

There can be little doubt that the various media of communication have played, and will continue to play, a crucial role in cultivating some sense of responsibility for our collective fate. They have helped to create a sense of responsibility which is not restricted to localized communities, but which is shared on a much wider scale. They have helped to set in motion a certain 'democratization of responsibility', in the sense that a concern for distant others becomes an increasing part of the daily lives of more and more individuals. It is difficult to watch images of civilians caught up in military conflict or of children dying of malnutrition without feeling that the plight of these individuals is – in some sense and to some degree – a matter for our concern. It is difficult to read reports of animal species threatened with extinction by the activities of poachers without feeling some sense of responsibility – mixed, perhaps, with feelings of sadness and guilt – for their fate.

Of course, such feelings do not by themselves constitute a process of moral-practical thinking, but their significance should not be underestimated. They attest to the possibility that the increasing diffusion of information and images through the media may help to stimulate and deepen a sense of responsibility for the non-human world of nature and for the universe of distant others who do not share one's own conditions of life.

It would be naive to suppose that, as a basis for the renewal of moral-practical thinking in the late twentieth century, this incipient sense of responsibility is anything other than precarious. We all know how fragile the sense of responsibility for distant others, how fleeting the pang of conscience, can be; we all know how easy it is, when others are far removed from the circumstances of our daily lives, to turn our attention away from their plight while we concern ourselves with those who benefit from the immediacy of face-to-face interaction. We know how the sheer scale and frequency of the calamities that take place in the world today can threaten to overwhelm us, giving rise to a kind of moral fatigue which can neutralize our capacity to feel compassion. We know how dramatic images can be cynically manipulated and exploited for the purposes of mobilizing sympathy or support on the part of viewing audiences. Above all, we know that there is a yawning chasm between a sense of responsibility, on the one hand, and a willingness and capacity to take effective action, on the other. Individuals may feel a deep sense of concern about the plight of distant others or about the destruction of the global environment; but given the enormous complexity of the processes that have produced the crises and predicaments we face today, and given the difficulty of intervening effectively in processes that are in many cases poorly understood, many people may feel reluctant or unable to translate their sense of concern into a determinate course of action.

Precarious, certainly; insignificant, certainly not. The development of communication media has fuelled a growing awareness of the very interconnectedness and interdependency which this development, among others, has helped to create. It has nourished a sense of responsibility, however fragile, for a humanity that is commonly shared and for a world that is collectively inhabited. It is this sense of responsibility which could form part of a new kind of moral-practical reflection which has broken free from the anthropocentric and spatial-temporal limitations of the traditional conception of ethics, a kind of reflection which might stand in some tolerably coherent relation to the realities of an increasingly interconnected world. This is a world, as Jonas observed,[27] in which our capacity to act at a distance, to set in motion processes that can have far-reaching consequences in space and in time, greatly exceeds our capacity to understand and to judge: the causal reach of our actions constantly outstrips our prescience. Whether we can develop our sense of responsibility into a form of moral-practical reflection which would provide some reasoned guidance for the conduct of human affairs, and whether we can gain sufficient understanding of complex humanly created processes to intervene effectively in them, it is difficult to say. But to attempt to do so might be the best – the only – option we have.

Notes

Introduction

1 Carlo Ginzburg, *The Cheese and the Worms: The Cosmos of a Sixteenth-Century Miller*, trans. John and Anne Tedeschi (London: Routledge and Kegan Paul, 1980), pp. 5–6. My discussion of this example is based on Ginzburg's brilliant, sleuth-like reconstruction of the life and world-view of Menocchio, a miller who was tried on two separate occasions for his heretical beliefs and eventually burned at the stake by order of the Holy Office.

2 See especially Max Horkheimer and Theodor W. Adorno, 'The Culture Industry: Enlightenment as Mass Deception', in their *Dialectic of Enlightenment*, trans. John Cumming (New York: Seabury Press, 1972), pp. 120–67; Theodor W. Adorno, *The Culture Industry: Selected Essays on Mass Culture*, ed. J. M. Bernstein (London: Routledge, 1991).

3 For critical appraisals of the contribution of the early critical theorists to the study of the media, see Douglas Kellner, *Critical Theory, Marxism and Modernity* (Cambridge: Polity Press, 1989), chs 5 and 6; John B. Thompson, *Ideology and Modern Culture: Critical Social Theory in the Era of Mass Communication* (Cambridge: Polity Press, 1990), ch. 2.

4 See Jürgen Habermas, *The Structural Transformation of the Public Sphere: An Inquiry into a Category of Bourgeois Society*, trans. Thomas Burger with Frederick Lawrence (Cambridge: Polity Press, 1989).

5 See Harold A. Innis, *Empire and Communications* (Oxford: Oxford University Press, 1950) and *The Bias of Communications* (Toronto: University of Toronto Press, 1951). For a sympathetic assessment of

Innis's contribution, see James W. Carey, 'Space, Time, and Communications: A Tribute to Harold Innis', in his *Communication as Culture: Essays on Media and Society* (Boston: Unwin Hyman, 1989), pp. 142–72.

6 See Joshua Meyrowitz, *No Sense of Place: The Impact of Electronic Media on Social Behavior* (New York: Oxford University Press, 1985).

7 See especially Hans-Georg Gadamer, *Truth and Method* (London: Sheed and Ward, 1975); Paul Ricoeur, *Hermeneutics and the Human Sciences: Essays on Language, Action and Interpretation*, ed. and trans. John B. Thompson (Cambridge: Cambridge University Press, 1981); Clifford Geertz, *The Interpretation of Cultures* (New York: Basic Books, 1973). On the relevance of this tradition to the study of the media, see Peter Dahlgren, 'The Modes of Reception: For a Hermeneutic of TV News', in Phillip Drummond and Richard Patterson (eds), *Television in Transition* (London: British Film Institute, 1985), pp. 235–49; Thompson, *Ideology and Modern Culture*, ch. 6.

Chapter 1 Communication and Social Context

1 For an elaboration of this notion of cultural analysis, see John B. Thompson, *Ideology and Modern Culture: Critical Social Theory in the Era of Mass Communication* (Cambridge: Polity Press, 1990), ch. 3.

2 Clifford Geertz, *The Interpretation of Cultures* (New York: Basic Books, 1973), p. 5.

3 See J. L. Austin, *How to Do Things with Words*, 2nd edn, ed. J. O. Urmson and Marina Sbisà (Oxford: Oxford University Press, 1976).

4 This account is developed in more detail in John B. Thompson, *Critical Hermeneutics: A Study in the Thought of Paul Ricoeur and Jürgen Habermas* (Cambridge: Cambridge University Press, 1981), ch. 4; and *Ideology and Modern Culture*, ch. 3.

5 On the concept of field, see Pierre Bourdieu, *Distinction: A Social Critique of the Judgement of Taste*, trans. Richard Nice (Cambridge: Harvard University Press, 1984); *The Logic of Practice*, trans. Richard Nice (Cambridge: Polity Press, 1990); and 'Some Properties of Fields', in his *Sociology in Question*, trans. Richard Nice (London: Sage, 1993), pp. 72–7.

6 See especially Michael Mann, *The Sources of Social Power*, vol. 1: *A History of Power from the Beginning to AD 1760* (Cambridge: Cambridge University Press, 1986). See also Ernest Gellner, *Plough, Sword and Book: The Structure of Human History* (London: Collins Harvill, 1988); Anthony Giddens, *The Nation-State and Violence:*

Volume Two of a Contemporary Critique of Historical Materialism (Cambridge: Polity Press, 1985).

Both Mann and Giddens distinguish four main types of power. Where my account differs most significantly from their work is in the analysis of what I call, following Bourdieu, 'symbolic power'. Used in a general way, the notion of symbolic power is better suited to capture some of the general features of symbolic activity than are Mann's notion of 'ideological power' or Giddens's notion (derived from Foucault) of 'surveillance'. The main problem with Mann's notion of ideological power is that it stretches the sense of the term 'ideology' too far, and thus loses the connection between ideology, domination and critique. It is better, in my view, to use the term 'ideology' in a more restricted fashion (see *Ideology and Modern Culture*, ch. 1), and to use the more general notion of symbolic power to grasp the ways in which symbolic forms are employed to influence and shape the course of events. The main problem with Giddens's notion of surveillance is that it highlights only one rather limited set of the uses to which symbolic forms are put – namely, the ways in which the state and other organizations gather information and employ it to control populations. But this notion places too much emphasis on the monitoring activities of the state and is not broad enough to grasp the many other ways that information and communication are used.

It is also noteworthy that authors such as Mann and Giddens have given relatively little direct and sustained consideration to the nature and impact of communication media in the modern world. The first volume of Mann's history of power mentions printing only in passing (pp. 442–3) and does not discuss its development or explore its implications, even though by 1760 (the end date of Mann's first volume) printing had existed for 300 years and printed materials were in general circulation in Europe and elsewhere. In the second volume, which covers the period 1760–1914, Mann attributes a more significant role to the diffusion of printed materials and to the development of what he calls 'discursive literacy'; however, his analysis of communication media is framed and limited by his overriding theoretical concern, which is to explain the rise of classes and nation-states and to examine their interconnections. (See Michael Mann, *The Sources of Social Power*, vol. 2: *The Rise of Classes and Nation-States, 1760–1914* (Cambridge: Cambridge University Press, 1993).) Somewhat similar comments could be made with regard to the work of Giddens, Bourdieu, Foucault and most other social theorists, social analysts and historical sociologists, though I shall not pursue this line of criticism here.

7 See Pierre Bourdieu, 'The Forms of Capital', trans. Richard Nice, in J. G. Richardson (ed.), *Handbook of Theory and Research for the*

Sociology of Education (Westport, Conn.: Greenwood Press, 1986), pp. 241–58; and *Distinction,* pp. 114ff.

8 The term 'symbolic power' is borrowed from Bourdieu; see especially his *Language and Symbolic Power,* ed. John B. Thompson, trans. Gino Raymond and Matthew Adamson (Cambridge: Polity Press, 1991). However, my use of this term differs in various respects from the way in which it is used by Bourdieu. Most importantly, I do not wish to imply, as Bourdieu does, that the exercise of symbolic power necessarily presupposes a form of 'misrecognition' (*méconnaissance*) on the part of those who are subjected to it. The exercise of symbolic power often does involve shared belief and active complicity, and in some cases these beliefs may be erroneous or rooted in a limited understanding of the social bases of power, but these should be regarded as contingent possibilities rather than necessary presuppositions.

9 See I. J. Gelb, *A Study of Writing: The Foundations of Grammatology* (London: Routledge and Kegan Paul, 1952); David Diringer, *Writing* (London: Thames and Hudson, 1962); Jack Goody, *The Domestication of the Savage Mind* (Cambridge: Cambridge University Press, 1977).

10 In England, the protection of copyright was not formally established in law until the early eighteenth century, but arrangements for protecting the right of printing books existed from the early sixteenth century. These arrangements had two principal sources: concern on the part of the Crown to suppress the printing of seditious and heretical material; and the concern of printers and booksellers to protect their sole and exclusive right to print particular works. During the first half of the sixteenth century the Crown claimed prerogative rights in certain classes of books and granted the sole privilege of printing them to its assigns. From the mid-sixteenth century, the task of regulating the activities of printers and booksellers was increasingly taken over by the Stationers' Company, created by a decree of the Star Chamber in 1556 and incorporated the following year. The Stationers' Company consisted of 97 named persons who were authorized to print books. The company kept a register of printers who acquired the right to copy books and other works; any unauthorized printing by a piratical printer could be stopped by the company, which had the power to seize and destroy books and to search and close down presses. The Stationers' 'copyright' (although the term was not generally used at the time) was effectively a mechanism for regulating the book trade in the interests of certain printers and booksellers and in partnership with the Crown; it was a way of protecting the right of commercial enterprises to print and sell copies of a work without fear of piracy. The modern idea of copyright as a right of the author did not develop until the eighteenth century,

following the enactment of the Statute of Anne in 1709. For further details see Thomas E. Scrutton, *The Laws of Copyright* (London: John Murray, 1883), ch. 4; Lyman Ray Patterson, *Copyright in Historical Perspective* (Nashville, Tenn.: Vanderbilt University Press, 1968); Sir Frank Mackinnon, 'Notes on the History of English Copyright', in Margaret Drabble (ed.), *The Oxford Companion to English Literature*, 5th edn (Oxford: Oxford University Press, 1985), pp. 1113-25.

11 The impact of enhanced reproducibility on the status of the traditional work of art was examined by Walter Benjamin in his classic essay, 'The Work of Art in the Age of Mechanical Reproduction', in his *Illuminations*, trans. Harry Zohn (London: Fontana, 1973), pp. 219-53.

12 The term 'distanciation' is derived from Paul Ricoeur; see especially his *Hermeneutics and the Human Sciences: Essays on Language, Action and Interpretation*, ed. and trans. John B. Thompson (Cambridge: Cambridge University Press, 1981). However, the way in which I use this term does not coincide with Ricoeur's use. For Ricoeur, 'distanciation' refers to the process by which written discourses, or texts, are severed from their original contexts of production; Ricoeur regards this as a distinctive feature of written, as opposed to spoken, discourse. I doubt, however, whether it is helpful to draw this broad distinction between spoken and written discourse and to restrict the notion of distanciation to the latter. How, on this account, would we deal with unwritten forms of mediated discourse, such as those transmitted via television? In my view, it is more fruitful to regard *all* kinds of symbolic production and exchange as involving varying degrees of distanciation in time and space. Any process of symbolic production and exchange – as well as other kinds of action – involves some degree of movement through time and space, however limited it may be. This more general notion of space-time distanciation has been elaborated in detail by Anthony Giddens; see especially his *A Contemporary Critique of Historical Materialism*, vol. 1: *Power, Property and the State* (London: Macmillan, 1981); *The Constitution of Society: Outline of the Theory of Structuration* (Cambridge: Polity Press, 1984); and *The Nation-State and Violence*.

13 Harold Innis was among the first to call attention to the ways in which technical media of communication enable individuals to exercise power across space and time; see his *Empire and Communications* (Oxford: Oxford University Press, 1950) and his *The Bias of Communication* (Toronto: University of Toronto Press, 1951).

14 For further discussion of this point see Thompson, *Ideology and Modern Culture*, pp. 154-62.

15 See Denis McQuail, 'Uncertainty about the Audience and the Organization of Mass Communication', in Paul Halmos (ed.), *The*

Sociology of Mass-Media Communicators, Sociological Review Monograph 13 (Keele: Keele University, 1969), pp. 75–84. For a more extended discussion of the ways in which television broadcasting organizations monitor their audiences, see Ien Ang, *Desperately Seeking the Audience* (London: Routledge, 1991).

16 See Helga Nowotny, *Time: The Modern and Postmodern Experience*, trans. Neville Plaice (Cambridge: Polity Press, 1994).

17 See Eviatar Zerubaval, 'The Standardization of Time: A Sociohistorical Perspective', *American Journal of Sociology*, 88 (1982), pp. 1–23.

18 See Stephen Kern, *The Culture of Time and Space 1880–1918* (London: Weidenfeld and Nicolson, 1983); Marshall Berman, *All That Is Solid Melts into Air: The Experience of Modernity* (London: Verso, 1983).

19 This term is explained in chapter 7.

20 See J. Crofts, *Packhorse, Waggon and Post: Land Carriage and Communications under the Tudors and Stuarts* (London: Routledge and Kegan Paul, 1967), p. 123: 'Coach-journeys were so dreary and exhausting that travellers were thankful to move by short stages, and to reckon their progress in days.'

21 See David Harvey, *The Condition of Postmodernity: An Enquiry into the Origins of Cultural Change* (Oxford: Blackwell, 1989), pp. 240ff. See also Janelle's discussion of the somewhat similar notion of 'time-space convergence': Donald G. Janelle, 'Global Interdependence and its Consequences', in Stanley D. Brunn and Thomas R. Leinbach (eds), *Collapsing Space and Time: Geographic Aspects of Communication and Information* (London: HarperCollins Academic, 1991), pp. 47–81.

22 See E. P. Thompson, 'Time, Work-Discipline and Industrial Capitalism', reprinted in his *Customs in Common: Studies in Traditional Popular Culture* (New York: New Press, 1991), pp. 352–403.

23 See Nowotny, *Time*, ch. 2.

24 The classic example of this kind of cultural criticism is Roland Barthes's *Mythologies*, trans. Annette Lavers (St Albans: Paladin, 1973). See also Judith Williamson, *Decoding Advertisements: Ideology and Meaning in Advertising* (London: Marion Boyars, 1978).

25 See, for example, Elihu Katz and Paul F. Lazarsfeld, *Personal Influence: The Part Played by People in the Flow of Mass Communications* (Glencoe, Ill.: Free Press, 1950); J. Klapper, *The Effects of Mass Communication* (New York: Free Press, 1960); J. G. Blumer and E. Katz (eds), *The Uses of Mass Communications* (London and Beverly Hills: Sage, 1974). For an overview of research on audiences and media effects, see Denis McQuail, *Mass Communication Theory: An Introduction*, 2nd edn (London and Beverly Hills: Sage, 1987), chs 8 and 9.

26 For a selection of recent studies, see Janice A. Radway, *Reading the Romance: Women, Patriarchy, and Popular Literature* (Chapel Hill: University of North Carolina Press, 1984); Tamar Liebes and Elihu Katz, *The Export of Meaning: Cross-Cultural Readings of 'Dallas'* (New York and Oxford: Oxford University Press, 1990); James Lull, *China Turned On: Television, Reform, and Resistance* (London: Routledge, 1990). For discussions of the relevance of ethnographic inquiry to media studies, see James Lull, *Inside Family Viewing: Ethnographic Research on Television's Audiences* (London: Routledge, 1990); David Morley, *Television, Audiences and Cultural Studies* (London: Routledge, 1992); Roger Silverstone, *Television and Everyday Life* (London: Routledge, 1994).

27 See Michel de Certeau, *The Practice of Everyday Life*, trans. Stephen Randall (Berkeley: University of California Press, 1984), especially chs 3 and 12.

28 See James Lull, *Inside Family Viewing*, ch. 5; David Morley, *Family Television: Cultural Power and Domestic Leisure* (London: Comedia, 1986).

29 'Readers are travellers,' remarked Michel de Certeau, 'they move across lands belonging to someone else, like nomads poaching their way across fields they did not write, despoiling the wealth of Egypt to enjoy it themselves' (*The Practice of Everyday Life*, p. 174).

30 The social differentiation of skills and competences, as well as schemata of judgement and taste, have been highlighted by Pierre Bourdieu in numerous studies. See especially Pierre Bourdieu, Alain Darbel and Dominique Schnapper, *The Love of Art: European Museums and their Public*, trans. C. Beattie and N. Merriman (Cambridge: Polity Press, 1990); Pierre Bourdieu, *The Field of Cultural Production: Essays on Art and Literature*, ed. Randal Johnson (Cambridge: Polity Press, 1993); and Bourdieu, *Distinction*.

31 See Hans-Georg Gadamer, *Truth and Method* (London: Sheed and Ward, 1975), pp. 235ff.

32 See Paul Ricoeur, *Hermeneutics and the Human Sciences*, ch. 7.

Chapter 2 The Media and the Development of Modern Societies

1 For more detailed accounts of the economic transformations associated with the rise of modern societies, see Immanuel Wallerstein, *The Modern World-System I: Capitalist Agriculture and the Origins of the European World-Economy in the Sixteenth Century* (New York: Academic Press, 1974) and *The Modern World-System II: Mercantilism and the Consolidation of the European World-Economy, 1600–1750*

(New York: Academic Press, 1980); see also Michael Mann, *The Sources of Social Power*, vol. 1: *A History of Power from the Beginning to AD 1760* (Cambridge: Cambridge University Press, 1986), chs 12–15.

2 See, for example, Charles Tilly (ed.), *The Formation of National States in Western Europe* (Princeton: Princeton University Press, 1975); Charles Tilly, *Coercion, Capital, and European States, AD 990–1990* (Oxford: Blackwell, 1990); Mann, *The Sources of Social Power*; Anthony Giddens, *The Nation-State and Violence: Volume Two of a Contemporary Critique of Historical Materialism* (Cambridge: Polity Press, 1985); Gianfranco Poggi, *The State: Its Nature, Development and Prospects* (Cambridge: Polity Press, 1990).

3 See Tilly, *Coercion, Capital and European States*, pp. 14–15 and *passim*.

4 See Poggi, *The State*, pp. 42ff.; Mann, *The Sources of Social Power*, pp. 475ff.

5 Anthony D. Smith, *National Identity* (Harmondsworth: Penguin, 1991), p. 14.

6 See Poggi, *The State*, pp. 40ff.; Mann, *The Sources of Social Power*, pp. 379ff.

7 See Thomas Francis Carter, *The Invention of Printing in China and its Spread Westward* (New York: Ronald Press Company, 1955); Joseph Needham, *Science and Civilisation in China*, vol. 5: *Chemistry and Chemical Technology*, part 1: *Paper and Printing*, by Tsien Tsuen-Hsuin (Cambridge: Cambridge University Press, 1985); Lucien Febvre and Henri-Jean Martin, *The Coming of the Book: The Impact of Printing 1450–1800*, trans. David Gerard (London: Verso, 1976), ch. 1.

8 See Carter, *The Invention of Printing in China*, ch. 22; Needham, *Science and Civilisation in China*, pp. 201–3.

9 See Carter, *The Invention of Printing in China*, chs 19 and 24; Needham, *Science and Civilisation in China*, pp. 303–19.

10 See S. H. Steinberg, *Five Hundred Years of Printing* (Harmondsworth: Penguin, 1974), pp. 17ff.; Febvre and Martin, *The Coming of the Book*, pp. 45ff.

11 Febvre and Martin, *The Coming of the Book*, pp. 186, 248–9. The estimate assumes an average pre-1500 print run of 500 copies per edition. The figures for the sixteenth century are even more striking. Febvre and Martin estimate that between 1500 and 1600 somewhere between 150,000 and 200,000 editions were produced. Assuming an average edition of 1,000 copies, then 150–200 million copies were produced in the sixteenth century (ibid., p. 262).

12 Ibid., pp. 249ff.

13 See Elizabeth L. Eisenstein, *The Printing Press as an Agent of Change: Communications and Cultural Transformations in Early-Modern Europe*,

vols 1 and 2 (Cambridge: Cambridge University Press, 1979), pp. 12ff.

14 Febvre and Martin, *The Coming of the Book*, p. 126.

15 Ibid., pp. 125–6. See also Eisenstein, *The Printing Press as an Agent of Change*, pp. 408–9, 443–5.

16 See Steinberg, *Five Hundred Years of Printing*, pp. 260–72; Febvre and Martin, The *Coming of the Book*, pp. 244–7, 297ff.

17 On the relation between printing and the Reformation, see Eisenstein, *The Printing Press as an Agent of Change*, ch. 4; Febvre and Martin, *The Coming of the Book*, pp. 287–319.

18 See Margaret Aston, *The Fifteenth Century: The Prospect of Europe* (London: Thames and Hudson, 1968), p. 76; 'In doing for Luther what the copyists had done for Wycliffe', remarks Aston, 'the printing presses transformed the field of communications and fathered an international revolt. It was a revolution.'

19 Febvre and Martin, *The Coming of the Book*, p. 291.

20 Ibid., p. 197.

21 See Peter Burke, *The Renaissance* (London: Macmillan, 1987), pp. 46–7.

22 See Eisenstein, *The Printing Press as an Agent of Change*, pp. 181ff.

23 On the relation between printing and the scientific revolution, see ibid., chs 5–8.

24 Ibid., p. 430.

25 See Natalie Zemon Davis, 'Printing and the People', in her *Society and Culture in Early Modern France* (Stanford: Stanford University Press, 1975), p. 210. For general discussions of literacy in early modern Europe, see Carlo M. Cipolla, *Literacy and Development in the West* (Harmondsworth: Penguin, 1969); R. A. Houston, *Literacy in Early Modern Europe: Culture and Education 1500–1800* (London: Longman, 1988).

26 See Peter Burke, *Popular Culture in Early Modern Europe* (London: Temple Smith, 1978), pp. 253–4.

27 Davis, 'Printing and the People', p. 211.

28 See Laurence Fontaine, *Histoire du colportage en Europe, XVe–XIXe siècle* (Paris: Albin Michel, 1993).

29 See Davis, 'Printing and the People', pp. 213–14; Roger Chartier, 'Figures of the "Other": Peasant Reading in the Age of Enlightenment', in his *Cultural History: Between Practices and Representations*, trans. Lydia G. Cochrane (Cambridge: Polity Press, 1988), pp. 151–71; Roger Chartier, 'Leisure and Sociability: Reading Aloud in Early Modern Europe', in Susan Zimmerman and Ronald F. E. Weissman (eds), *Urban Life in the Renaissance* (Newark: University of Delaware Press, 1989), pp. 105–20; Robert Darnton, 'History of Reading', in Peter Burke (ed.), *New Perspectives on Historical Writing* (Cambridge: Polity Press, 1991), pp. 140–67.

30 Febvre and Martin, *The Coming of the Book*, pp. 319–22.
31 Despite this broad pattern of decline, Latin did not suddenly disappear: it was still spoken and written in some contexts well into the nineteenth and twentieth centuries. See Peter Burke, '"Heu Domine, Adsunt Turcae": A Sketch for a Social History of Post-Medieval Latin', in his *The Art of Conversation* (Cambridge: Polity Press, 1993), pp. 34–65.
32 Hugh Seton-Watson, *Nations and States: An Inquiry into the Origins of Nations and the Politics of Nationalism* (London: Methuen, 1977), p. 48.
33 See Eugen Weber, *Peasants into Frenchmen: The Modernization of Rural France 1870–1914* (London: Chatto and Windus, 1979), especially ch. 6; Pierre Bourdieu, *Language and Symbolic Power*, ed. John B. Thompson, trans. Gino Raymond and Matthew Adamson (Cambridge: Polity Press, 1991), pp. 46ff.
34 See Benedict Anderson, *Imagined Communities: Reflections on the Origin and Spread of Nationalism*, rev. edn (London: Verso, 1991), especially pp. 43–6. Of course, Anderson was not the first to point to a possible connection between the development of printing and the rise of nationalism. For earlier discussions see, among others, Harold A. Innis, *Empire and Communications* (Oxford: Oxford University Press, 1950), pp. 211ff.; Marshall McLuhan, *The Gutenberg Galaxy: The Making of Typographic Man* (Toronto: University of Toronto Press, 1962), pp. 216ff.
35 See Howard Robinson, *The British Post Office: A History* (Princeton: Princeton University Press, 1948), p. 4.
36 For an account of the 'Thurn und Taxis' postal service, as it became known, see Martin Dallmeier, *Quellen zur Geschichte des Europäischen Postwesens, 1501–1806*, Part 1: *Quellen-Literatur-Einleitung* (Kallmünz: Michael Lassleben, 1977), pp. 49–220.
37 Robinson, *The British Post Office*, chs 1–3; J. Crofts, *Packhorse, Waggon and Post: Land Carriage and Communications under the Tudors and Stuarts* (London: Routledge and Kegan Paul, 1967), chs 8–17.
38 The identification of what could be called 'the first newspaper' is a matter of dispute, though most historians would agree that something resembling the modern newspaper first appeared around 1610. See Eric W. Allen, 'International Origins of the Newspapers: The Establishment of Periodicity in Print', *Journalism Quarterly*, 7 (1930), pp. 307–19; Joseph Frank, *The Beginnings of the English Newspaper, 1620–1660* (Cambridge, Mass.: Harvard University Press, 1961), ch. 1.
39 Frank, *The Beginnings of the English Newspaper*, p. 3.
40 Folke Dahl, *A Bibliography of English Corantos and Periodical Newsbooks, 1620–1642* (London: Bibliographical Society, 1952), p. 22.

41 Frank, *The Beginnings of the English Newspaper*, pp. 21–2.

42 Anthony Smith, *The Newspaper: An International History* (London: Thames and Hudson, 1979), pp. 56–7.

43 For more detailed discussions of the history of political control and censorship of the press, see F. S. Siebert, *Freedom of the Press in England, 1476–1776* (Urbana: University of Illinois Press, 1952); A. Aspinall, *Politics and the Press, c.1780–1850* (Brighton: Harvester, 1973); Smith, *The Newspaper*, chs 3–5.

44 See especially James Mill, 'Liberty of the Press', in his *Essays on Government, Jurisprudence, Liberty of the Press and Law of Nations* (New York: Kelly, 1967); John Stuart Mill, 'On Liberty', in his *Utilitarianism, On Liberty and Considerations on Representative Government*, ed. H. B. Acton (London: Dent, 1972). I shall return to these issues in chapter 8.

45 See Jürgen Habermas, *The Structural Transformation of the Public Sphere: An Inquiry into a Category of Bourgeois Society*, trans. Thomas Burger with the assistance of Frederick Lawrence (Cambridge: Polity Press, 1989). For more detailed exposition and critical discussion of Habermas's argument, see Craig Calhoun (ed.), *Habermas and the Public Sphere* (Cambridge, Mass.: MIT Press, 1992); John B. Thompson, 'The Theory of the Public Sphere', *Theory, Culture and Society*, 10 (1993), pp. 173–89.

46 See Oskar Negt and Alexander Kluge, *Öffentlichkeit und Erfahrung. Zur Organisationsanalyse von bürgerlicher und proletarischer Öffentlichkeit* (Frankfurt: Suhrkamp, 1972); Günther Lottes, *Politische Aufklärung und plebejisches Publikum. Zur Theorie und Praxis des englischen Radikalismus im späten 18. Jahrhundert* (Munich: Oldenbourg, 1979); Geoff Eley, 'Nations, Publics, and Political Cultures: Placing Habermas im the Nineteenth Century', in Calhoun (ed.), *Habermas and the Public Sphere*, pp. 289–339; Arlette Farge, *Subversive Words: Public Opinion in Eighteenth-Century France*, trans. Rosemary Morris (Cambridge: Polity Press, 1994).

47 See especially E. P. Thompson, *The Making of the English Working Class* (Harmondsworth: Penguin, 1968); and Christopher Hill, *The World Turned Upside Down* (Harmondsworth: Penguin, 1975).

48 Eley, 'Nations, Publics, and Political Cultures', pp. 306, 321.

49 See Jürgen Habermas, 'Further Reflections on the Public Sphere', trans. Thomas Burger, in Calhoun (ed.), *Habermas and the Public Sphere*, pp. 421–61.

50 See Habermas's preface to *The Structural Transformation of the Public Sphere*, p. xviii.

51 For a brief and somewhat cryptic allusion to this issue, see Jürgen Habermas, 'Concluding Remarks', in Calhoun (ed.), *Habermas and the Public Sphere*, pp. 464–5.

52 See, for example, Joan Landes, *Women and the Public Sphere in the*

Age of the French Revolution (Ithaca, N.Y.: Cornell University Press, 1988); Mary P. Ryan, *Women in Public: Between Banners and Ballots, 1825–1880* (Baltimore: Johns Hopkins University Press, 1990); Carole Pateman, *The Sexual Contract* (Cambridge: Polity Press, 1988); Catherine Hall, *White, Male and Middle Class: Explorations in Feminism and History* (Cambridge: Polity Press, 1992).
53 Habermas, 'Further Reflections on the Public Sphere', p. 428.
54 See Alan J. Lee, *The Origins of the Popular Press in England 1855–1914* (London: Croom Helm, 1976).
55 For a brief selection of relevant works, see George Boyce, James Curran and Pauline Wingate (eds), *Newspaper History from the Seventeenth Century to the Present Day* (London: Constable, 1978); James Curran and Jean Seaton, *Power Without Responsibility: The Press and Broadcasting in Britain*, 4th edn (London: Routledge, 1991); Ben H. Bagdikian, *The Media Monopoly*, 4th edn (Boston: Beacon Press, 1992); Jeremy Tunstall and Michael Palmer, *Media Moguls* (London: Routledge, 1991); Alfonso Sánchez-Tabernero, *Media Concentration in Europe: Commercial Enterprise and the Public Interest* (Dusseldorf: European Institute for the Media, 1993). For a summary of the main trends, see John B. Thompson, *Ideology and Modern Culture: Critical Social Theory in the Age of Mass Communication* (Cambridge: Polity Press, 1990), especially pp. 193–205.
56 'From Press Baron to Media Mogul', *Labour Research* (Nov. 1993), pp. 11–12. The four groups are Rupert Murdoch's News International (which owns the *Sun*, *The Times*, *Today*, *News of the World* and *Sunday Times*); the Mirror Group (formerly Robert Maxwell's empire, this group owns the *Daily Mirror*, *Sunday Mirror*, *People*, *Sporting Life*, *Sunday Mail* and *Daily Record*); United Newspapers (*Daily Express*, *Sunday Express*, *Daily Star*); and Viscount Rothermere's Daily Mail and General Trust (*Daily Mail*, *Mail on Sunday*).
   The patterns of concentration vary from country to country and from one sector of the industry to another, reflecting the differing conditions under which the media industries have developed. In the United States, for instance, there are few (if any) national newspapers, but there are around 1,600 locally or regionally based daily newspapers. By the late 1980s, 14 large corporations controlled more than half of the daily newspaper business in the US. (See Bagdikian, *The Media Monopoly*, pp. 17ff.)
57 The British television industry offers a good example of this coexistence. While the BBC and the major ITV companies remain the dominant organizations and control a large proportion of the resources, there are many small, independent production companies, based primarily in London, which produce programmes on a commissioned basis for Channel Four and, increasingly, for the BBC and ITV. See Jeremy Tunstall, *Television Producers* (London: Routledge,

1993); Scott Lash and John Urry, *Economies of Signs and Space* (London and Thousand Oaks, Calif.: Sage, 1994), ch. 5.

58 For further details on the technical innovations, see M. MacLaren, *The Rise of the Electrical Industry during the Nineteenth Century* (Princeton: Princeton University Press, 1943); D. G. Tucker, 'Electrical Communication', in T. I. Williams (ed.), *A History of Technology*, vol. 6: *The Twentieth Century c.1900 to c.1950* (Oxford: Oxford University Press, 1978).

59 See W. R. Maclauren, *Invention and Innovation in the Radio Industry* (New York: Macmillan, 1949); S. G. Sturmey, *The Economic Development of Radio* (London: Duckworth, 1958).

60 See Peter Hall and Paschall Preston, *The Carrier Wave: New Information Technology and the Geography of Innovation, 1846–2003* (London: Unwin Hyman, 1988), especially part 4.

Chapter 3   The Rise of Mediated Interaction

1 This term is similar to the expression used by Horton and Wohl: in an early and insightful article, they suggested that mass communication gives rise to a new type of social relationship which they call 'para-social interaction'. See Donald Horton and R. Richard Wohl, 'Mass Communication and Para-Social Interaction: Observations on Intimacy at a Distance', *Psychiatry*, 19 (1956), pp. 215–29.

2 Of course, there are ways in which a reader can respond to an author: he or she can write to the author (if the author is still alive), or write a review of the book which the author is likely to see, or simply refuse to read anything else written by the author. But these modes of response are limited in character and are quite different from the kind of dialogical exchange characteristic of face-to-face and mediated interaction.

3. The use of computer technology in combination with telecommunications systems may give rise to forms of communication and interaction which diverge in some respects from the characteristics of mediated interaction and quasi-interaction. For example, computer networks allow for the possibility of two-way communication which is not oriented towards specific others but which is 'many-to-many' in character (conferencing, bulletin boards, etc.). For further discussion of these and other forms of 'computer-mediated communication' or interaction, see the contributions by Linda S. Harasim, John S. Quarterman and Howard Rheingold in Linda S. Harasim (ed.), *Global Networks: Computers and International Communication* (Cambridge, Mass.: MIT Press, 1993), part 1.

4 See Roger Chartier, *The Order of Books: Readers, Authors, and Librar-*

ies in Europe between the Fourteenth and Eighteenth Centuries, trans. Lydia G. Cochrane (Cambridge: Polity Press, 1993), especially pp. 8ff.

5 See Paul Saenger, 'Silent Reading: Its Impact in Late Medieval Script and Society', *Viator: Medieval and Renaissance Studies*, 13 (1982), pp. 364–414; Robert Darnton, 'History of Reading', in Peter Burke (ed.), *New Perspectives on Historical Writing* (Cambridge: Polity Press, 1991), pp. 140–67.

6 See especially Erving Goffman, *The Presentation of Self in Everyday Life* (Harmondsworth: Penguin, 1969). Goffman's work has been imaginatively applied to the analysis of the media by various authors. See Joshua Meyrowitz, *No Sense of Place: The Impact of Electronic Media on Social Behavior* (New York: Oxford University Press, 1985); David L. Altheide, *Media Power* (Beverly Hills: Sage, 1985); Richard V. Ericson, Patricia M. Baranek and Janet B. L. Chan, *Negotiating Control: A Study of News Sources* (Toronto: University of Toronto Press, 1989).

7 Goffman, *The Presentation of Self in Everyday Life*, pp. 100ff.

8 See A. A. L. Reid, 'Comparing Telephone with Face-to-Face Contact', in Ithiel de Sola Pool (ed.), *The Social Impact of the Telephone* (Cambridge, Mass.: MIT Press, 1977), pp. 386–414.

9 See Horton and Wohl, 'Mass Communication and Para-Social Interaction', pp. 216ff.

10 Ronald Reagan was, of course, one of the more accomplished practitioners of this conversational form of public discourse. For a perceptive analysis of his rhetorical style, see Kathleen Hall Jamieson, *Eloquence in an Electronic Age: The Transformation of Political Speechmaking* (New York: Oxford University Press, 1988), especially chs 6 and 7. Jamieson argues that the advent of television has extended and consolidated a broad shift in the nature of public speaking: 'Where once we expected messages laced with impassioned appeals, now we respond positively to a cooler, more conversational art; where once audiences expected to be conquered by an art bent on battle, today's television viewer expects instead an intimate rhetoric of conciliation' (p. 44).

11 Some of these examples are thoughtfully discussed by Meyrowitz, particularly in relation to the changing role and perception of political leaders; see *No Sense of Place*, ch. 14.

12 For a more detailed analysis of TV chat shows and related forms of audience discussion programmes, see Sonia Livingstone and Peter Lunt, *Talk on Television: Audience Participation and Public Debate* (London: Routledge, 1994).

13 See Daniel Dayan and Elihu Katz, *Media Events: The Live Broadcasting of History* (Cambridge, Mass.: Harvard University Press, 1992).

14 For a more detailed analysis of media events, see the perceptive

account of Dayan and Katz. I shall return to some of these issues in chapter 6, where I examine the transformation of royal rituals by the media.

15 To say this is not to claim, of course, that the media coverage and the anti-war movement were principal causes of the shift in the policy of the American government towards the war, nor is it to suggest – as some commentators have done over the years – that the media coverage 'lost the war' for the United States. There are plenty of reasons to doubt such claims and suggestions. For instance, it seems clear that, at least in the period prior to the Tet offensive of 1968, American television coverage of Vietnam was strongly supportive of US policy and of the American conduct of the War. (See Daniel C. Hallin, *The 'Uncensored War': The Media and Vietnam* (Oxford and New York: Oxford University Press, 1986).) A shift in television's portrayal of the war began to appear at the time of the Tet offensive. But it seems quite likely that this shift was due not so much to the adoption of a more adversarial stance on the part of the broadcasting media, but rather to the fact that the Administration itself was increasingly divided about the war. As Hallin remarks, 'for the most part television was a follower rather than a leader: it was not until the collapse of consensus was well under way that television's coverage began to turn around; and when it did, it only turned so far' (p. 163).

16 For a detailed analysis of media coverage of the Gulf War, see Douglas Kellner, *The Persian Gulf TV War* (Boulder, Colo.: Westview Press, 1992). See also Bruce Cumings, *War and Television* (London: Verso, 1992), ch. 4.

17 Thus, at the beginning of the Gulf War, ex-President Reagan's former Director of Communications, Pat Buchanan, urged the Bush Administration and the Pentagon to keep the blood off the screens: 'Thus far, we have been spared pictures of the carnage created by our air strikes. It would not be a bad thing if this continues. We did not suffer in the Second World War by not having live footage of the horrors of Guadalcanal, Anzio or Normandy' (*New York Post*, quoted in the *Guardian*, 24 January 1991).

18 For a thoughtful discussion of the role of communication media in the upheavals of 1989, see Deirdre Boden, 'Reinventing the Global Village: Communication and the Revolutions of 1989', in Anthony Giddens (ed.), *Human Societies: An Introductory Reader in Sociology* (Cambridge: Polity Press, 1992), pp. 327–31.

Chapter 4 *The Transformation of Visibility*

1 For more detailed accounts of the history of the public–private distinction, see Jürgen Habermas, *The Structural Transformation of the* .

Public Sphere: An Inquiry into a Category of Bourgeois Society, trans. Thomas Burger with the assistance of Frederick Lawrence (Cambridge: Polity Press, 1989), ch. 1; Norberto Bobbio, *Democracy and Dictatorship: The Nature and Limits of State Power*, trans. Peter Kennealy (Cambridge: Polity Press, 1989), ch. 1.

2 See Bobbio, *Democracy and Dictatorship*, ch. 2; see also John Keane, *Democracy and Civil Society* (London: Verso, 1988), especially ch. 2.

3 For a more detailed analysis of intermediate organizations and their growing significance in modern societies, see Alan Ware, *Between Profit and State: Intermediate Organizations in Britain and the United States* (Cambridge: Polity Press, 1989).

4 See Bobbio, *Democracy and Dictatorship*, pp. 17ff. See also Norberto Bobbio, *The Future of Democracy: A Defence of the Rules of the Game*, ed. Richard Bellamy, trans. Roger Griffin (Cambridge: Polity Press, 1987), pp. 79ff.

5 See Simon Hornblower, 'Creation and Development of Democratic Institutions in Ancient Greece', in John Dunn (ed.), *Democracy: The Unfinished Journey, 508 BC to AD 1993* (Oxford: Oxford University Press, 1992), pp. 1–16.

6 Bobbio, *Democracy and Dictatorship*, p. 19; and *The Future of Democracy*, pp. 86–9. Early writings on the *raison d'état* include works by Machiavelli, Botero and other sixteenth-century Italian authors. For a more detailed discussion, see Friedrich Meinecke, *Machiavellism: The Doctrine of Raison d'État and its Place in Modern History*, trans. Douglas Scott (London: Routledge and Kegan Paul, 1957).

7 Habermas, *The Structural Transformation of the Public Sphere*, p. 42.

8 Ibid., pp. 163–5.

9 Ibid., p. 164.

10 A similar criticism could be made of the work of other social theorists whose accounts of the changing character of public life converge in certain respects with Habermas's view. See, for example, Richard Sennett, *The Fall of Public Man* (Cambridge: Cambridge University Press, 1974), especially pp. 282ff.; Alvin W. Gouldner, *The Dialectic of Ideology and Technology: The Origins, Grammar, and Future of Ideology* (London: Macmillan, 1976), especially chs 6–8.

11 See Michel Foucault, *Discipline and Punish: The Birth of the Prison*, trans. Alan Sheridan (Harmondsworth: Penguin, 1977), especially pp. 170ff. For an extended discussion of the role of vision and visibility in Foucault's work, see Martin Jay, *Downcast Eyes: The Denigration of Vision in Twentieth-Century French Thought* (Berkeley: University of California Press, 1993), pp. 381–416.

12 See Jeremy Bentham, *Panopticon; or the Inspection House* (London: T. Payne, 1791); Foucault, *Discipline and Punish*, pp. 200ff.

13 For more detailed discussions of Foucault's work in relation to contemporary forms of surveillance, see Mark Poster, *The Mode of Information: Poststructuralism and Social Context* (Cambridge: Polity

Press, 1990); David Lyon, *The Electronic Eye: The Rise of Surveillance Society* (Cambridge: Polity Press, 1994).

14 As Kantorowicz has shown, the fusing together of mortal and divine elements in the person of the ruler was a key feature of medieval and early modern political thought (see Ernst H. Kantorowicz, *The King's Two Bodies: A Study in Mediaeval Political Theology* (Princeton: Princeton University Press, 1957)). For example, in the pamphlets of the Norman Anonymous written around AD 1100, the king was portrayed as a *persona mixta* which combined temporal and spiritual elements. 'We thus have to recognize [in the king] a *twin person*, one descending from nature, the other from grace . . .' (quoted in ibid., p. 46). In Kantorowicz's account, the doctrine of the *persona mixta* was a theological precursor of the legal fiction, subsequently elaborated by English jurists in the Tudor and later periods, of the 'King's Two Bodies' in which the 'Body natural' and the 'Body politic' were fused indivisibly in 'one Person'.

15 See Clifford Geertz, 'Centers, Kings, and Charisma: Reflections on the Symbolics of Power', in his *Local Knowledge: Further Essays in Interpretive Anthropology* (New York: Basic Books, 1983), pp. 121–46.

16 See S. R. F. Price, *Rituals and Power: The Roman Imperial Cult in Asia Minor* (Cambridge: Cambridge University Press, 1984), especially chs 1, 5 and 9.

17 See Peter Burke, *The Fabrication of Louis XIV* (New Haven, Conn., and London: Yale University Press, 1992); J. H. Elliott, 'Power and Propaganda in the Spain of Philip IV', in Sean Wilentz (ed.), *Rites of Power: Symbolism, Ritual, and Politics since the Middle Ages* (Philadelphia: University of Pennsylvania Press, 1985), pp. 145–73.

18 Burke, *The Fabrication of Louis XIV*, p. 17.

19 The construction of Nixon's image in the 1968 campaign was analysed by Joe McGuinniss in his now-classic study, *The Selling of the President, 1968* (London: Andre Deutsch, 1970).

20 These strategies have been well documented by Mark Hertsgaard, whose work I draw on here; see Mark Hertsgaard, *On Bended Knee: The Press and the Reagan Presidency* (New York: Farrar Straus Giroux, 1988). See also John Anthony Maltese, *Spin Control: The White House Office of Communications and the Management of Presidential News*, 2nd edn (Chapel Hill: University of North Carolina Press, 1994).

21 David Gergen, quoted in Hertsgaard, *On Bended Knee*, p. 32.

22 Ibid., p. 140.

23 Hertsgaard, *On Bended Knee*, p. 52.

24 Goffman insightfully analyses some of the sources of trouble in broadcast talk, but his analysis is concerned primarily with conversational faults; he does not explore the broader social and political

aspects of mediated troubles. See Erving Goffman, 'Radio Talk', in his *Forms of Talk* (Oxford: Blackwell, 1981), pp. 197–327.

25 This example is interestingly discussed by Samuel L. Popkin in *The Reasoning Voter: Communication and Persuasion in Presidential Campaigns* (Chicago: University of Chicago Press, 1991), pp. 1–6.

26 For further discussion of this example, see Colin Seymour-Ure, *The Political Impact of Mass Media* (London: Constable, 1974), p. 59.

27 In June 1992, Dan Quayle was invited to supervise a 'spelling bee' competition at an elementary school in Trenton, New Jersey. The class of 12-year-olds had been drilled beforehand on the words they would be asked to spell, and Quayle had been given a set of cards on which the words were printed. Quayle asked one of the children to spell 'potato', and he printed P-O-T-A-T-O on the blackboard. 'That's fine phonetically,' said Mr Quayle, 'but you're missing just a little bit.' He gave the puzzled child a hint, and the child added a final 'E'. Laughter broke out among reporters at the back of the classroom, who could hardly believe the story they had been given. Quayle's potato gaffe provided the material for countless jokes, cartoons and derogatory comments and fuelled the debate about his suitability for the post of Vice President.

28 Edwina Currie was prone to making ill-judged remarks to the media. But on 3 December 1988 she made a comment that eventually led to her downfall. While being interviewed on television news, she said that most UK egg production was contaminated by salmonella. The comment resulted in a dramatic slump in egg sales and provoked a furious public row – including sharp criticism from the government's own back benches. Numerous writs for damages were issued against Mrs Currie by egg producers. On 16 December she was forced to resign. 'Tory MPs saw her departure as an inevitable consequence of the gaffe which has devastated the poultry and egg industry and threatened costly claims against the Government' (*Guardian*, 17 December 1988, p. 1). The government was obliged to mount a £40 million salvage operation which included the purchase of vast quantities of eggs at taxpayers' expense.

29 A more thorough analysis of scandal would have to take into account a range of other considerations, including cultural variations in codes of behaviour, differences between political systems, and the commercial interests of media organizations. It would also require a more careful differentiation between various types of scandal. Anthony King usefully distinguishes between three types of scandal – those involving sex, those involving money, and those involving power – while recognizing that these three categories often overlap. (See Anthony King, 'Sex, Money, and Power', in Richard Hodder-Williams and James Ceaser (eds), *Politics in Britain and the United*

States: Comparative Perspectives (Durham, N.C.: Duke University Press, 1986), pp. 173–222.)

Although scandals are a pervasive feature of contemporary political life, there is a dearth of good critical literature on the subject. The comparative study of political scandals is, as King rightly observes, still in its infancy. In addition to King's important article, see Manfred Schmitz, *Theorie und Praxis des politischen Skandals* (Frankfurt: Campus Verlag, 1981); Andrei S. Markovits and Mark Silverstein (eds), *The Politics of Scandal: Power and Process in Liberal Democracies* (New York: Holmes and Meier, 1988).

30 One could cite numerous other examples of Parkinson's predicament. Consider, for example, the case of Tim Yeo, a Conservative Member of Parliament and junior minister for the environment in John Major's government. In January 1994 he was forced to resign as environment minister shortly after it had been disclosed in a tabloid newspaper that he had fathered a child in an extramarital affair. This revelation came at a time when John Major's government was pursuing a 'back to basics' policy and placing particular emphasis on 'traditional family values'. Although several members of the government publicly supported Yeo when news of the affair initially broke, the hypocritical potential of the situation was such that his position became, in the end, untenable.

31 Hertsgaard, *On Bended Knee*, p. 323.

Chapter 5 The Globalization of Communication

1 For a review of different usages, see Roland Robertson, *Globalization: Social Theory and Global Culture* (London and Newbury Park, Calif.: Sage, 1992), especially ch. 1.

2 See Immanuel Wallerstein, *The Modern World-System I: Capitalist Agriculture and the Origins of the European World-Economy in the Sixteenth Century* (New York: Academic Press, 1974); Michael Mann, *The Sources of Social Power*, vol. 1: *A History of Power from the Beginning to AD 1760* (Cambridge: Cambridge University Press, 1986), chs 12–15; Peter Dicken, *Global Shift: The Internationalization of Economic Activity*, 2nd edn (London: Paul Chapman, 1992), especially pp. 11–14.

3 See Daniel R. Headrick, *The Tools of Empire: Technology and European Imperialism in the Nineteenth Century* (Oxford: Oxford University Press, 1981), ch. 11; Bernard S. Finn, *Submarine Telegraphy: The Grand Victorian Technology* (Margate: Thanet Press, 1973).

4 Headrick, *The Tools of Empire*, p. 130.

5 For more detailed accounts of the development of the major news

agencies, see Graham Storey, *Reuters' Century 1851–1951* (London: Max Parrish, 1951); Oliver Boyd-Barrett, *The International News Agencies* (London: Constable, 1980); Anthony Smith, *The Geopolitics of Information: How Western Culture Dominates the World* (London: Faber, 1980).

6 The growth and diversification of Reuters in the 1970s and 1980s was particularly pronounced. In 1963, two-thirds of Reuters' revenue of £3 million came from media subscribers. In 1989, the media accounted for only 7 per cent of Reuters' revenue; 55 per cent was derived from the money market, 19 per cent from securities, 8 per cent from commodities and 11 per cent from client services. By 1990 Reuters' overall revenue had risen to £1,369 million, of which 82.5 per cent was earned overseas. (See Jeremy Tunstall and Michael Palmer, *Media Moguls* (London and New York: Routledge, 1991), p. 56.)

7 For a detailed account of the NWICO debate and the role of UNESCO, see Thomas L. McPhail, *Electronic Colonialism: The Future of International Broadcasting and Communication*, 2nd edn (Newbury Park, Calif.: Sage, 1987).

8 On the development of news agencies and other mechanisms of information exchange in Third World countries, see Oliver Boyd-Barrett and Daya Kishan Thussu, *Contra-Flow in Global News: International and Regional News Exchange Mechanisms* (London: John Libbey, 1992).

9 See above, pp. 78–9.

10 For further discussion of the institutional frameworks of broadcasting, see John B. Thompson, *Ideology and Modern Culture: Critical Social Theory in the Era of Mass Communication* (Cambridge: Polity Press, 1991), pp. 183–92.

11 See McPhail, *Electronic Colonialism*, ch. 5; John Howkins, 'The Management of the Spectrum', *InterMedia*, 7.5 (Sept. 1979), pp. 10–22.

12 Howkins, 'The Management of the Spectrum', p. 14.

13 Among the most important and influential of the early studies were the UNESCO-sponsored surveys carried out by Nordenstreng and Varis in 1971–3 and by Varis in 1983. See Kaarle Nordenstreng and Tapio Varis, *Television Traffic – A One-Way Street? A Survey and Analysis of the International Flow of Television Programme Material*, Reports and Papers on Mass Communication, no. 70 (Paris: UNESCO, 1974); Tapio Varis, *International Flow of Television Programmes*, Reports and Papers on Mass Communication, no. 100 (Paris: UNESCO, 1986). Numerous other studies have been carried out. For useful discussions of the relevant literature, see Jeremy Tunstall, *The Media are American: Anglo-American Media in the World* (London: Constable, 1977); Ehihu Katz and George Wedell, *Broadcasting in the Third World: Promise and Performance* (Cambridge,

Mass.: Harvard University Press, 1977); Smith, *The Geopolitics of Information*; Ralph Negrine and S. Papathanassopoulos, *The Internationalization of Television* (London: Pinter, 1990); Preben Sepstrup, *Transnationalization of Television in Europe* (London: John Libbey, 1990); Annabelle Sreberny-Mohammadi, 'The Global and the Local in International Communications', in James Curran and Michael Gurevitch (eds), *Mass Media and Society* (London: Edward Arnold, 1991); Geoffrey Reeves, *Communications and the 'Third World'* (London: Routledge, 1993).

14 See above, pp. 76–8.

15 A recent UNESCO report on world communications showed that, of the 78 largest communication conglomerates ranked according to total media turnover, 39 were based in the United States, 25 in Western Europe, 8 in Japan, 5 in Canada and 1 in Australia; none were based in the Third World. (See *World Communication Report* (Paris: UNESCO, 1989), pp. 104–5.)

16 See, for example, Ben H. Bagdikian, *The Media Monopoly*, 4th edn (Boston: Beacon Press, 1992); Anthony Smith, *The Age of Behemoths: The Globalization of Mass Media Firms* (New York: Priority Press, 1991); Tunstall and Palmer, *Media Moguls*.

17 For further discussion of historical and technical aspects of satellite communications, see Abram Chayes, James Fawcett, Masami Ito, Alexandre-Charles Kiss et al., *Satellite Broadcasting* (London: Oxford University Press, 1973); Jonathan F. Galloway, *The Politics and Technology of Satellite Communications* (Lexington, Mass.: D. C. Heath, 1972).

18 Nordenstreng and Varis, *Television Traffic – A One Way Street?*; see also Tapio Varis, 'Global Traffic in Television', *Journal of Communication*, 24 (1974), pp. 102–9.

19 See Varis, *International Flow of Television Programmes*; Annabelle Sreberny-Mohammadi, 'The "World of the News" Study: Results of International Cooperation', *Journal of Communications*, 34 (1984), pp. 121–34; Sepstrup, *Transnationalization of Television in Europe*.

20 Some commentators have argued that the influence of Western-based news agencies has been exaggerated. See, for example, Robert L. Stevenson, 'The "World of the News" Study: Pseudo Debate', *Journal of Communications*, 34 (1984), pp. 134–8; Michael Tracey, 'The Poisoned Chalice? International Television and the Idea of Dominance', *Daedalus*, 114 (1985), pp. 17–55.

21 See Katz and Wedell, *Broadcasting in the Third World*, ch. 1.

22 For a discussion of some of the issues involved in studying patterns of consumption in relation to the globalization of communication, see Sepstrup, *Transnationalization of Television in Western Europe*, ch. 4.

23 For a concise overview of the theoretical debates, see Sreberny-

Mohammadi, 'The Global and the Local in International Communications', pp. 119–22.

24 See especially Herbert I. Schiller, *Mass Communications and American Empire* (New York: Augustus M. Kelley, 1969). A second edition of this book appeared in 1992 with a substantial new chapter by Schiller in which he reflects on the relevance of the work in the changing global conditions of the late twentieth century; see Schiller, 'A Quarter-Century Retrospective', in *Mass Communications and American Empire*, 2nd edn (Boulder, Colo.: Westview Press, 1992), pp. 1–43. For work in a similar vein see, for example, A. F. Wells, *Picture Tube Imperialism? The Impact of US Television on Latin America* (New York: Orbis, 1972); A. Dorfman and A. Mattelart, *How to Read Donald Duck: Imperialist Ideology in the Disney Comic* (New York: International General Editions, 1975); Herbert I. Schiller, *Communication and Cultural Domination* (White Plains, N.Y.: International Arts and Sciences Press, 1976); Kaarle Nordenstreng and Herbert I. Schiller (eds), *National Sovereignty and International Communication* (Norwood, N.J.: Ablex, 1979); Cees J. Hamelink, *Cultural Autonomy in Global Communications: Planning National Information Policy* (London: Centre for the Study of Communication and Culture, 1988).

25 A distinction is sometimes drawn between 'cultural imperialism' and 'media imperialism', but I shall not pursue this distinction here. (See, for example, Oliver Boyd-Barrett, 'Media Imperialism: Towards an International Framework for the Analysis of Media Systems', in James Curran, Michael Gurevitch and Janet Woollacott (eds), *Mass Communication and Society* (London: Edward Arnold, 1977), pp. 116–35.)

26 The critical literature is extensive. For helpful commentaries, see Tunstall, *The Media are American*, ch. 2; John Tomlinson, *Cultural Imperialism: A Critical Introduction* (London: Pinter, 1991); Reeves, *Communications and the 'Third World'*, ch. 3.

27 This reconstruction of Schiller's argument is based on the original 1969 edition of *Mass Communications and American Empire*.

28 See Dicken, *Global Shift*, especially ch. 2.

29 Ibid., p. 316.

30 See Janet Wasko, *Hollywood in the Information Age: Beyond the Silver Screen* (Cambridge: Polity Press, 1994), ch. 4.

31 See Schiller, 'A Quarter-Century Retrospective'.

32 Ibid., p. 39.

33 Schiller, *Mass Communications and American Empire* (1969 edn), p. 109.

34 See Tunstall, *The Media are American*, pp. 57–9.

35 For a perceptive account of the different forms of cultural encounter and conflict associated with European expansion, see Urs Bitterli, *Cultures in Conflict: Encounters Between European and Non-European*

Cultures, 1492–1800, trans. Ritchie Robertson (Cambridge: Polity Press, 1989).

36 See, for example, Nathan Wachtel's classic study of the Spanish conquest of Peru, *The Vision of the Vanquished: The Spanish Conquest of Peru Through Indian Eyes, 1530–1570*, trans. Ben and Sian Reynolds (Hassocks, Sussex: Harvester Press, 1977); see also Serge Gruzinski, *The Conquest of Mexico: The Westernization of Indian Societies from the Sixteenth to the Eighteenth Century*, trans. Eileen Corrigan (Cambridge: Polity Press, 1993).

37 For further discussion of this point, see Tomlinson, *Cultural Imperialism*, pp. 45–64; Sreberny-Mohammadi, 'The Global and the Local in International Communications', pp. 130–4.

38 See Thompson, *Ideology and Modern Culture*, especially pp. 24–5, 105, 291.

39 See Tamar Liebes and Elihu Katz, *The Export of Meaning: Cross-Cultural Readings of 'Dallas'*, 2nd edn (Cambridge: Polity Press, 1993). See also Daniel Miller's discussion of the significance of soap operas in Trinidad in his *Modernity – An Ethnographic Approach: Dualism and Mass Consumption in Trinidad* (Oxford: Berg, 1994), pp. 247–53.

40 See Annabelle Sreberny-Mohammadi and Ali Mohammadi, *Small Media, Big Revolution: Communication, Culture, and the Iranian Revolution* (Minneapolis: University of Minnesota Press, 1994).

41 Ibid., pp. 186–8.

42 See James Lull, *China Turned On: Television, Reform, and Resistance* (London: Routledge, 1991).

43 Ibid., p. 23.

44 Quoted in ibid., p. 171.

45 Quoted in ibid., pp. 174–5.

46 See Lila Abu-Lughod, 'Bedouins, Cassettes and Technologies of Public Culture', *Middle East Report*, 159.4 (1989), pp. 7–11, 47.

Chapter 6   *The Re-mooring of Tradition*

1 The most significant exception is probably the work of Shils; see Edward Shils, *Tradition* (London: Faber and Faber, 1981). A more recent work – which expresses, however, many of the 'traditional' ways of thinking about tradition – is David Gross, *The Past in Ruins: Tradition and the Critique of Modernity* (Amherst: University of Massachusetts Press, 1992). Of course, the notion of tradition has been discussed more extensively by anthropologists; for a recent example, see P. Boyer, *Tradition as Truth and Communication* (Cambridge: Cambridge University Press, 1990).

2 Karl Marx and Frederick Engels, *Manifesto of the Communist Party*, in *Selected Works in One Volume* (London: Lawrence and Wishart, 1968), p. 38. For an elaboration of this theme, see Marshall Berman, *All That is Solid Melts Into Air: The Experience of Modernity* (London: Verso, 1982).

3 See especially Max Weber, *The Protestant Ethic and the Spirit of Capitalism*, trans. Talcott Parsons (London: Unwin, 1930), pp. 180–3.

4 See especially Ulrich Beck, *Risk Society: Towards a New Modernity*, trans. Mark Ritter (London and Newbury Park, Calif.: Sage, 1992); Anthony Giddens, *Modernity and Self-Identity: Self and Society in the Late Modern Age* (Cambridge: Polity Press, 1991); Ulrich Beck, Anthony Giddens and Scott Lash, *Reflexive Modernization: Politics, Tradition and Aesthetics in the Modern Social Order* (Cambridge: Polity Press, 1994).

5 See Shils, *Tradition*, p. 12.

6 See Martin Heidegger, *Being and Time*, trans. John Macquarrie and Edward Robinson (Oxford: Blackwell, 1962), especially sections 31–3; Hans-Georg Gadamer, *Truth and Method* (London: Sheed and Ward, 1975), especially pp. 235–74.

7 See Max Weber, *Economy and Society: An Outline of Interpretive Sociology*, vol. 1, ed. Guenther Roth and Claus Wittich (Berkeley: University of California Press, 1978), pp. 212ff.

8 Daniel Lerner, *The Passing of Traditional Society: Modernizing the Middle East* (Glencoe, Ill.: Free Press, 1958).

9 Wilbur Schramm, *Mass Media and National Development* (Stanford, Calif.: Stanford University Press, 1964).

10 Lerner, *The Passing of Traditional Society*, p. 405.

11 See Annabelle Sreberny-Mohammadi and Ali Mohammadi, *Small Media, Big Revolution: Communication, Culture, and the Iranian Revolution* (Minneapolis: University of Minnesota Press, 1994).

12 See Gilles Kepel, *The Revenge of God: The Resurgence of Islam, Christianity and Judaism in the Modern World*, trans. Alan Braley (Cambridge: Polity Press, 1994), ch. 1.

13 The contours of this implicit set of concepts, values and beliefs have been charted perceptively (and provocatively) by Zygmunt Bauman among others; see especially his *Modernity and Ambivalence* (Cambridge: Polity Press, 1991).

14 See Eric Hobsbawm and Terence Ranger (eds), *The Invention of Tradition* (Cambridge: Cambridge University Press, 1983).

15 Hugh Trevor-Roper, 'The Invention of Tradition: The Highland Tradition of Scotland', in ibid., pp. 15–41.

16 David Cannadine, 'The Context, Performance and Meaning of Ritual: The British Monarchy and the "Invention of Tradition", *c.*1820–1977', in ibid., pp. 101–64.

17 Ibid., p. 117.
18 Ibid., p. 142; see also J. C. W. Reith, *Into the Wind* (London: Hodder and Stoughton, 1949); Andrew Boyle, *Only the Wind Will Listen: Reith of the BBC* (London: Hutchinson, 1972).
19 For a discussion of the coronation as a mediated ritual, see David Chaney, 'A Symbolic Mirror of Ourselves: Civic Ritual in Mass Society', *Media, Culture and Society*, 5 (1983), pp. 119–35. See also Daniel Dayan and Elihu Katz, *Media Events: The Live Broadcasting of History* (Cambridge, Mass.: Harvard University Press, 1992).
20 For a recent version of this argument, see Gross, *The Past in Ruins*, ch. 4. Surprisingly, however, Gross does not refer to the work of Hobsbawm and his associates on the invention of tradition.
21 See Marie Gillespie, 'Technology and Tradition: Audio-Visual Culture among South Asian Families in West London', *Cultural Studies*, 3 (1989), pp. 226–39; see also Arjun Appadurai, 'Disjuncture and Difference in the Global Cultural Economy', in Mike Featherstone (ed.), *Global Culture: Nationalism, Globalization and Modernity* (London and Newbury Park, Calif.: Sage, 1990), pp. 295–310.
22 Quoted in Gillespie, 'Technology and Tradition', p. 238.
23 See Néstor García Canclini, *Culturas híbridas: Estrategias para entrar y salir de la modernidad* (Mexico, D.F.: Grijalbo, 1989); Jesús Martín-Barbero, *Communication, Culture and Hegemony: From the Media to Mediations*, trans. Elizabeth Fox and Robert A. White (London and Newbury Park, Calif.: Sage, 1993), ch. 9; Stuart Hall, 'The Local and the Global: Globalization and Ethnicity' and 'Old and New Identities, Old and New Ethnicities', in Anthony D. King (ed.), *Culture, Globalization and the World-System* (Basingstoke: Macmillan, 1991), pp. 19–39 and 41–68; James Lull, *Media, Communication, Culture: A Global Approach* (Cambridge: Polity Press, 1994), ch. 5.

Chapter 7 Self and Experience in a Mediated World

1 See especially Paul Ricoeur, 'The Question of the Subject: The Challenge of Semiology', trans. Kathleen McLaughlin, in his *The Conflict of Interpretations: Essays in Hermeneutics*, ed. Don Ihde (Evanston, Ill.: Northwestern University Press, 1974), pp. 236–66. I also draw loosely on other writings by Ricoeur, including *Freud and Philosophy: An Essay on Interpretation*, trans. Denis Savage (New Haven and London: Yale University Press, 1970); *Hermeneutics and the Human Sciences: Essays on Language, Action and Interpretation*, ed. and trans. John B. Thompson (Cambridge: Cambridge University Press, 1981); and *Oneself as Another*, trans. Kathleen Blamey (Chicago: University of Chicago Press, 1992).

2 This point is emphasized and well documented by Bourdieu among others. A central theme of Bourdieu's theory of practice is that the dispositions (or 'habitus') which shape individuals' ways of acting, perceiving, etc., are structured by the differentiated social conditions under which they were acquired. (See especially Pierre Bourdieu, *The Logic of Practice*, trans. Richard Nice (Cambridge: Polity Press, 1990), pp. 52ff.) The emphasis on the social conditions of practice is important, but it is also important to conceptualize these conditions in a way that enriches rather than undermines the notion of the self as a creative, constructive project.

3 Clifford Geertz, *Local Knowledge: Further Essays in Interpretive Anthropology* (New York: Basic Books, 1983).

4 The reflexive character of the self is insightfully explored by Anthony Giddens; see his *Modernity and Self-Identity: Self and Society in the Late Modern Age* (Cambridge: Polity Press, 1991), especially pp. 75ff.

5 James Lull, *China Turned On: Television, Reform, and Resistance* (London: Routledge, 1991), pp. 170ff.

6 See John B. Thompson, *Ideology and Modern Culture: Critical Social Theory in the Era of Mass Communication* (Cambridge: Polity Press, 1990).

7 Ibid., ch 6; and John B. Thompson, 'Depth Hermeneutics and the Analysis of Symbolic Forms', *Sociology*, 25 (1991), pp. 395–401.

8 For a perceptive discussion of this paradox, see Ulrich Beck, *Risk Society: Towards a New Modernity*, trans. Mark Ritter (London and Newbury Park, Calif.: Sage, 1992), especially ch. 5.

9 See Elihu Katz and Paul F. Lazarsfeld, *Personal Influence: The Part Played by People in the Flow of Mass Communications* (Glencoe, Ill.: Free Press, 1955). Of course, this study is rather dated now, and there are many aspects of the analysis which can be questioned. But the central idea of their model of the two-step flow of communication – that media messages are commonly filtered through particular individuals who act as a source of expert advice for others – retains some relevance today.

10 See Janice A. Radway, *Reading the Romance: Women, Patriarchy, and Popular Literature* (Chapel Hill: University of North Carolina Press, 1984).

11 See Anthony Giddens, *The Consequences of Modernity* (Cambridge: Polity Press, 1990), pp. 27ff.; Zygmunt Bauman, *Modernity and Ambivalence* (Cambridge: Polity Press, 1991), pp. 199ff.

12 Clifford Geertz, *The Interpretation of Cultures* (New York: Basic Books, 1973), p. 449.

13 Donald Horton and R. Richard Wohl, 'Mass Communication and Para-Social Interaction: Observations on Intimacy at a Distance', *Psychiatry*, 19 (1956), pp. 215–29.

14 This is one of many accounts recorded by Fred and Judy Vermorel in *Starlust: The Secret Life of Fans* (London: W. H. Allen, 1985), pp. 11–12.

15 See, for example, Henry Jenkins, *Textual Poachers: Television Fans and Participatory Culture* (London and New York: Routledge, 1992). See also the various contributions to Lisa A. Lewis (ed.), *The Adoring Audience: Fan Culture and Popular Media* (London and New York: Routledge, 1992).

16 For a detailed account of the transformative practices of *Star Trek* fans, see Jenkins, *Textual Poachers*, chs 5–8.

17 Quoted in Vermorel and Vermorel, *Starlust*, p. 106.

18 Ibid.

19 This development has been analysed very effectively by Foucault and others. See especially Michel Foucault, *Discipline and Punish: The Birth of the Prison*, trans. Alan Sheridan (Harmondsworth: Penguin, 1977); David Rothman, *The Discovery of the Asylum: Social Order and Disorder in the New Republic* (Boston: Little, Brown, 1971); Michael Ignatieff, *A Just Measure of Pain: The Penitentiary in the Industrial Revolution, 1750–1850* (London: Macmillan, 1978); Stanley Cohen and Andrew Scull (eds), *Social Control and the State: Historical and Comparative Essays* (Oxford: Blackwell, 1983).

20 See Wilhelm Dilthey, *Selected Writings*, ed. and trans. H. P. Rickman (Cambridge: Cambridge University Press, 1976), pp. 184ff., 210ff. See also Hans-Georg Gadamer, *Truth and Method* (London: Sheed and Ward, 1975), pp. 55–63; Richard E. Palmer, *Hermeneutics: Interpretation Theory in Schleiermacher, Dilthey, Heidegger, and Gadamer* (Evanston, Ill.: Northwestern University Press, 1969), pp. 107–11.

21 The analysis of experience in terms of relevance structures was developed by Husserl and Schutz, among others. See especially Alfred Schutz, *Reflections on the Problem of Relevance*, ed. Richard M. Zaner (New Haven, Conn.: Yale University Press, 1970); and Alfred Schutz and Thomas Luckmann, *The Structures of the Life World*, trans. Richard M. Zaner and H. Tristram Engelhardt Jr (London: Heinemann, 1974), pp. 182–229.

22 Jean Baudrillard is perhaps the most well-known proponent of this view. Baudrillard claims that today we have entered a new phase in the history of the subject, a phase that he describes as a new form of schizophrenia: 'In spite of himself the schizophrenic is open to everything and lives in the most extreme confusion . . . Stripped of a stage and crossed over without the least obstacle, the schizophrenic cannot produce the limits of his very being, he can no longer produce himself as a mirror. He becomes a pure screen, a pure absorption and resorption surface of the influent networks.' (Jean Baudrillard, *The Ecstasy of Communication*, trans. Bernard and Caroline Schutze, ed. Sylvère Lotringer (New York: Semiotext(e), 1988), p. 27.)

23 See, for example, Fredric Jameson, *Postmodernism, or, The Cultural Logic of Late Capitalism* (London: Verso, 1991), especially ch. 1.

24 Graham Bamford was a 48-year-old lorry driver who lived in Macclesfield. He had watched the television reports of the civil war in the former Yugoslavia and, according to his father, he had been 'very upset by the film of the massacre in Vitez'. Just after 4 p.m. on 29 April 1993, as the House of Commons was debating what to do about Bosnia, 'Graham walked calmly on to the green at Parliament Square, doused himself in petrol, and struck a match. After the air ambulance had taken him to Queen Mary's Hospital, Roehampton, where he was to die later that evening, police officers discovered a German-language guide to Sarajevo on the grass. Across the flyleaf Graham had written that he thought Britain should do more than stand by as a guard of honour to the Balkan tragedy' (*Guardian*, 12 May 1993).

Chapter 8 The Reinvention of Publicness

1 See especially James Mill, 'Liberty of the Press', in his *Essays on Government, Jurisprudence, Liberty of the Press and Law of Nations* (New York: Kelly, 1967); John Stuart Mill, 'On Liberty', in his *Utilitarianism, On Liberty and Considerations on Representative Government*, ed. H. B. Acton (London: Dent, 1972).

2 See John Stuart Mill, 'On Liberty', p. 150.

3 This point is well argued by David Held. See his 'Democracy, the Nation-State and the Global System', in David Held (ed.), *Political Theory Today* (Cambridge: Polity Press, 1991), pp. 197–235; and 'Democracy: From City-states to a Cosmopolitan Order?', in David Held (ed.), *Prospects for Democracy: North, South, East, West* (Cambridge: Polity Press, 1993), pp. 13–52.

4 See Graham Murdock and Peter Golding, 'The Structure, Ownership and Control of the Press, 1914–76', in George Boyce, James Curran and Pauline Wingate (eds), *Newspaper History from the Seventeenth Century to the Present Day* (London: Constable, 1978), pp. 130–48; James Curran and Jean Seaton, *Power Without Responsibility: The Press and Broadcasting in Britain*, 4th edn (London: Routledge, 1991), especially ch. 7; Jeremy Tunstall, *The Media in Britain* (London: Constable, 1983), ch. 7; Ralph Negrine, *Politics and the Mass Media in Britain* (London: Routledge, 1989), ch. 4.

5 See John B. Thompson, *Ideology and Modern Culture: Critical Social Theory in the Era of Mass Communication* (Cambridge: Polity Press, 1990), pp. 261–2.

6 The principle of regulated pluralism thus stands opposed to those proponents of 'deregulation' and others who advocate a free market

approach to the information and communication industries. See, for instance, Ithiel de Sola Pool, *Technologies of Freedom* (Cambridge, Mass.: Harvard University Press, 1983).

7 It is important to emphasize that the state can impinge on media organizations not only through overt forms of censorship and control, but in diverse and subtle ways. Consider, for instance, the observations of Greg Dyke, former head of London Weekend Television, who argues that the relationship between the government and broadcasting organizations in Britain has, in recent years, increasingly become a dependent one, giving rise to a kind of 'dependency culture, in which broadcasters are increasingly dependent on the actions of government in some cases for their very existence and, in the commercial sector, for their financial success' (Greg Dyke, MacTaggert Lecture at the Edinburgh Television Festival, reported in the *Guardian*, 27 August 1994, p. 27).

8 In this respect, I wish to distinguish the principle of regulated pluralism from the view – put forward by a number of media critics on the left in recent years – that a public sphere can be reconstituted today only through the maximum possible 'decommodification' of communication media. This is the view developed, for instance, by John Keane in *The Media and Democracy* (Cambridge: Polity Press, 1991). Keane argues for a 'revised public service model of communications' which 'implies the development of a publicly funded self-organizing and cosmopolitan civil society which is genuinely pluralist precisely because it is not dominated by commodity production and exchange. Public service media require a *post-capitalist* civil society guaranteed by democratic state institutions' (p. 152). The main problem with this kind of argument is that it presupposes too strong an opposition between pluralism, on the one hand, and commodity production and exchange, on the other. The cultivation of pluralism may require one to regulate the media industries in various ways, but it does not follow that media organizations can contribute to a 'genuinely pluralist' culture only if they are 'post-capitalist' in some sense.

9 To see that the illusion of the conversation writ large continues to exercise considerable power over the contemporary political imagination, one need only consider the attention bestowed on Ross Perot's call for the creation of an 'electronic town hall'. Perot envisages a situation in the near future in which, by virtue of interactive media, the electorate can enter quite freely into conversation with candidates and political figures. Hence, 'without ever leaving your home, you can register your views and the electorate officials can see literally what the people are thinking' (Ross Perot, interviewed by Martin Jacques, *Guardian*, 25 October 1993).

10 See especially David Held, *Models of Democracy* (Cambridge: Polity Press, 1987); David Held (ed.), *Prospects for Democracy*; John Dunn

(ed.), *Democracy: The Unfinished Journey, 508 BC to AD 1993* (Oxford: Oxford University Press, 1992).

11 See John Dunn, 'Conclusion', in *Democracy*, pp. 248ff.

12 See especially Max Weber, 'Politics as a Vocation' and 'Bureaucracy', in *From Max Weber: Essays in Sociology*, trans. and ed. H. H. Gerth and C. Wright Mills (London: Routledge and Kegan Paul, 1948), pp. 77–128, 196–244. For a more recent analysis which has some affinity to Weber's account, see Pierre Bourdieu, 'Political Representation: Elements for a Theory of the Political Field', in his *Language and Symbolic Power*, ed. John B. Thompson, trans. Gino Raymond and Matthew Adamson (Cambridge: Polity Press, 1991), pp. 171–202.

13 See Anthony Giddens, *The Transformation of Intimacy: Sexuality, Love and Eroticism in Modern Societies* (Cambridge: Polity Press, 1992); Ulrich Beck and Elisabeth Beck-Gernsheim, *The Normal Chaos of Love*, trans. Mark Ritter and Jane Wiebel (Cambridge: Polity Press, 1995).

14 See Held, 'Democracy, the Nation-State and the Global System' and 'Democracy: From City-states to a Cosmopolitan Order?'.

15 The limitations of the classical model and its inapplicability to conditions of large-scale social organization have, of course, been discussed by many authors in the tradition of liberal democratic thought; see, for example, John Stuart Mill, 'Representative Government', in his *Utilitarianism*, especially pp. 217–18. For a more recent discussion which highlights the significance of the model of face-to-face interaction implicit in Greek political thought and its legacy, see Peter Laslett, 'The Face to Face Society', in Peter Laslett (ed.), *Philosophy, Politics and Society* (Oxford: Blackwell, 1956), pp. 157–84.

16 The idea of deliberative democracy has been discussed by a number of authors in recent years. See, for example, Bernard Manin, 'On Legitimacy and Political Deliberation', trans. Elly Stein and Jane Mansbridge, *Political Theory*, 15 (1987), pp. 338–68; Joshua Cohen, 'Deliberation and Democratic Legitimacy', in Alan Hamlin and Philip Pettit (eds), *The Good Polity: Normative Analysis of the State* (Oxford: Blackwell, 1989), pp. 17–34; David Miller, 'Deliberative Democracy and Social Choice', in David Held (ed.), *Prospects for Democracy*, pp. 74–92; John S. Dryzek, *Discursive Democracy: Politics, Policy, and Political Science* (Cambridge: Cambridge University Press, 1990); James S. Fishkin, *Democracy and Deliberation: New Directions for Democratic Reform* (New Haven and London: Yale University Press, 1991); Seyla Benhabib, 'Deliberative Rationality and Models of Democratic Legitimacy', *Constellations*, 1 (1994), pp. 26–52. Much of the literature on deliberative democracy draws inspiration from Habermas's recent work on communicative rationality and

discourse ethics, but I shall defer discussion of Habermas's recent work until the following section.

17 Bernard Manin expresses this point well: 'a legitimate decision does not represent the *will* of all, but is one that results from the *deliberation of all*. It is the process by which everyone's will is formed that confers its legitimacy on the outcome, rather than the sum of already formed wills' ('On Legitimacy and Political Deliberation', p. 352).

18 See Manin, 'On Legitimacy and Political Deliberation', p. 359; Benhabib, 'Deliberative Rationality and Models of Democratic Legitimacy', p. 33.

19 In this respect, one might have reservations about James Fishkin's otherwise thoughtful and innovative proposals for democratic reform. Fishkin proposes the development of 'deliberative opinion polls' in which a statistically representative sample of the population would be brought together and allowed to discuss specific issues over an extended period of time. The polls would seek to create a direct, participatory form of democracy among a group of participants who, 'as a statistical microcosm of the society, represent or stand for the deliberations of the whole' (*Democracy and Deliberation*, p. 93). Deliberative opinion polls would thus 'provide the possibility of recreating the conditions of the face-to-face society in a manner that serves democracy in the large-scale nation-state' (pp. 92–3). But, quite apart from the problems of assuming that the deliberations of a statistically representative sample can stand for the deliberations of the whole, why should one insist, as Fishkin does, that deliberation requires face-to-face dialogue?

20 As Joshua Cohen aptly remarks, 'In the absence of a realistic account of the functioning of citizen assemblies, we cannot simply assume that large gatherings with open-ended agendas will yield any deliberation at all, or that they will encourage participants to regard one another as equals in a free deliberative procedure' ('Deliberation and Democratic Legitimacy', p. 30).

21 For a sober assessment of some of the issues raised by the potential uses of new communication technologies for democratic reform, see F. Christopher Anterton, *Teledemocracy: Can Technology Protect Democracy?* (Newbury Park, Calif.: Sage, 1987).

22 See Jürgen Habermas, *The Structural Transformation of the Public Sphere: An Inquiry into a Category of Bourgeois Society*, trans. Thomas Burger with the assistance of Frederick Lawrence (Cambridge: Polity Press, 1989), especially pp. 102ff.

23 See especially Jürgen Habermas, *The Theory of Communicative Action*, vol. 1: *Reason and the Rationalization of Society*, trans. Thomas McCarthy (Cambridge: Polity Press, 1984); 'Discourse Ethics: Notes on a Program of Philosophical Justification', in his *Moral Consciousness and Communicative Action*, trans. Christian Lenhardt

and Shierry Weber Nicholsen (Cambridge: Polity Press, 1990), pp. 43–155; *Justification and Application: Remarks on Discourse Ethics*, trans. Ciaran P. Cronin (Cambridge: Polity Press, 1993); and *Faktizität und Geltung: Beiträge zur Diskurstheorie des Rechts und des demokratischen Rechtsstaats* (Frankfurt: Suhrkamp, 1992).

24 See, for example, Seyla Benhabib and Fred Dallmayr (eds), *The Communicative Ethics Controversy* (Cambridge, Mass.: MIT Press, 1990); Thomas McCarthy, 'Practical Discourse: On the Relation of Morality to Politics', in his *Ideals and Illusions: On Reconstruction and Deconstruction in Contemporary Critical Theory* (Cambridge, Mass.: MIT Press, 1991), pp. 181–99.

25 See Hans Jonas, 'Technology and Responsibility: Reflections on the New Tasks of Ethics', in his *Philosophical Essays: From Ancient Creed to Technological Man* (Englewood Cliffs, N.J.: Prentice-Hall, 1974), pp. 3–20; and his *The Imperative of Responsibility: In Search of an Ethics for the Technological Age*, trans. Hans Jonas with the collaboration of David Herr (Chicago: University of Chicago Press, 1984). See also Zygmunt Bauman, *Postmodern Ethics* (Oxford: Blackwell, 1993), especially pp. 217ff.

26 On the distinction between formal and substantive responsibility, see Jonas, *The Imperative of Responsibility*, pp. 90ff. See also Richard J. Bernstein, 'Rethinking Responsibility', *Social Research*, 61.4 (1994), pp. 833–52; Bernstein offers a perceptive analysis of the strengths and limitations of Jonas's work, an analysis which has influenced my account.

27 Jonas, 'Technology and Responsibility', p. 18; *The Imperative of Responsibility*, pp. 21–2, 117–22.

Index

Index compiled by Meg Davies
(Society of Indexers)